IMAGES
of America

NORTH PLATTE

CITY BETWEEN TWO RIVERS

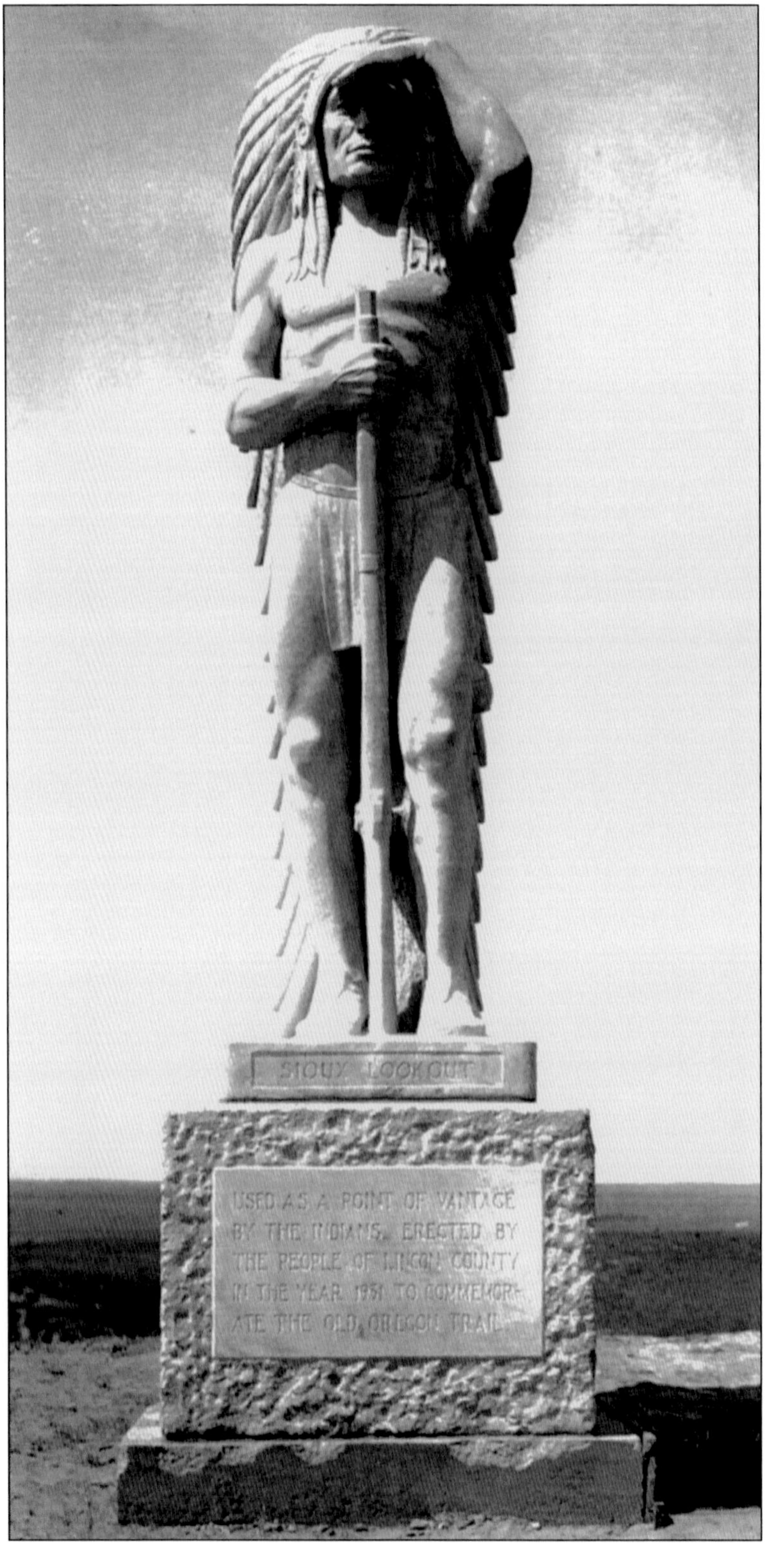

Sioux Lookout, about seven miles southeast of North Platte, was a popular place for the Indians to watch for the wagon trains on their way west. Sioux Lookout is the highest point in Lincoln County. For 75 years there was a statue of a Sioux Indian located at the top of the hill. It was placed there in 1931 by a committee of pioneers led by Loren Sturgess, Theodore Lowe, Charles Hendy, Robert McMurray, and Cyrus Fox. All of these men were either Civil War or Indian War veterans. The statue had been vandalized so many times that it was taken down and restored. It is now located on the southeast corner of the courthouse square.

IMAGES
of America

NORTH PLATTE

CITY BETWEEN TWO RIVERS

Jim Beckius

ARCADIA
PUBLISHING

ISBN 978-0-7385-1988-3

Published by Arcadia Publishing
Charleston, South Carolina

Printed in the United States of America

Library of Congress Catalog Card Number: 2002107363

For all general information contact Arcadia Publishing at:
Telephone 843-853-2070
Fax 843-853-0044
E-mail sales@arcadiapublishing.com
For customer service and orders:
Toll-Free 1-888-313-2665

Visit us on the Internet at www.arcadiapublishing.com

This book is dedicated to Phyllis, my lovely wife of 52 years.
I would also like to thank our son John, his wife Wendy, and their sons;
and our daughter Marsha, her husband Rex, and their sons.

Also to my many friends who have encouraged me
to publish a book on North Platte.
Without their help, advice, and loaned pictures, this would not have been possible.

All of the pictures of pioneers, merchants, bankers, and ranchers were taken from The History of Lincoln County, Vol. II *by Ira Bare and William McDonald.*

CONTENTS

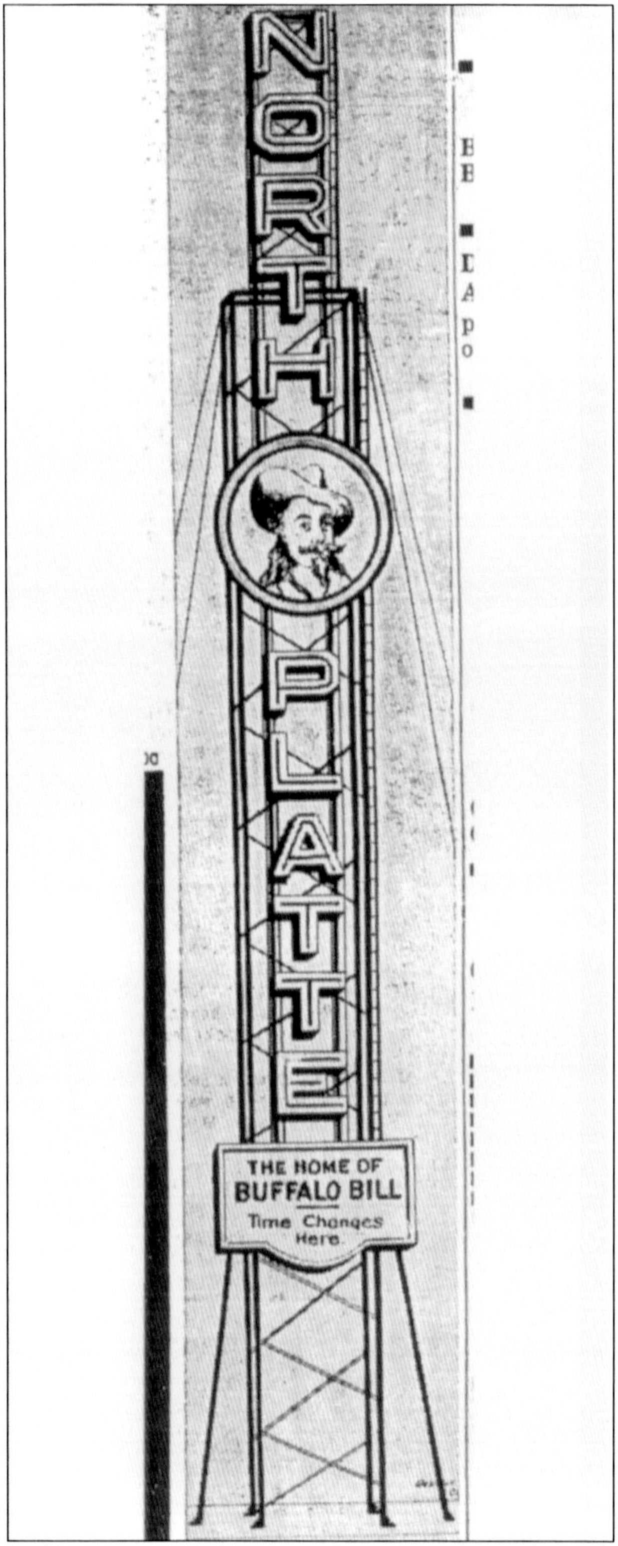

On April 20, 1940, this North Platte sign, complete with a picture of Buffalo Bill, was erected on the east end of the city on the old Lincoln Highway. It was about where Wheeler's farm equipment is now located. This sign was only up for about three years before it blew over and was never repaired.

Introduction

When the first Union Pacific train rumbled across the new bridge over the North Platte River, it continued for another two and a half miles, and when it stopped, construction of the Union Pacific halted until the spring of 1867. Weather and a shortage of supplies, including railroad ties, were the biggest reasons.

This area had been visited much earlier. In 1541, a group of Spanish explorers traveled as far as the south fort of the South Platte River, almost directly across from where North Platte is now located. There was a Spanish Padre who accompanied them, and he said mass there. This is commemorated with an annual event every June.

In 1842, the United States government sent John Freemont to find a route through the Rocky Mountains and on to California. It was a year and a half before he reached the area of Sacramento.

The discovery of gold in California in 1848 changed the whole civilization of the United States. People from the east sold all of their belongings and bought wagons and oxen in hope of making a better life. It is hard to believe that they knew what a difficult trip was in store for them. Supplies were hard to come by, and wood for making fires was difficult to find. When Fort McPherson was built just west of the settlement at Cottonwood Springs, some protection from the Indians was provided. Soldiers said that more than one thousand wagons would pass the fort every day. Many of the people would never live to see their destination. Cholera and smallpox were the worst of the diseases. Surprisingly, Indians were not the main cause of death among the travelers. It is estimated that there is a grave for every mile traveled, most of which are unmarked. Bodies were buried and then the wagons and stock were driven over the grave to hide it from the Indians. People believed they would be dug up and mutilated.

Sioux Lookout, about seven miles southeast of North Platte, was a popular place for the Indians to watch the wagons on their way west. Sioux Lookout is the highest point in Lincoln County. For 75 years there was a statue of an Indian located there, but it had been vandalized so many times it was taken down and restored and is now located on the southeast corner of the courthouse square.

About four miles west of Sioux Lookout was Jack Morrows' road ranch. Morrow was an unsavory character who had a crew of men and some Indians who worked for him. He ran an extensive rustling ring that was highly profitable. When a wagon train came in to camp for the night, he would have his crew run off their stock. Then in the morning he would act surprised and offer to sell them extra stock he had on hand. Of course they had come from the previous train, so it was all profit. Soon the wagon trains were warned about him and began to bypass his place, so he hired a crew to dig a deep ditch from the river to his yard, and the process would start all over again. The ditch is still there to this day, and you pass over it every time you travel this road.

With a steady population of about 25,000, North Platte has the largest rail yard in the world, and the number of trains exceeds 150 per day. Today, construction has begun on an 8-story observation tower and museum, and it will soon allow visitors to observe the rail operation.

Many changes have taken place over the years, among them the loss of many historic buildings, including all of those on Front Street, and the Union Pacific Depot that housed the famous North Platte Canteen of World War II. It served over 6 million servicemen and women between December 25, 1941 and April 1, 1946. Many of the men and women who enjoyed the canteen still write to the mayor or historical society to thank them, after 57 years. In 2002, North Platte citizens are building a 20th Century Veterans' Memorial to be located just off I-80 on the south side of the eastbound ramp. Its completion is scheduled for the fall of 2003. A huge granite memorial will be placed there to commemorate the canteen. The names of over one hundred towns that supported and worked at the canteen will be engraved on the back of the granite. Remember, they used their own sugar, gas, tires, and other rationed items to make cakes, donuts, cookies, and most other things the troops so much enjoyed. Also there were free cigarettes, magazines, music, and entertainment. Now nothing marks the depot except a small memorial wall; the entire depot was razed in 1973.

Two rivers hem in North Platte. The North Platte River heads up in northern Colorado and flows northeast into Wyoming through Saratoga, Fort Laramie and Torrington to Scottsbluff, Nebraska, past Chimney Rock, Ash Hollow, and then to North Platte, meeting the South Platte River three miles east of North Platte. The South Platte River begins north of Colorado Springs, Colorado, around Tarryall, and flows southeast to Denver, Fort Morgan, Sterling, and Julesburg, then to Ogallala, Nebraska, to North Platte. After the rivers join, the Platte River flows past Kearney, Grand Island, and then flows on to the Missouri River, which is the border between Nebraska and Iowa.

One

The 19th Century

1870–1899

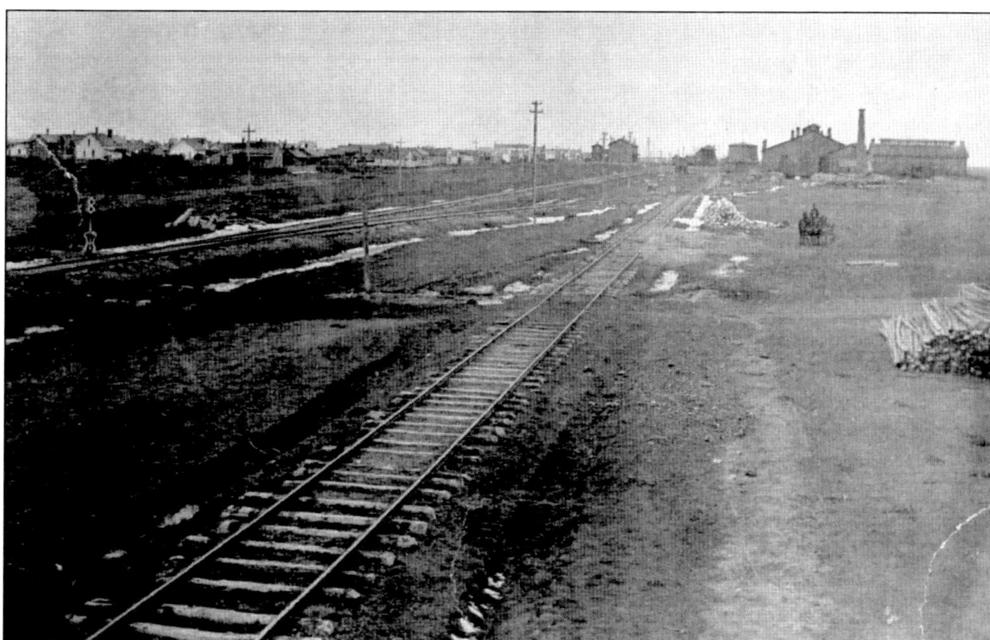

Pictured here is a western view of North Platte around 1871. The Union Pacific Depot and Hotel can be seen in background, and the U.P. shops and roundhouse sit on the right side of the tracks.

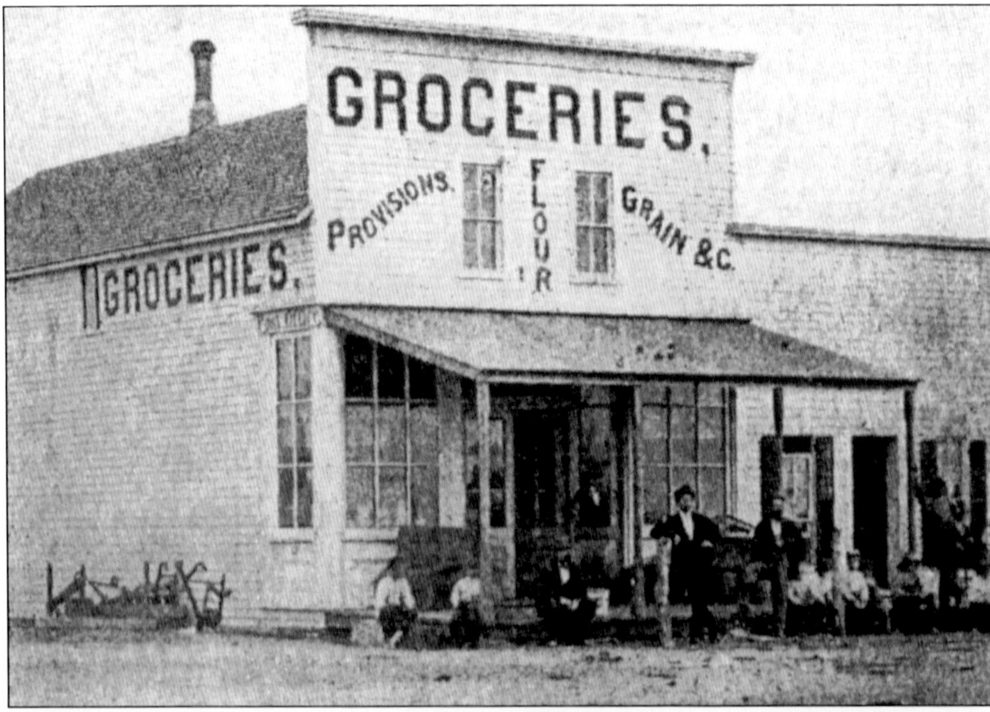

The first store in North Platte was founded when William Peniston and Andrew Miller learned that the Union Pacific was going to declare North Platte a division point. They moved their trading post from Cold Springs, west of Fort McPherson, to a site one and one half miles west of the North Platte River, and set up the store. It was later bought by Charles McDonald.

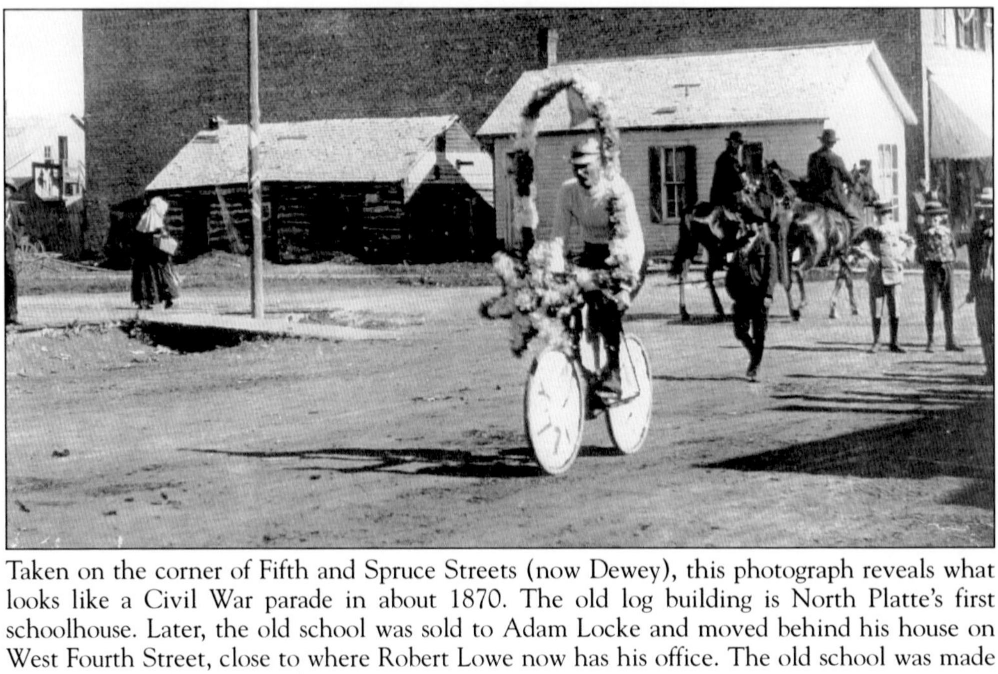

Taken on the corner of Fifth and Spruce Streets (now Dewey), this photograph reveals what looks like a Civil War parade in about 1870. The old log building is North Platte's first schoolhouse. Later, the old school was sold to Adam Locke and moved behind his house on West Fourth Street, close to where Robert Lowe now has his office. The old school was made into a stable and later torn down.

The first high school building in North Platte was located between Third and Fourth Streets on Spruce Street (Dewey). Built in 1873, it only lasted until 1899 when it was torn down due to earthquake damage. Notice the two doors in front—one for the girls and one for the boys.

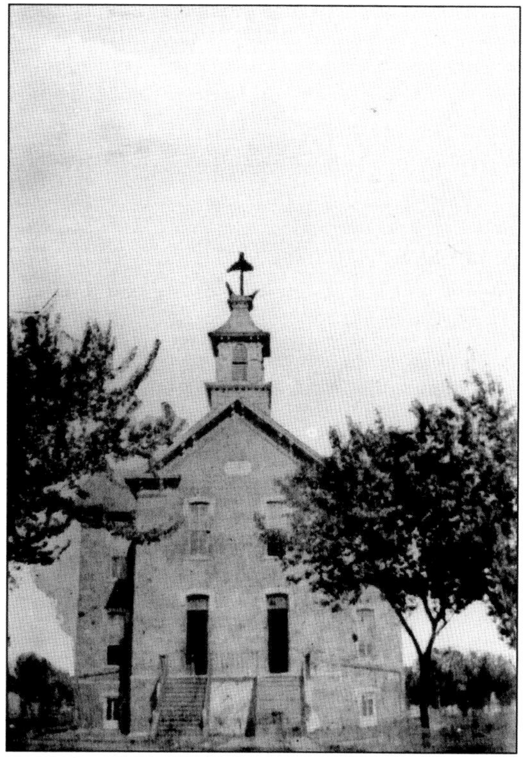

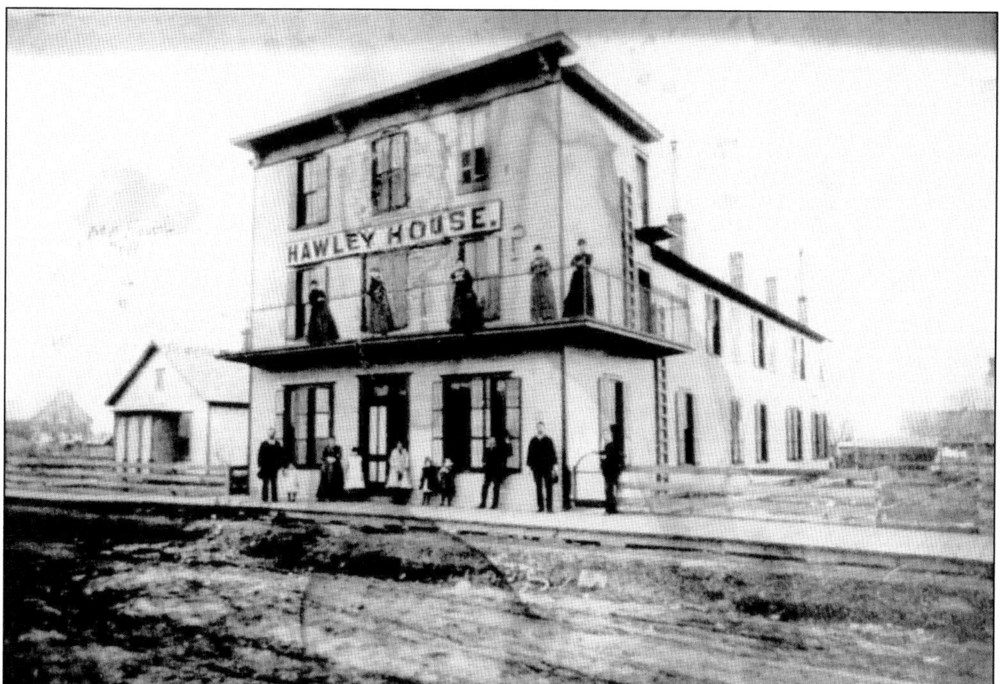

Pictured here is the Hawly House at 216 East Fifth Street in 1886. Located just west of the Maloney Furniture Store and Undertaking Parlor, this site later housed the north end of the Woolworth Dime Store.

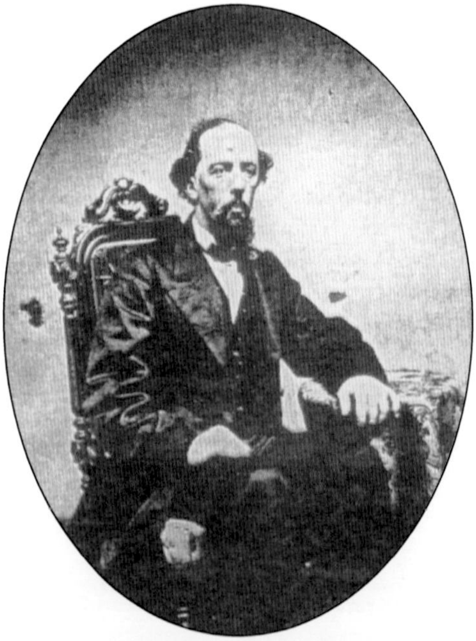

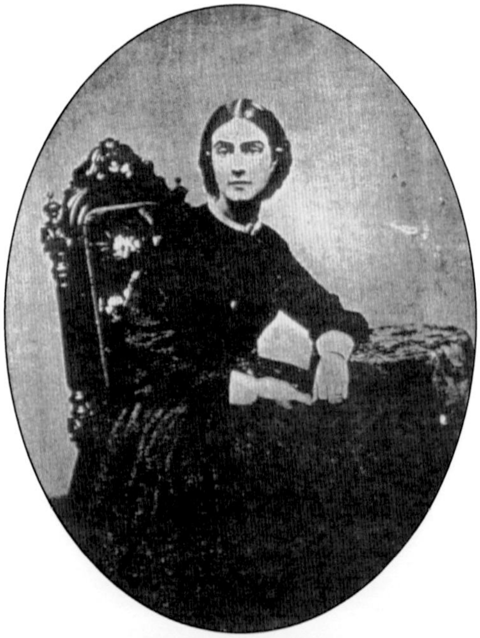

William S. Peniston and Ann A. Webb Peniston were married in 1865. William was born November 20, 1834 in Yorkshire, England, and died October 14, 1906. Anna was born June 9, 1840 and died March 6, 1908. Both are buried in North Platte Cemetery.

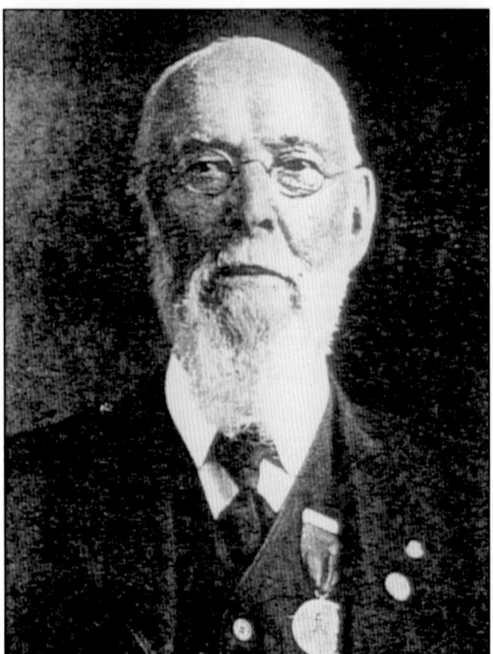

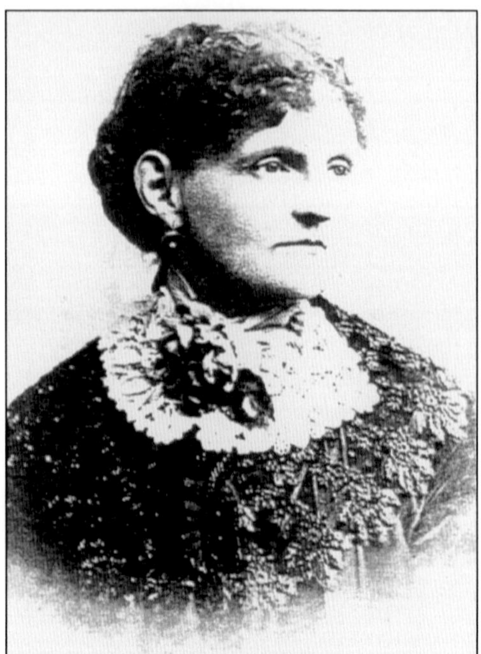

Charles McDonald and Orra B. Henry McDonald were married on October 24, 1858 in Omaha. Charles was born in Tennessee on October 25, 1826 and died April 22, 1919. Orra was born March 8, 1840 in Hamilton, New York, and died December 28, 1898. They are both buried in the North Platte Cemetery.

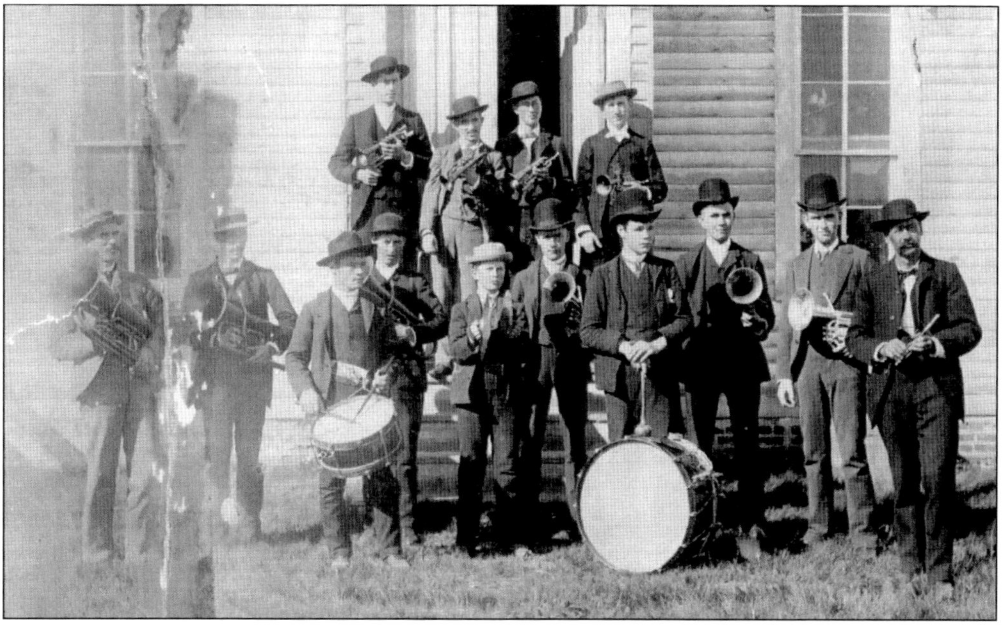

This is a photograph of the first North Platte band in 1887, taken in front of the first Catholic Church, which was built in 1875. They are, from left to right: (top row) Tom Keliher, Tom Loftus, and Joe, Danell, and Dennis Redmand, along with (bottom row) Frank Redmand, Pat Browney, William Moran, Joe Grace, E. Grandy, John Sullivan, John Lonegan, Art Reish, Charles Whalen, and Joe Fillion.

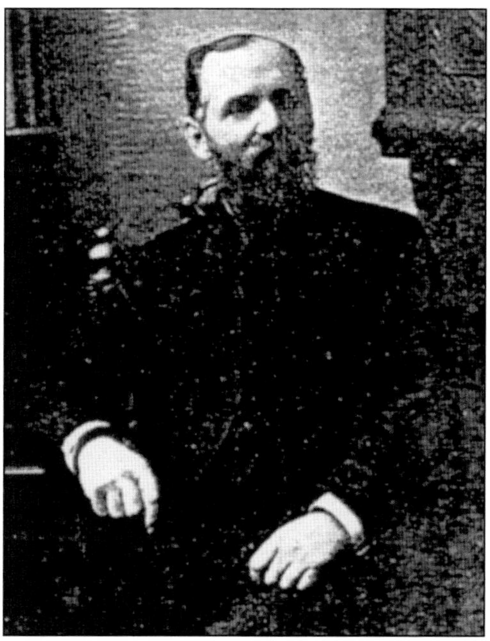

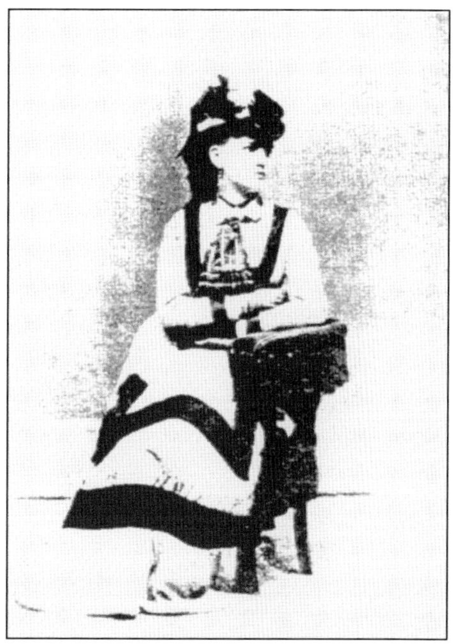

John Bratt, one of the largest cattle ranchers in the state, is pictured here with his wife, Elizabeth Burke Bratt. They were married May 18, 1875. John Bratt was born August 9, 1842 in Leek, England, and died June 15, 1918 at North Platte. Elizabeth Burke Bratt was born in Illinois on November 14, 1852, and died August 29, 1937 in North Platte.

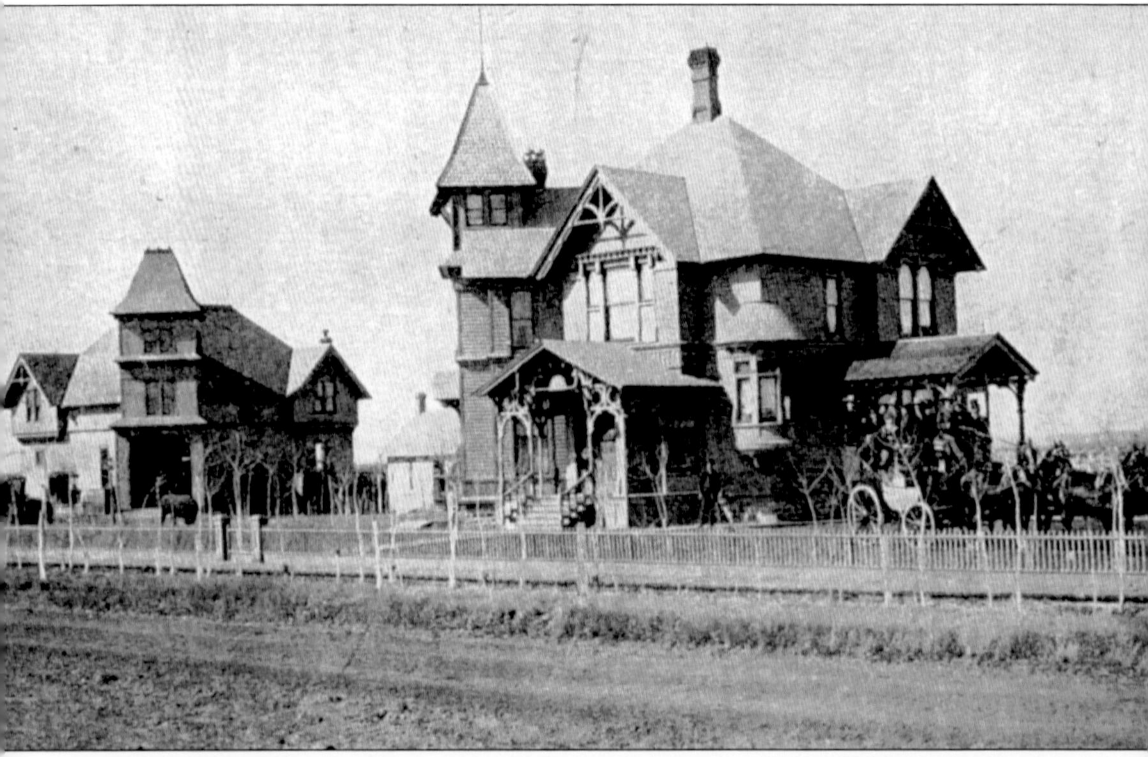

Buffalo Bill's Welcome Wigwam Town House was located in the 1200 block of West Fourth Street. Cody bought this house from a silk merchant and later added the carriage house in the back. The carriage house burned down in about 1893, and the house was torn down in 1934.

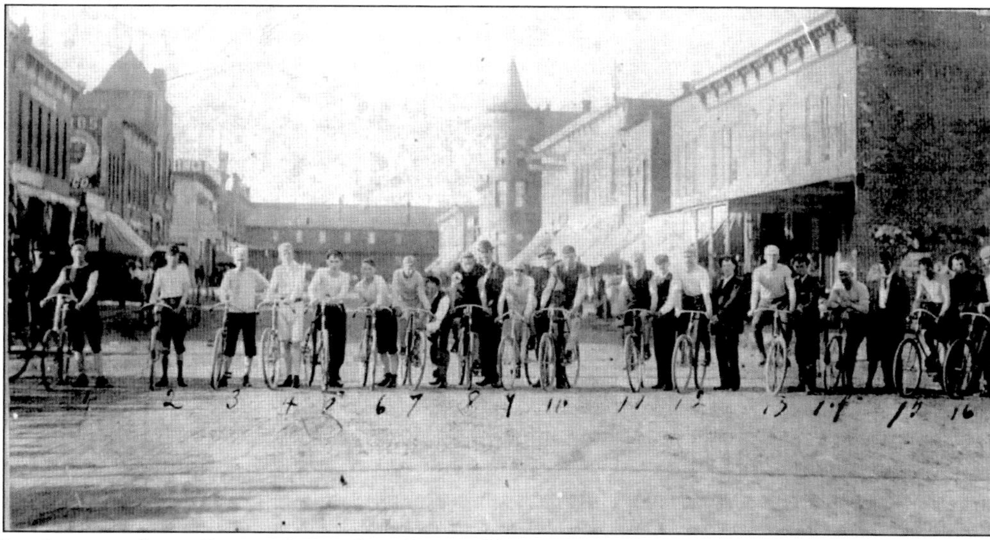

Looking north on Spruce Street from East Fifth in 1895, the old First National Bank and the Union Pacific Hotel and Depot are visible in the background. This photo celebrates an 18-mile road race. The winners of the race were as follows: Walker Hainline, Johnnie Ell, John Dugan, and Joe Ellison. Riders are identified as the following: 1. Eddie Friend, 2. Joe Fillion, 3. Eugene Picard, 4. Harry Dixon, 5. Henry Loneragan, 6. Billy Moran, 7. Frank Creek, 8. Walker Hainline, 9. Johnnie Ell, 10. Elay McGinn, 11. John Dugan, 12. Johnnie Gulliaum, 13. Andy Therman, 14. Lem Steel, 15. Eddie March, 16. Arthur Ruan, and 17. Billie Baker.

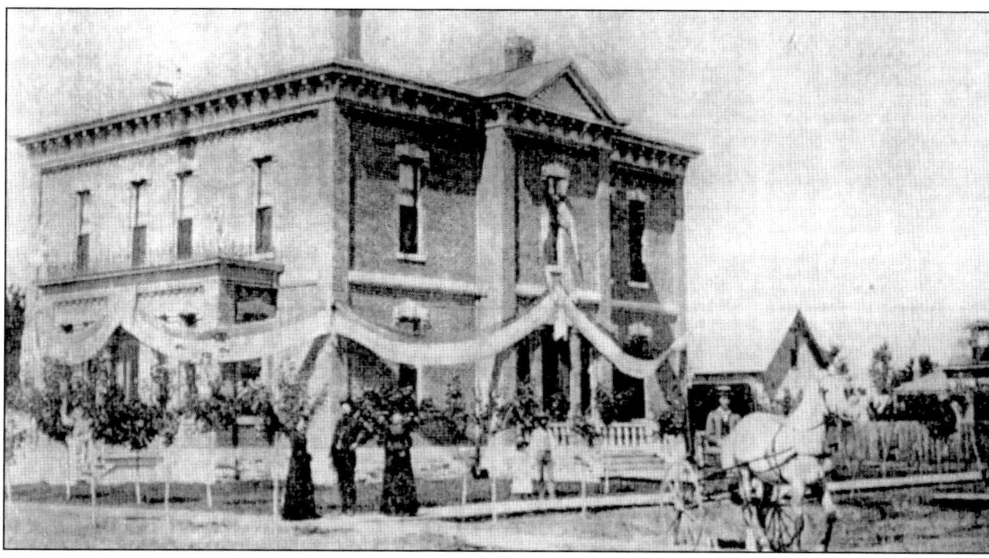

In the pioneer days, Lincoln County had a big strong modern brick jail—but no paved streets. Pictured here is Elmer Baker in his buggy with his renowned driving horse, White Eagle, outside of the Lincoln County Jail in 1896. Fourth of July strollers, from left to right, are as follows: Mrs. D.A. Baker, sister of Ed. Wheelock, and D.A. Baker, who was Lincoln County sheriff from 1888 to 1896, Emma Van Slyke, Ida Ottenstein (Mrs. Ed. Todenhoff), and her father, John Ottenstein. The frame building next to the jail is now the North Platte Public Library. The building on the far right is the old Pennington house where the Baptist Church was later located.

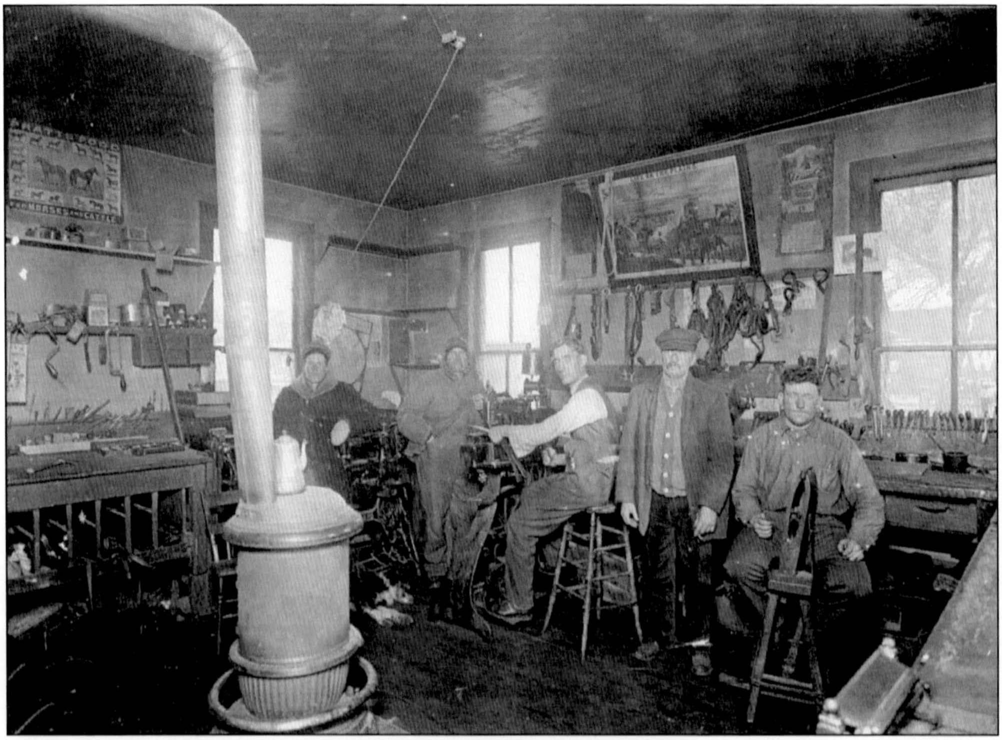

This picture was taken in March of 1899 in front of Fink Harness and Saddlery at 505 North Dewey. The people are not identified.

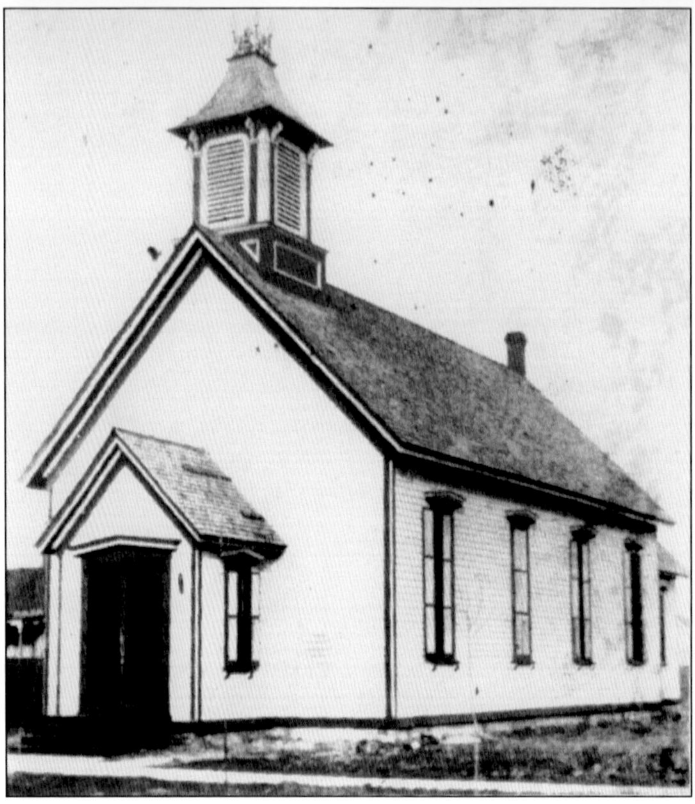

Here is a 1903 image of the First Presbyterian Church at 412 North Dewey. It was located just south of the post office at Fifth and Dewey.

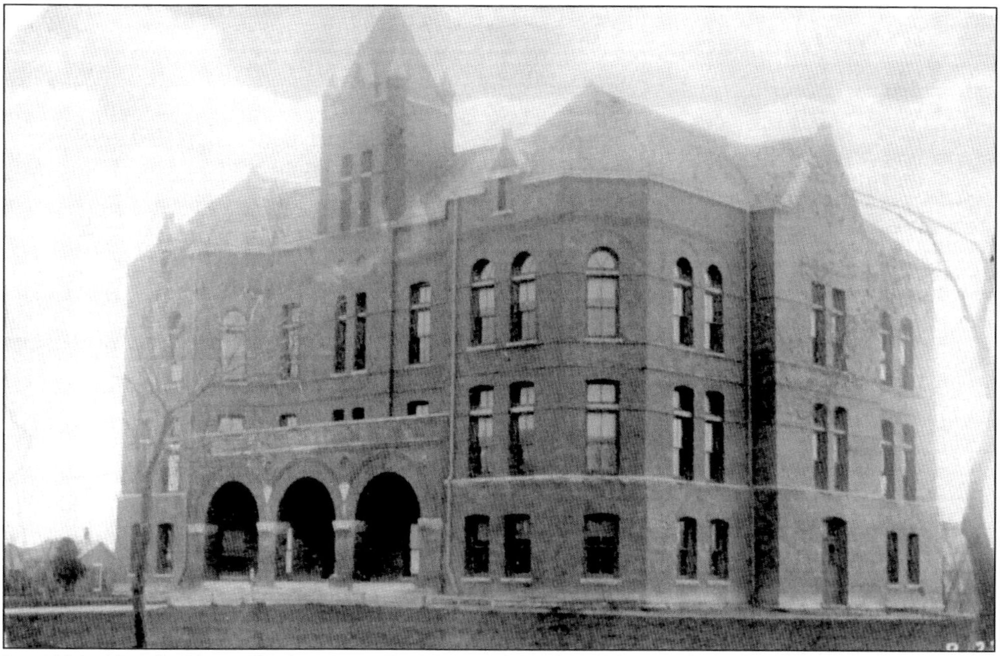

In 1901, North Platte had a new Senior High School located between Third and Fourth Streets at North Dewey.

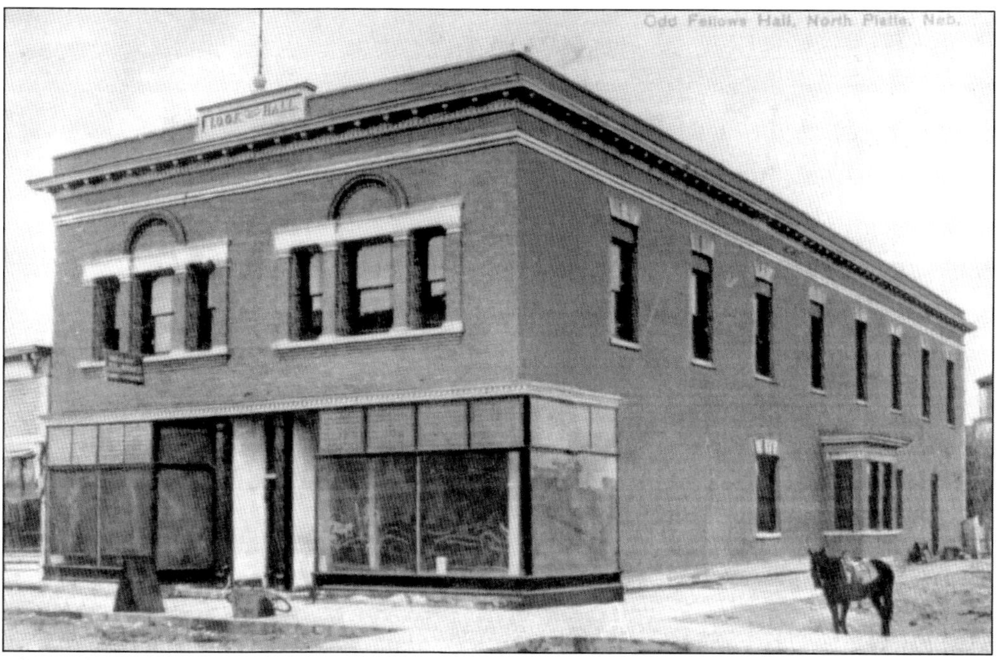

The Independent Order of Odd Fellows Hall on the corner of Fifth and Dewey Streets once housed the post office, Platte Valley Bank, and McDonald State Bank. Currently, the American Mortgage Company occupies it. This image of the building was captured in 1903.

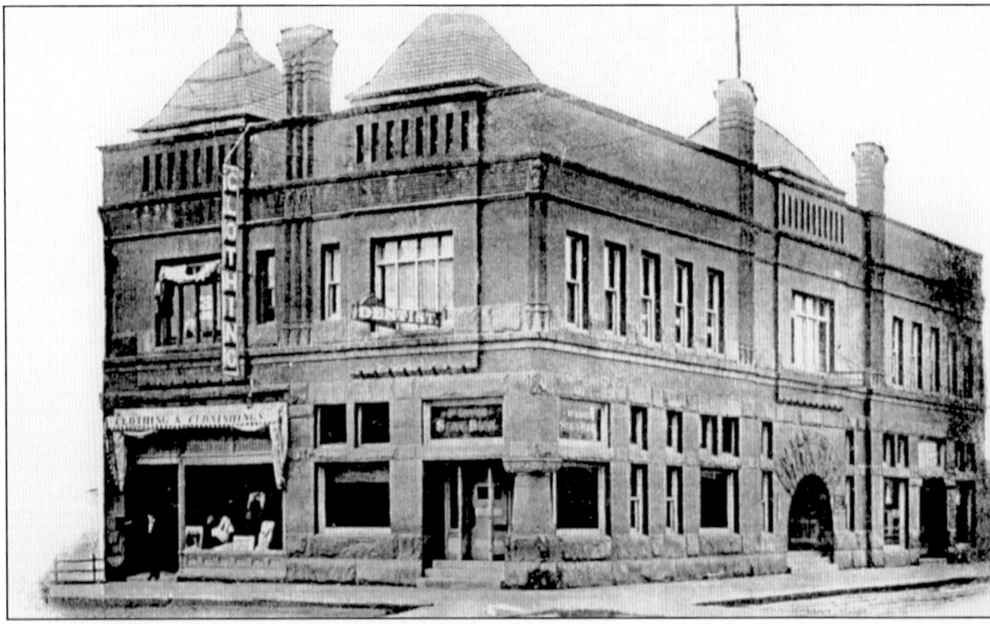

This building was erected by A. Schatz at the southwest corner of Sixth and Dewey in 1889. Shatz Clothing and McDonald State Bank were located at 520 and 522 North Dewey, respectively. The water fountain in Cody Park is the round column that held the corner of the building up. This is how the site appeared in 1907.

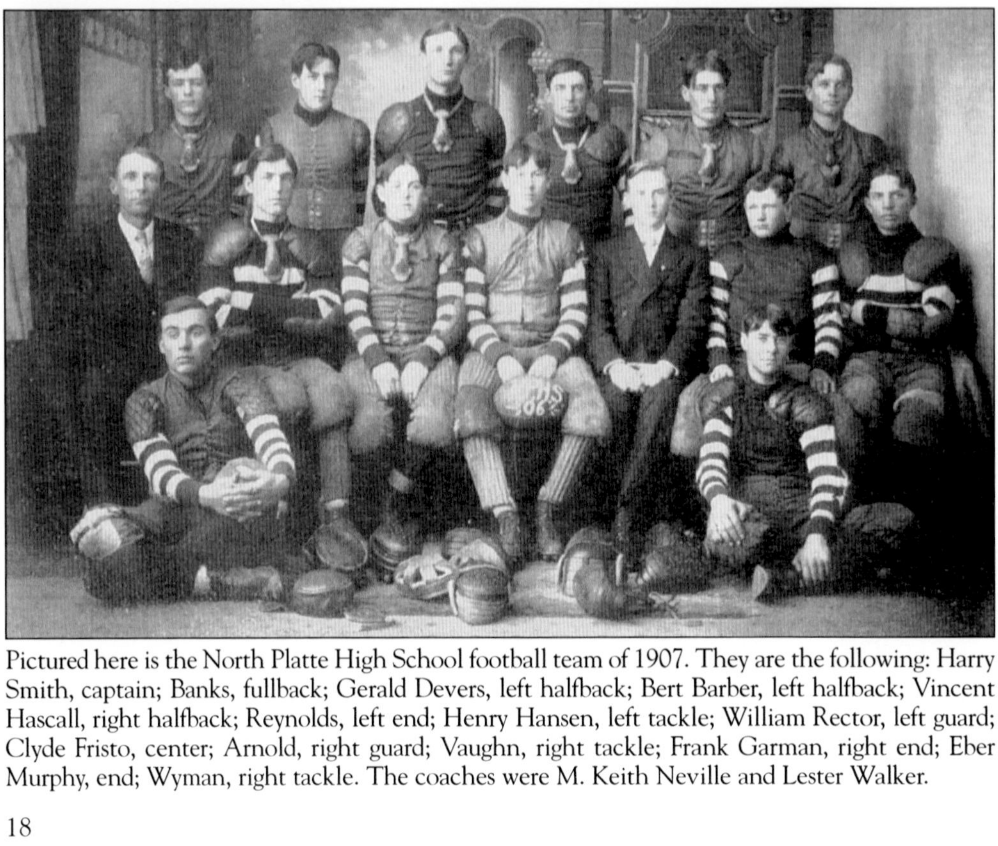

Pictured here is the North Platte High School football team of 1907. They are the following: Harry Smith, captain; Banks, fullback; Gerald Devers, left halfback; Bert Barber, left halfback; Vincent Hascall, right halfback; Reynolds, left end; Henry Hansen, left tackle; William Rector, left guard; Clyde Fristo, center; Arnold, right guard; Vaughn, right tackle; Frank Garman, right end; Eber Murphy, end; Wyman, right tackle. The coaches were M. Keith Neville and Lester Walker.

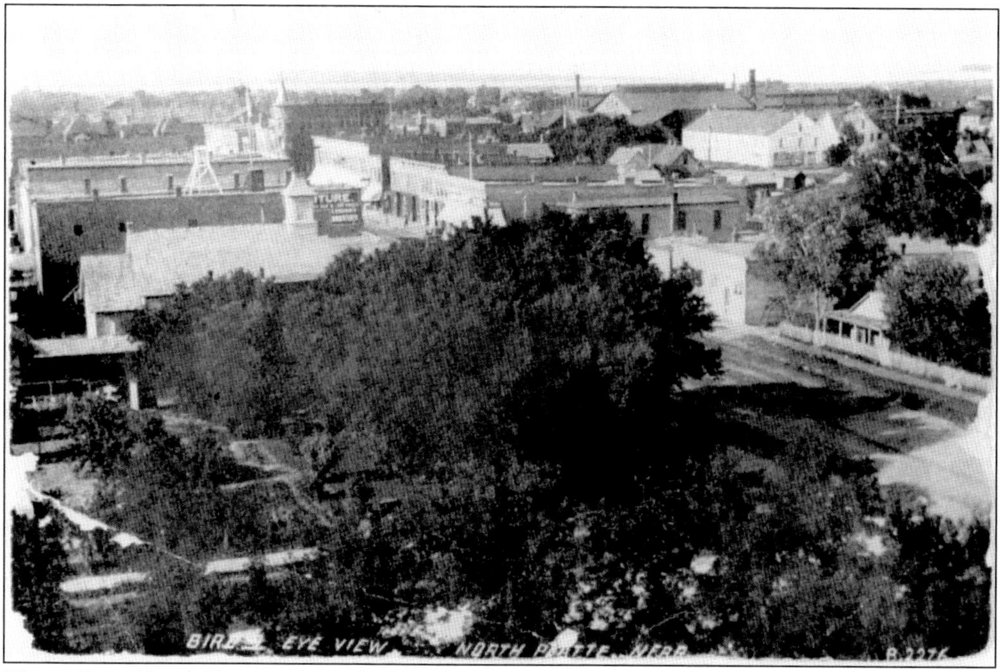

This is how North Dewey Street looked from East Fourth Street in 1903. Beside the house in the foreground is Howe and Maloney Undertaking Parlor. Across the street is the Presbyterian Church and post office. The large white building at the top right is Lloyd's Opera House.

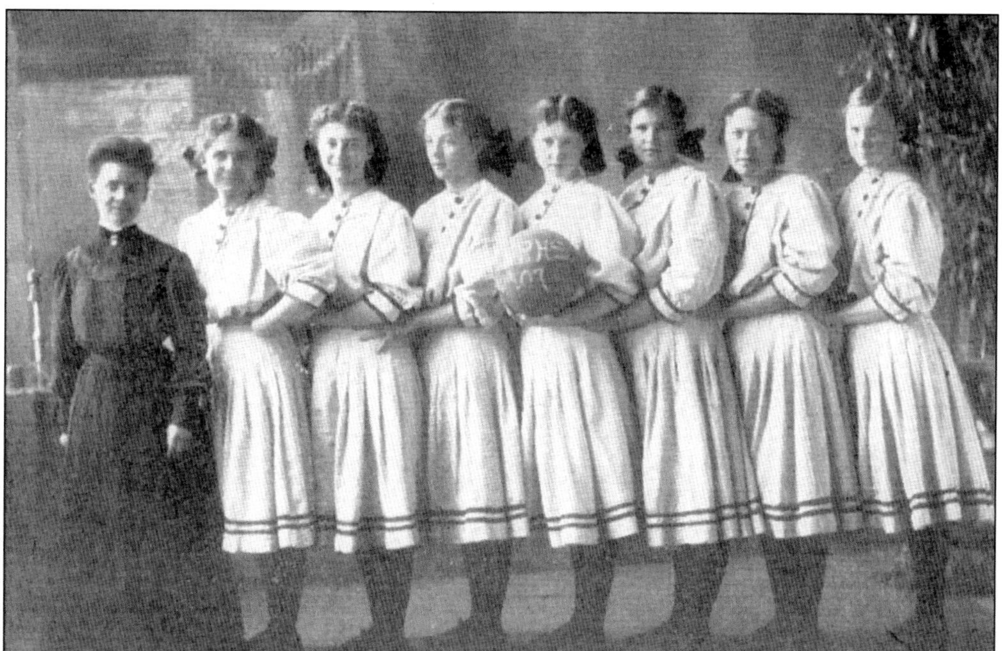

Members of the 1907 North Platte High School girls' basketball team are identified, from left to right, as follows: Coach Grafton, Mabel Duke, Mary Guilliaume, Alice Rnnie, Hazel Minshall, Captain Helen Davidson, and Marie Salisbury.

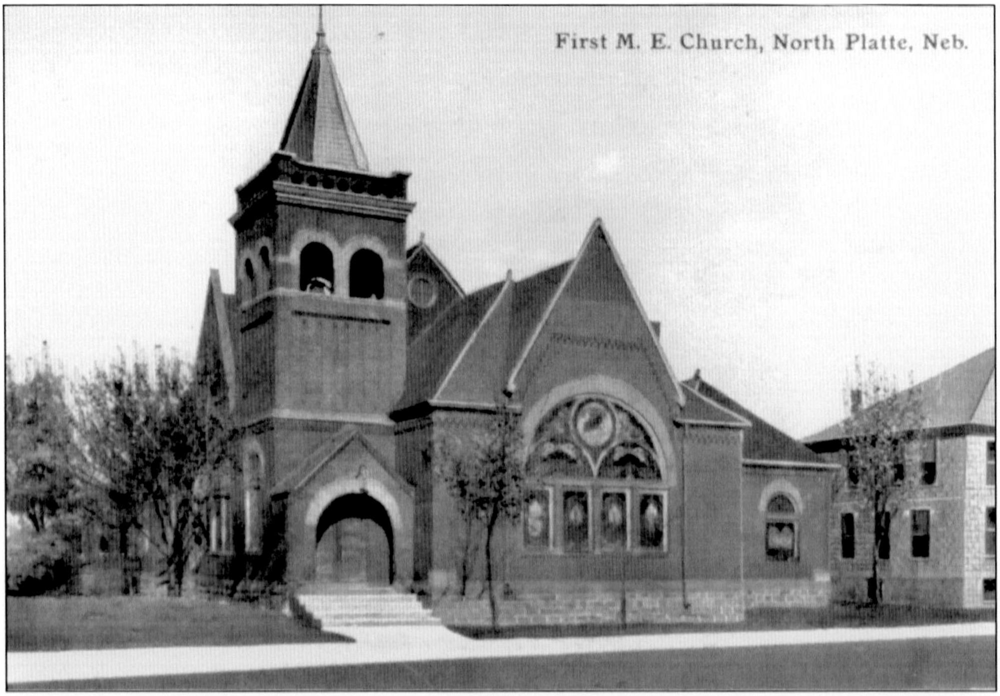

The Methodist Episcopal Church sat at 119 West Sixth Street. The first frame church burned on December 7, 1898, and it was rebuilt and dedicated on July 23, 1899. The second church, pictured, featured stained glass windows furnished by Buffalo Bill Cody. One window depicted his son, Kit Carson Cody. The church was torn down in 1963.

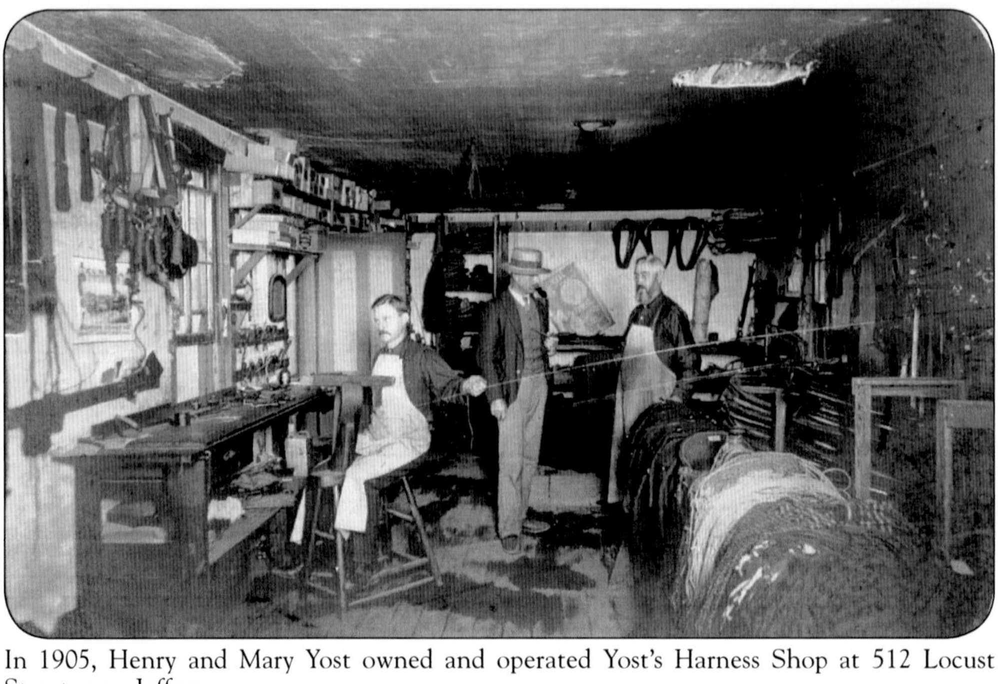

In 1905, Henry and Mary Yost owned and operated Yost's Harness Shop at 512 Locust Street, now Jeffers.

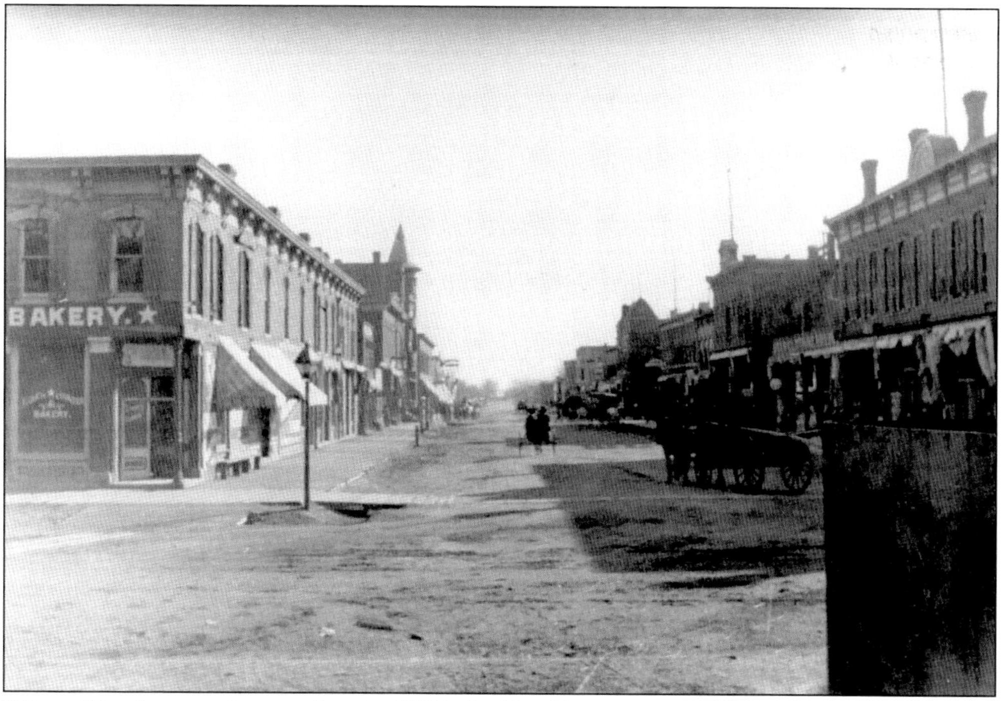

When this photograph was taken in 1900, the Star Restaurant and Bakery was owned by J.C. Federhoof. This is a view of North Dewey Street, looking south from Front Street.

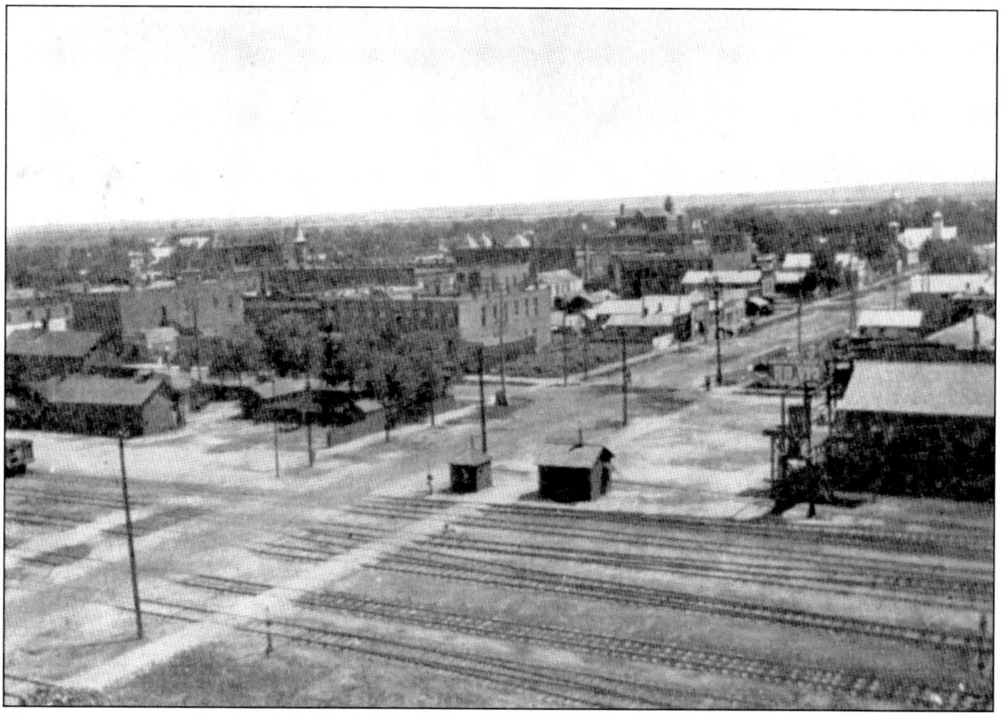

This picture provides a southern view of Locust Street as it looked on May 21, 1906. When a train crossed the road, a man on site flagged the cars to a stop.

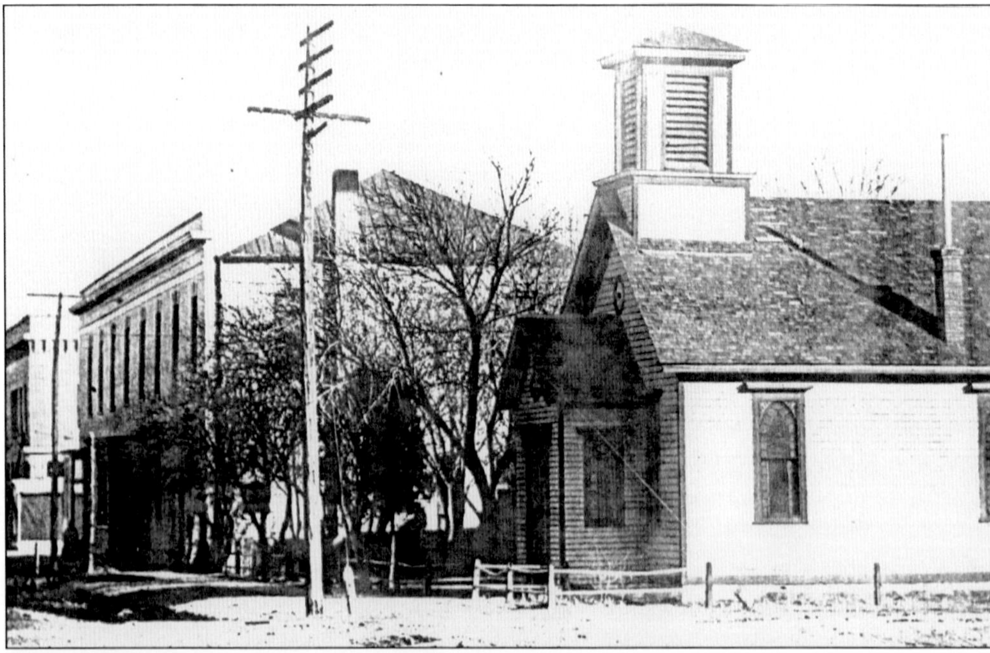

Here is a view of the old Baptist Church and the post office, as seen from the one hundred block of East Fifth Street in 1906. The church sat where the old Mutual Building and Loan office was built. The post office later became the Platte Valley Bank. The new Baptist church was later built on the corner of Fourth and Jeffers, where the Unitarian Hall had been. Now it houses the Drive-In Pharmacy.

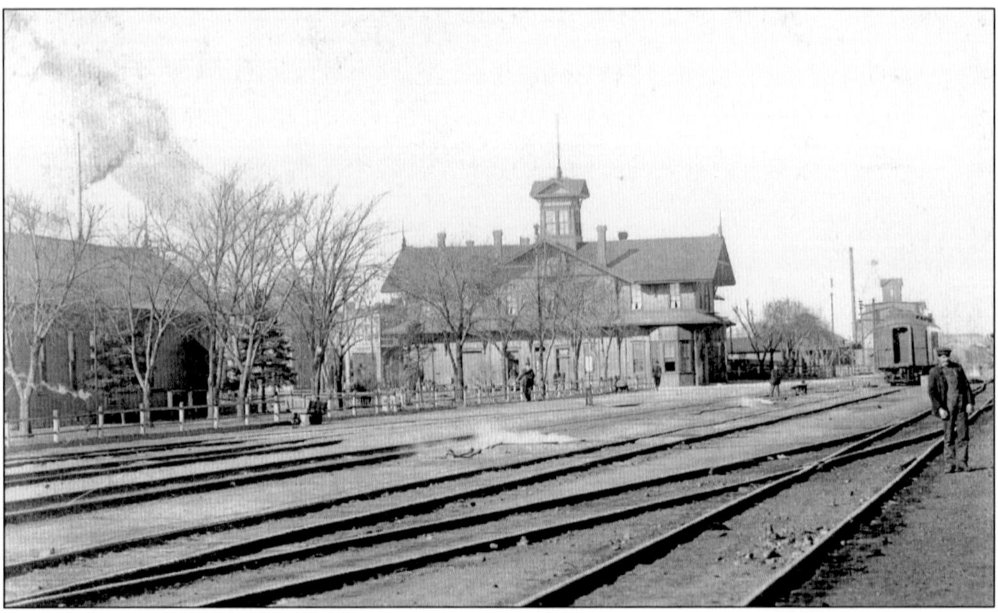

The Union Pacific Depot and Hotel at Front and Dewey had many famous visitors, including William F. Cody (Buffalo Bill), the Grand Duke Alexis of Russia, George A. Custer, Generals Sheridan and Sherman, Bat Masterson, and Teddy Roosevelt. This depot and hotel opened in December of 1869, and was destroyed by fire on November 17, 1915.

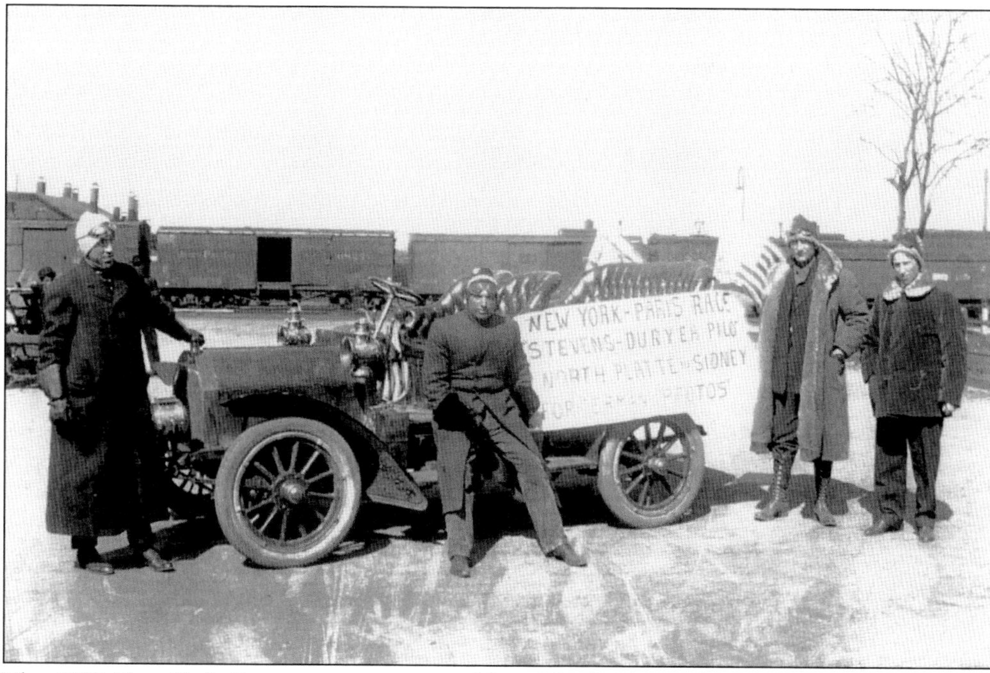

The 1907 New York–Paris race was captured by a North Platte photographer. There were no graded roads or highways at the time.

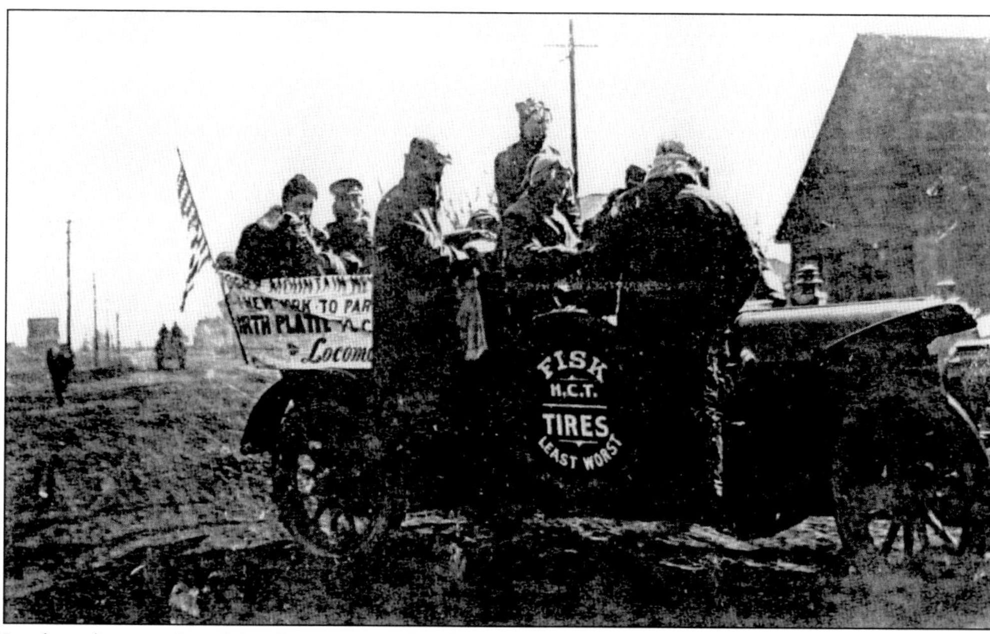

In this photo, taken March 10, 1908, Explorer Hanson and Montague Robert participate in a cross-country auto race. They drove a Thomas Flyer. The Locomobile from Denver carried a news crew for the occasion. The cars were stored in Salisbury's livery stable overnight at the corner of Front and Pine Streets. The Palace Hotel livery stable was later built on this corner, but burned down in 1915. The cars were gassed up at Fillion's station in North Platte, the only gas station in town, located at 111 East Fifth Street.

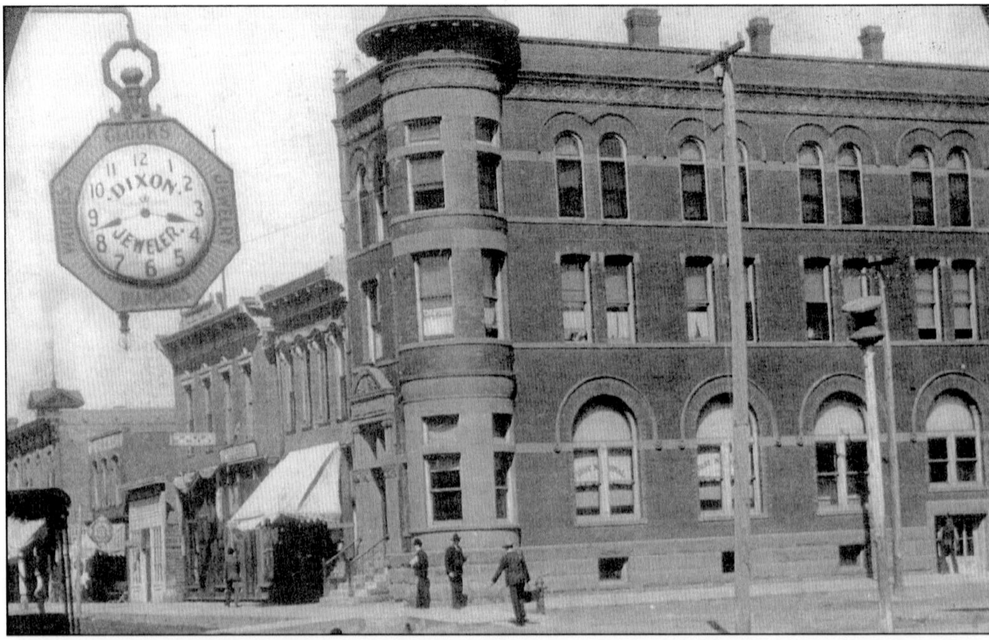

This is a northern view of Sixth and Dewey Streets in 1907. Businesses on the east side of the street include the confectionary, owned by John F. Federhoof; Fred Waltemath's saloon; Lem Bailey's barber shop; John F. Brocker's tailor shop; Henry J. Rebhausen's saloon; Thomas L. Green's billiard parlor; the North Platte Pharmacy, owned by Dan F. Barber; and the First National Bank, overseen by Arthur McNamara, President.

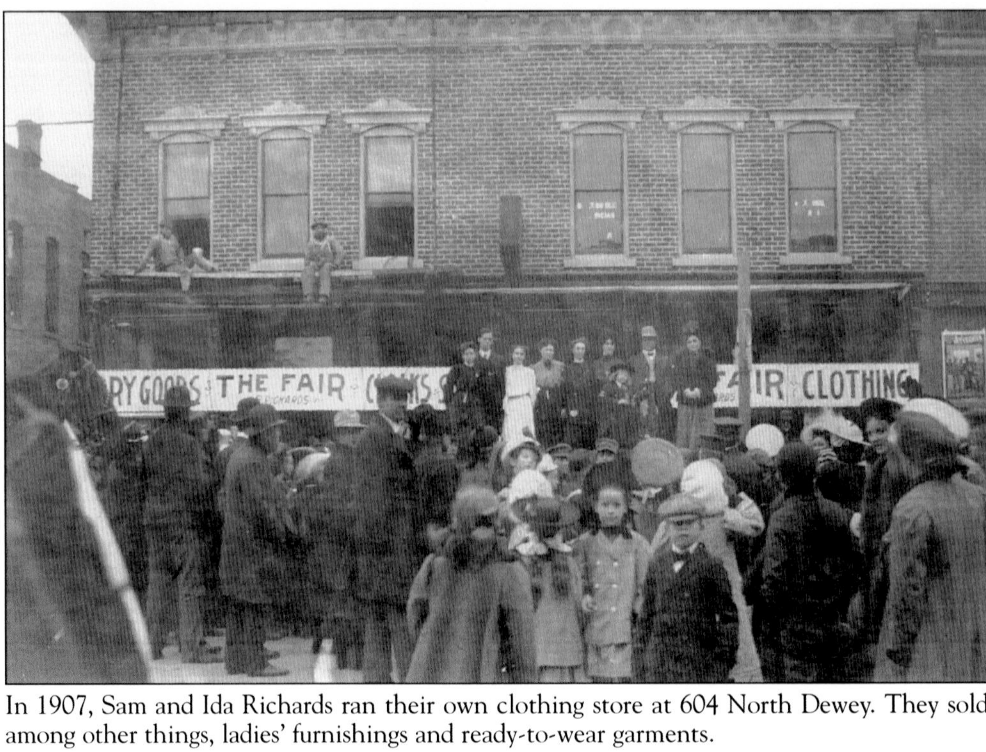

In 1907, Sam and Ida Richards ran their own clothing store at 604 North Dewey. They sold, among other things, ladies' furnishings and ready-to-wear garments.

Two

North Platte Expansion

1908–1942

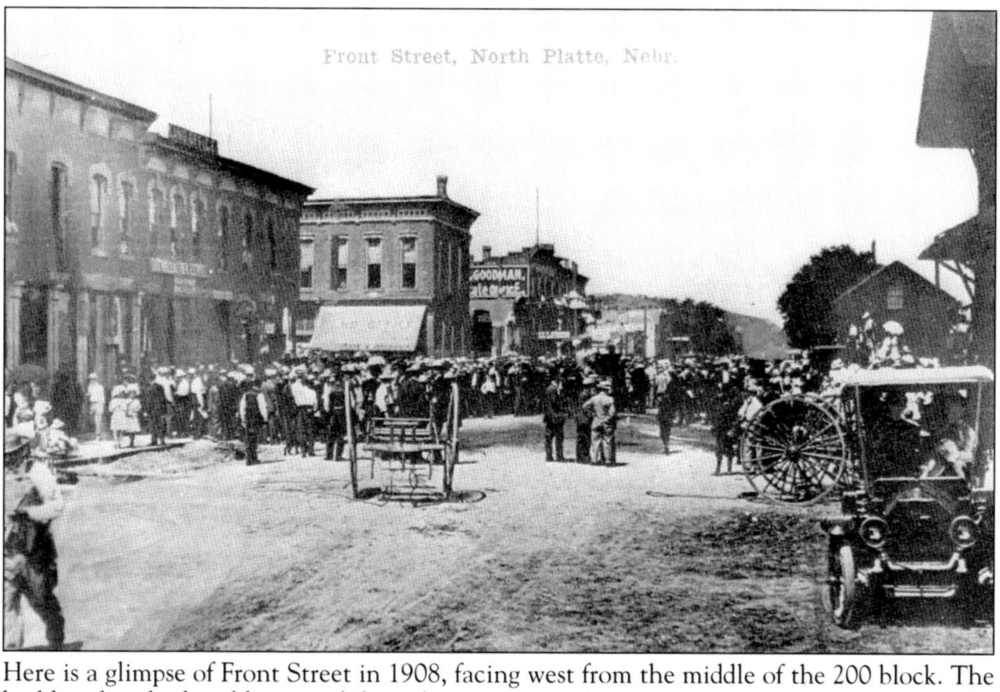

Here is a glimpse of Front Street in 1908, facing west from the middle of the 200 block. The building beside the old automobile is the Union Pacific Depot and Hotel. Just west, on the same side of the street, is the hotel laundry.

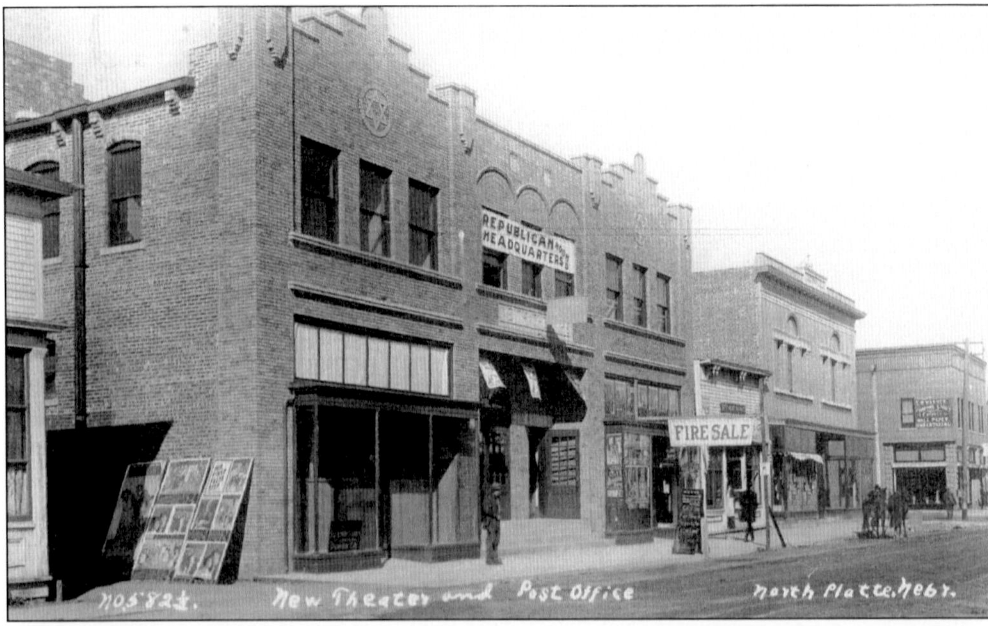

This is a 1909 image of the west side of North Dewey Street. Local businesses pictured here, starting at 412 and moving northward, are as follows: the North Platte Electric Light and Power, managed by Lester Walker; the Keith Theatre Building, managed by Charles and Anna Stamp; the City Meat Market, Henry Schreiber, Proprietor; Buchanan and Company Grocery, managed by Frank and Perry Buchanan; and the United States Post Office, where R.D. Thompson served as postmaster.

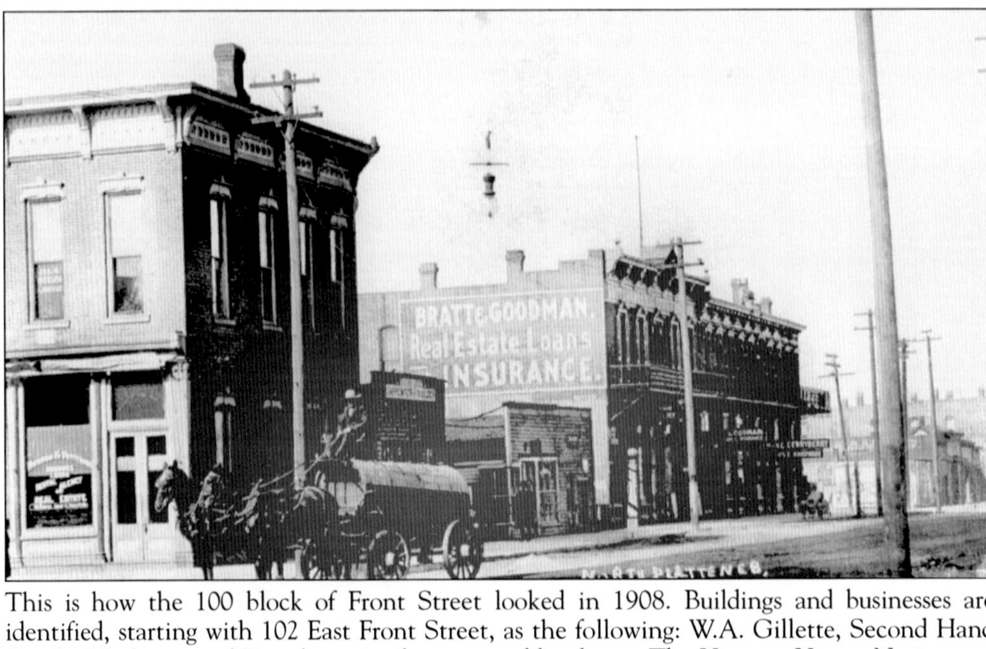

This is how the 100 block of Front Street looked in 1908. Buildings and businesses are identified, starting with 102 East Front Street, as the following: W.A. Gillette, Second Hand Goods; Workman and Derryberry implements and hardware; The Hinman House, Norine and Schrader; Bratt and Goodman, real estate; Tramp Grocery, owned by Ernest Tramp; O.W. Sizemore, barber; and James A. McMichael, contractor.

St. Patrick's Church was located on the corner of Fourth and Chestnut. The church was built around 1881 when Father Conway replaced Father Lynch. It was then torn down in 1949.

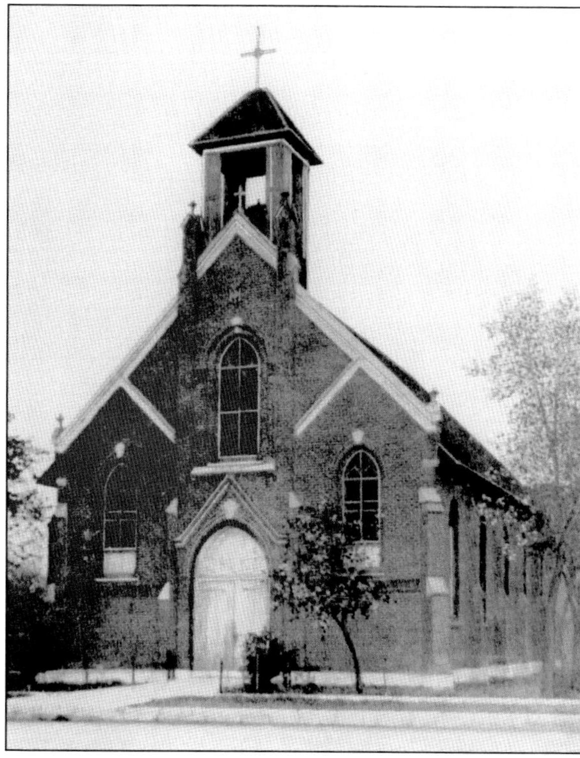

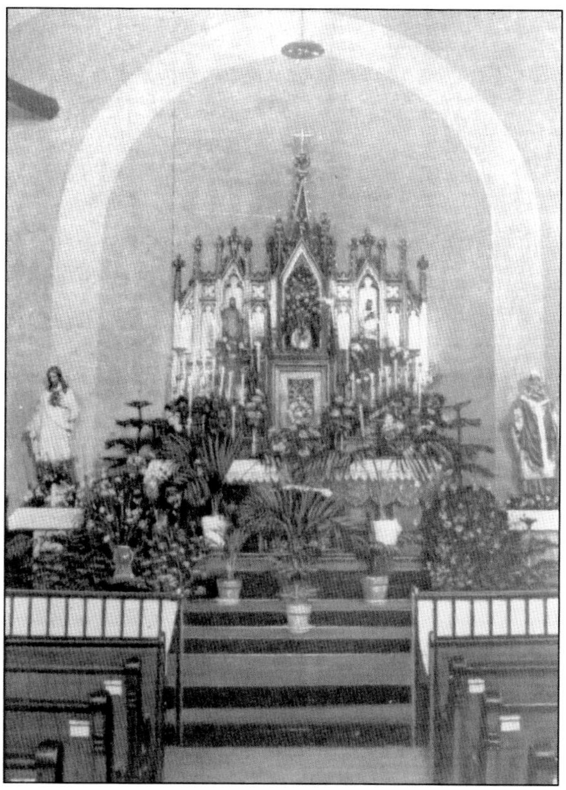

This is the interior of St. Patrick's Church on the corner of Fourth and Chestnut.

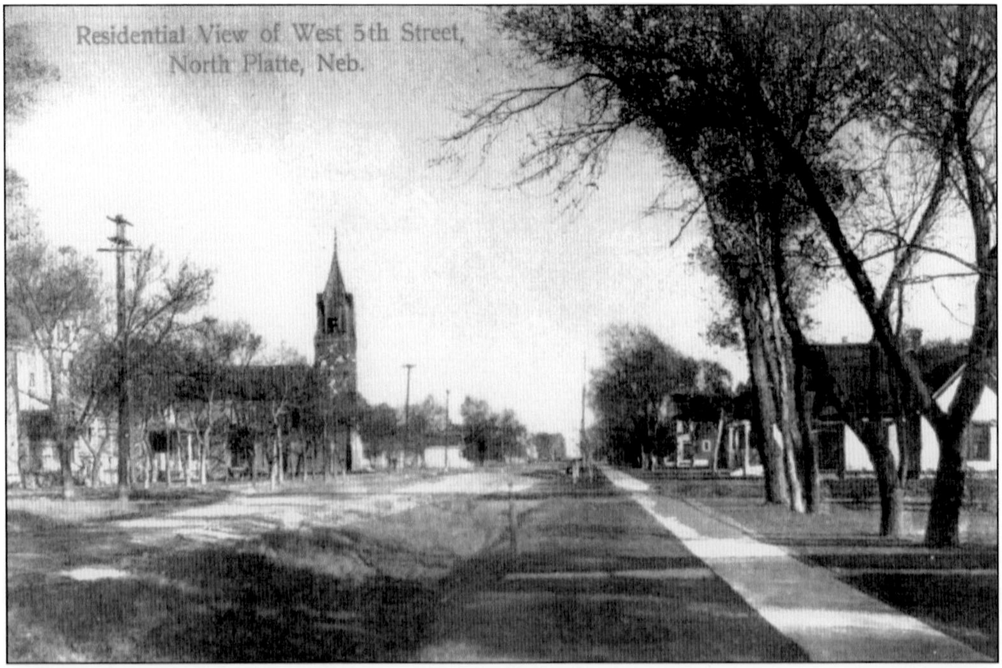

A look west on Fifth Street shows the earlier First Lutheran church. The negative has been reversed so that the church appears to be on the south side of the street. This picture was taken on November 12, 1910. The church was torn down on May 9, 1918, and rebuilt at the same location.

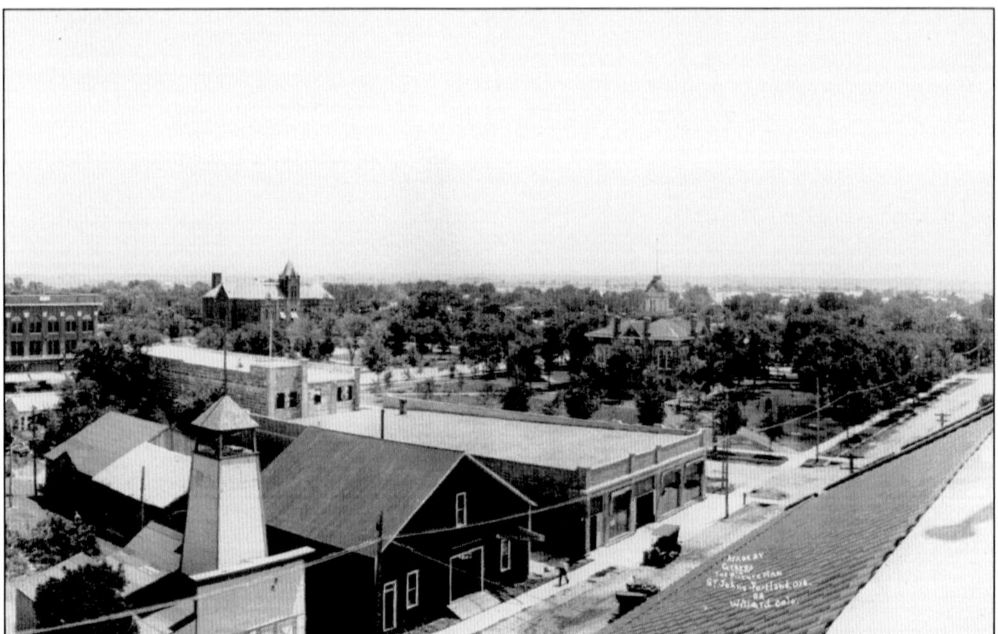

This photograph of North Locust (Jeffers) Street, taken in 1913 from the top of the new post office, provides a view of the courthouse and senior high. In the foreground are the J.S. Davis Auto Company, Adam Lock's Livery Stable, and Fire Hose Company Number One.

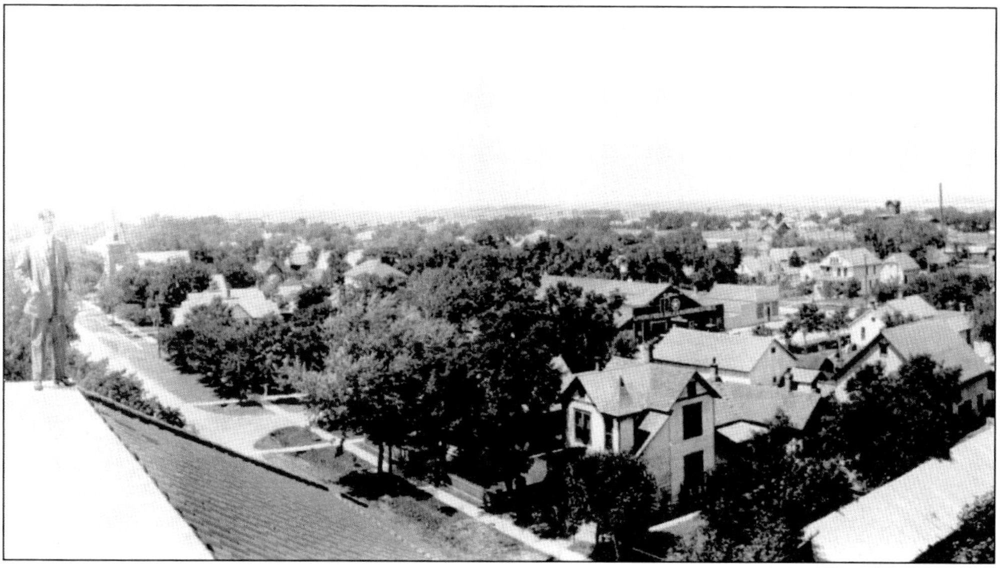

This picture, taken in 1913, provides a view looking west on Fifth Street and north on Vine Street. The two houses on Fifth Street belong to Joseph Hershey and J.L. Sinclair. In background on Vine Street is the Star Livery Barn, where Eakes Office Supply is now located. The man on the roof of the post office is J.S. Davis.

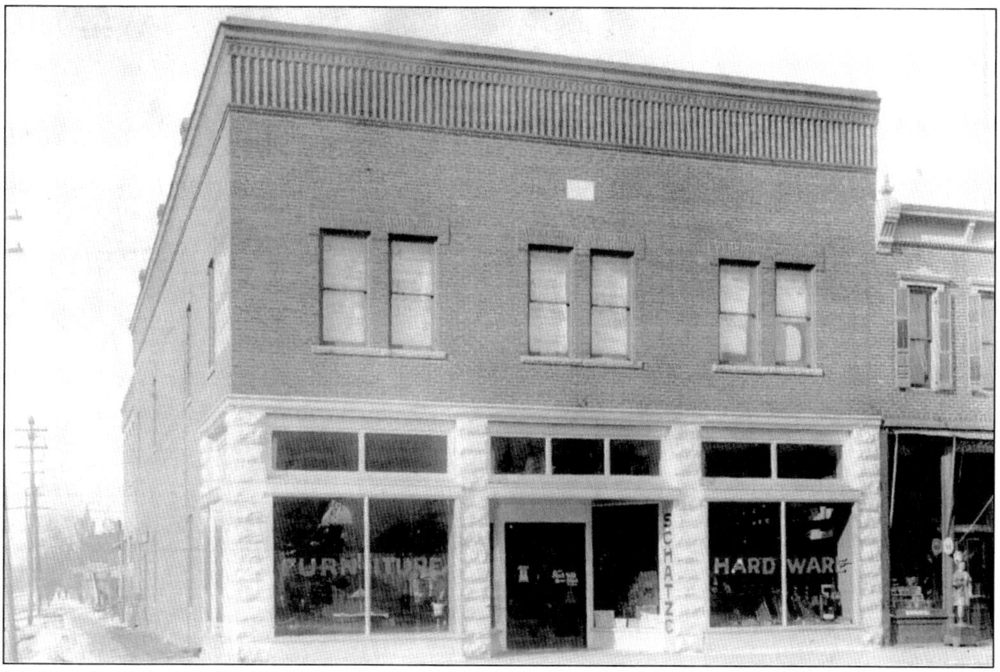

This is the Warner Building on the northwest corner of Fifth and Dewey. This building was occupied by various businesses, including Ginn and White Furniture and Hardware, in 1907; Derryberry and Forbes' Furniture and Hardware, in 1910; Higbee and Keyes, in 1921; and the J.C. Penney Company in 1935. The building was then torn down during urban renewal. A new building was built and occupied by Brown Shoe Fit. The building just next door, shown here, was occupied by J. Fred and Mary Schmalzried, cigar manufacturers.

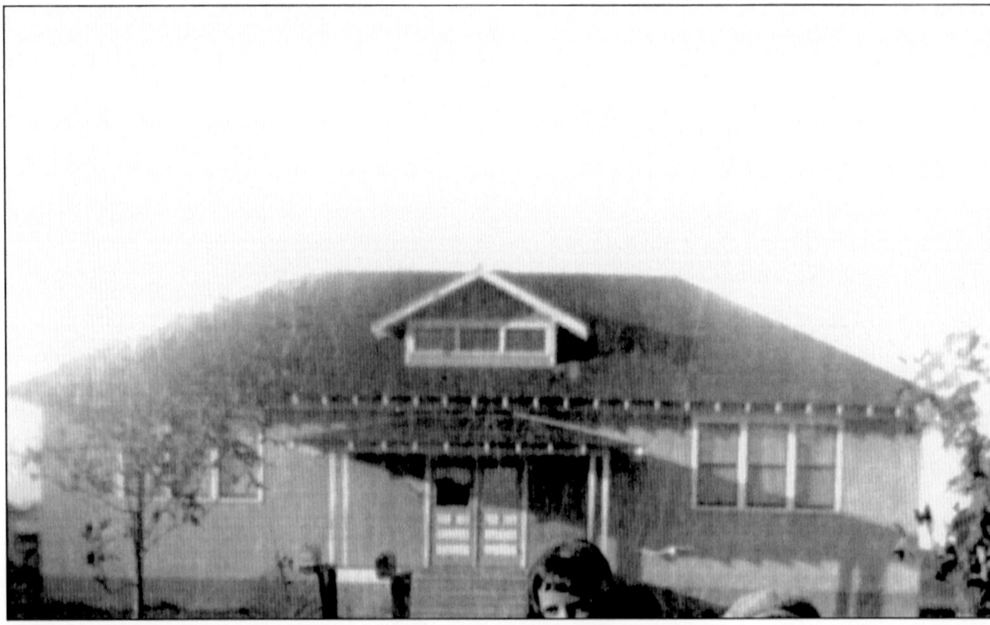

The old Cody school was located on the north side of the 1800 block of West Fourth Street. The girl in this picture, taken in 1927, is Irene Muchlinski.

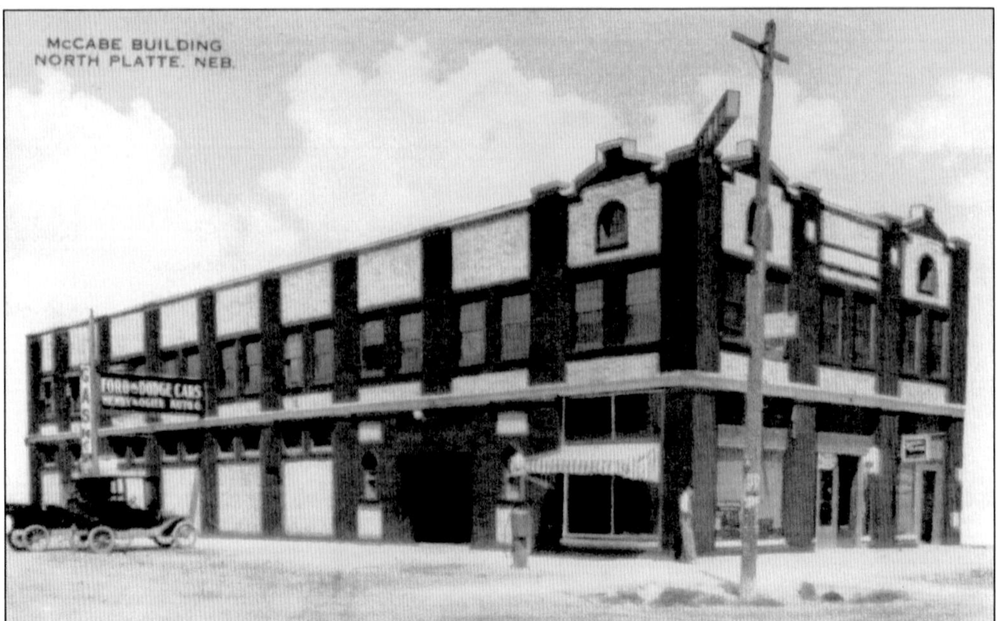

The McCabe Building, pictured in this 1914 photograph, was on the northwest corner of Fourth and Dewey Streets. This building is where Hendy-Ogier started their first Ford and Dodge Agency.

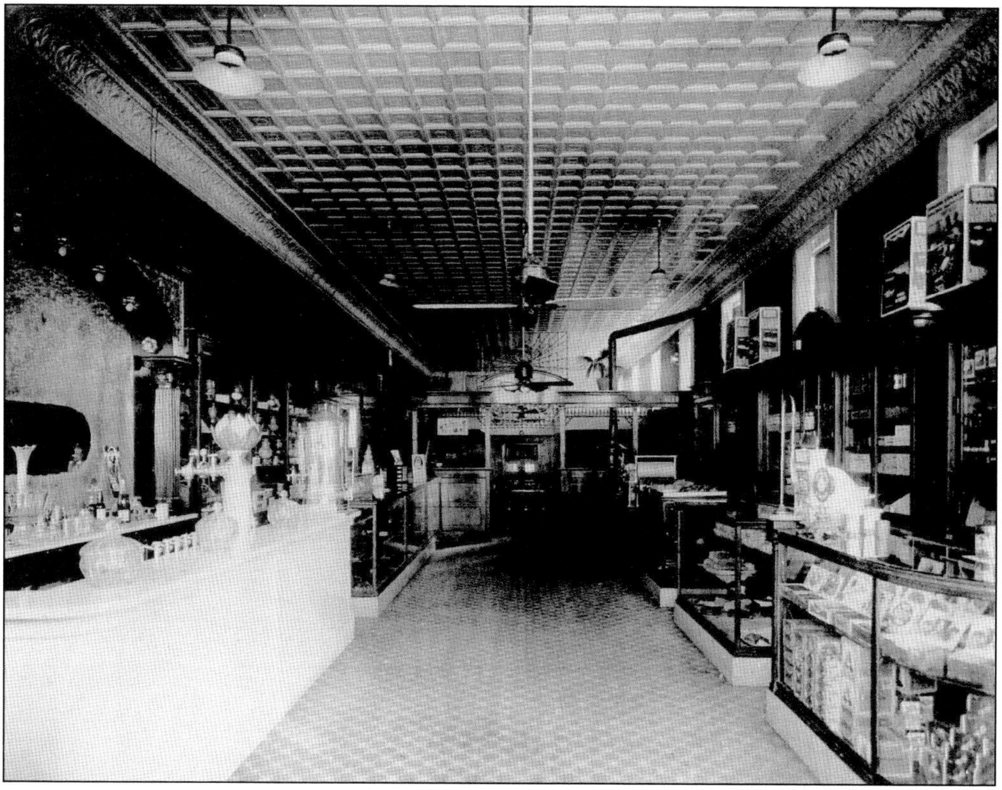

This photo of the Dickey Ice Cream Parlor, a confectionary and ice cream manufacturer, was taken in 1915. Owners Robert R. and La Vanche Dickey also sold pianos. Dickey's Ice Cream remained until 1921, when it was replaced by the King Fong Café. King Fong closed in 1973, and the site is now home to Stephanie's.

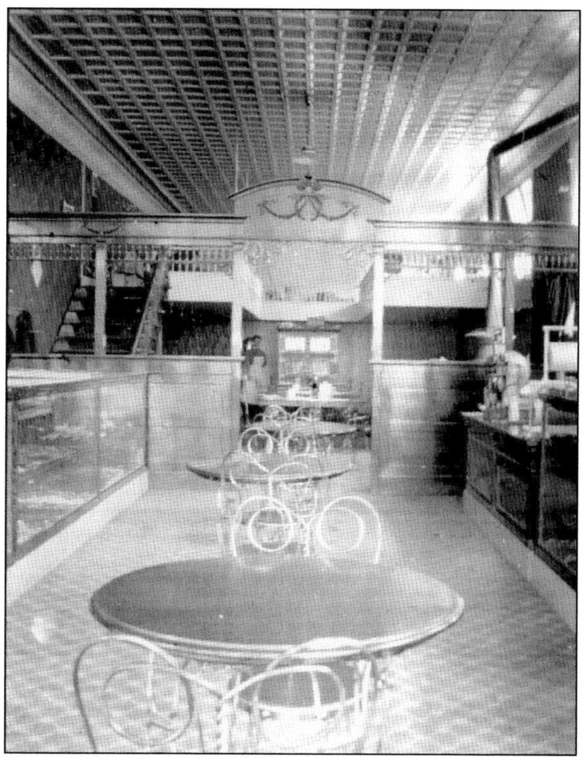

The dining room of Dickey's Ice Cream Parlor, at 501 North Dewey, is seen here as it appeared in 1915.

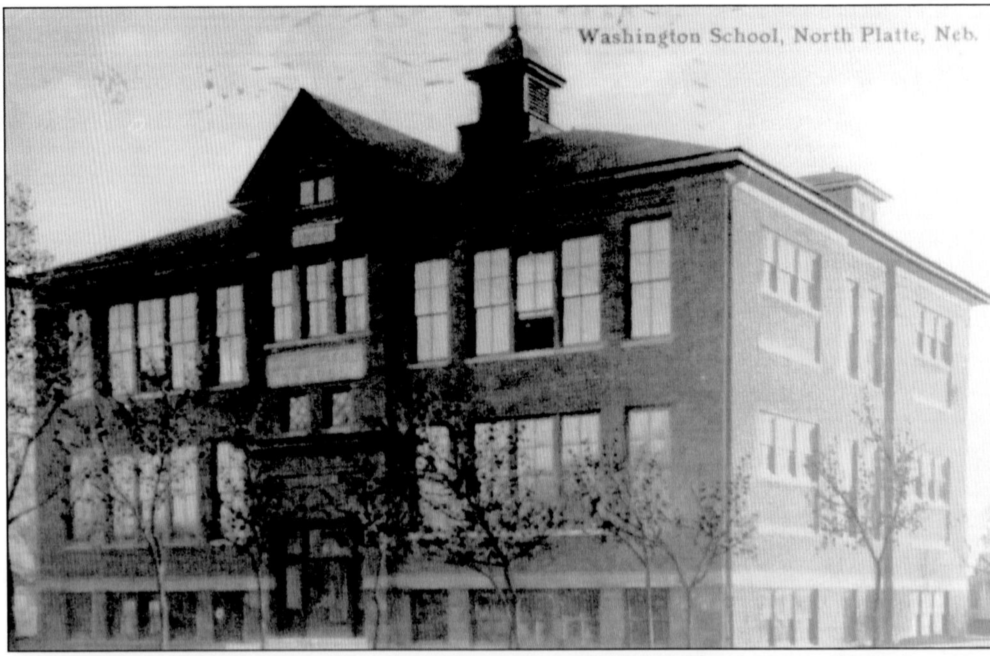

The Washington Elementary School was located at 600 West Third Street. This photo was taken in 1909.

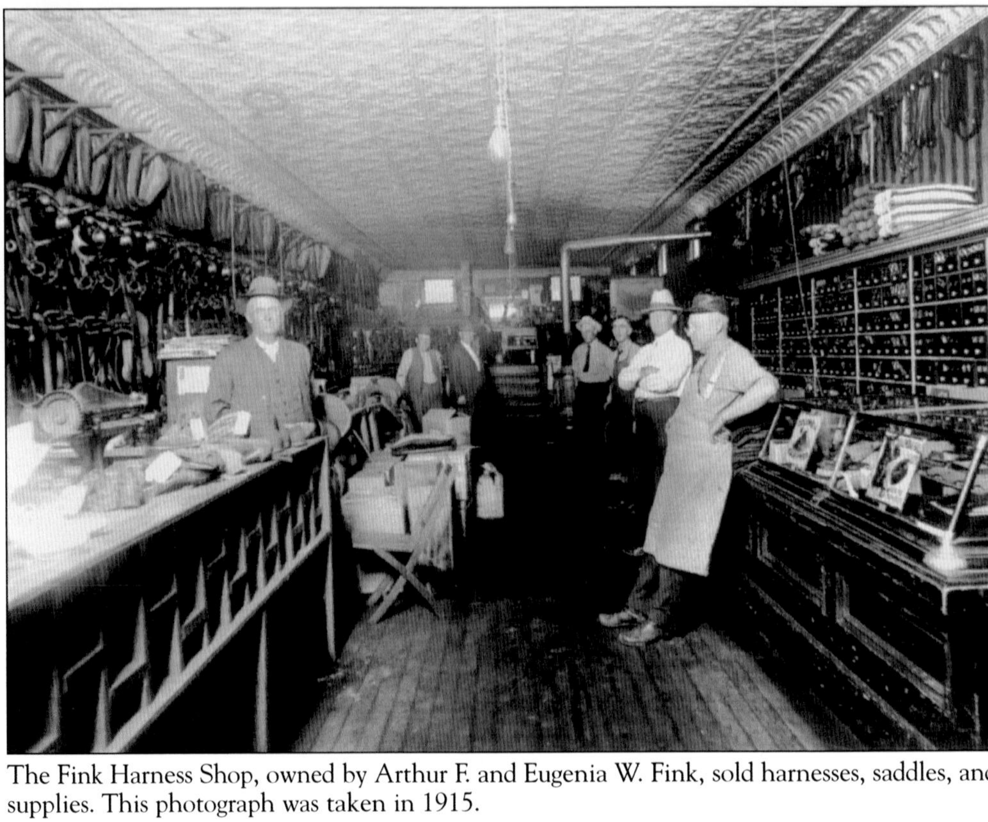

The Fink Harness Shop, owned by Arthur F. and Eugenia W. Fink, sold harnesses, saddles, and supplies. This photograph was taken in 1915.

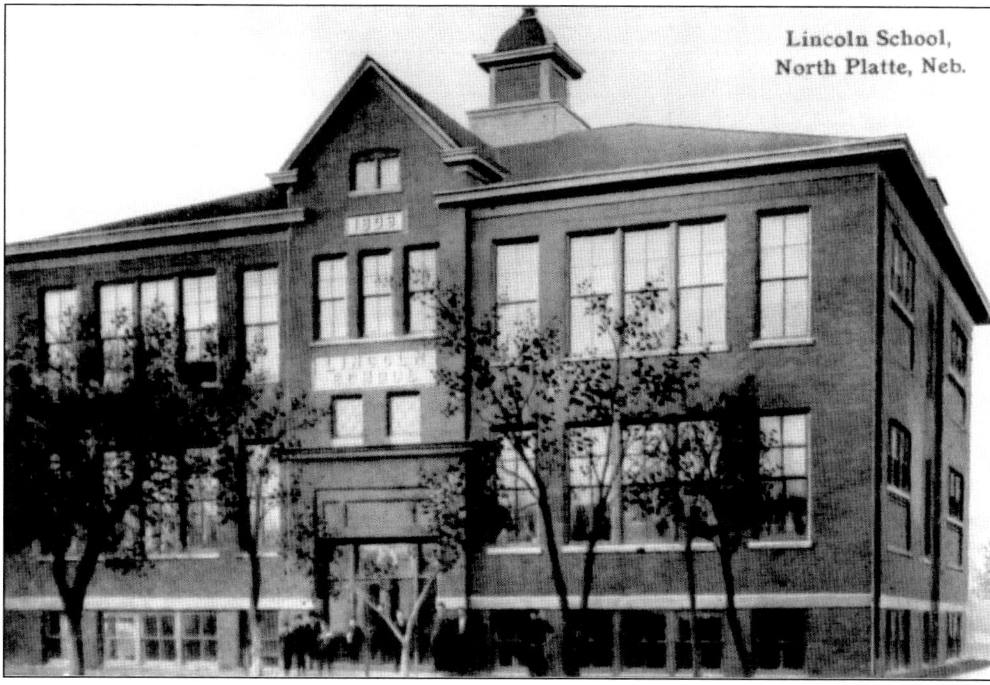

The Lincoln Elementary School, which was built in 1909, was located at 200 West Ninth Street.

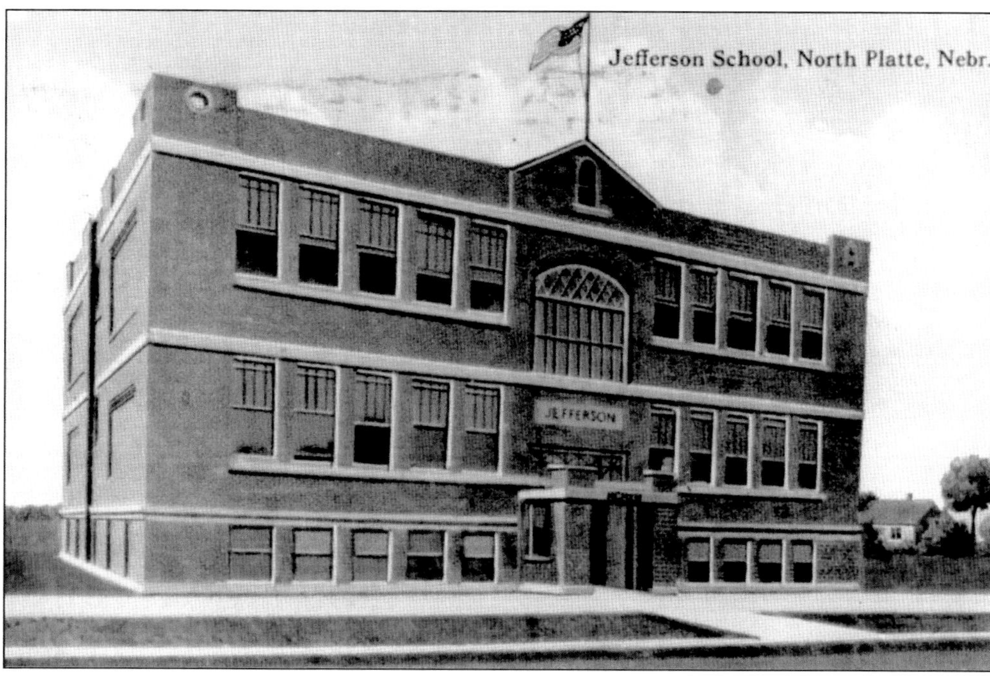

Built in 1914, the Jefferson Elementary School was located at 700 East Third Street.

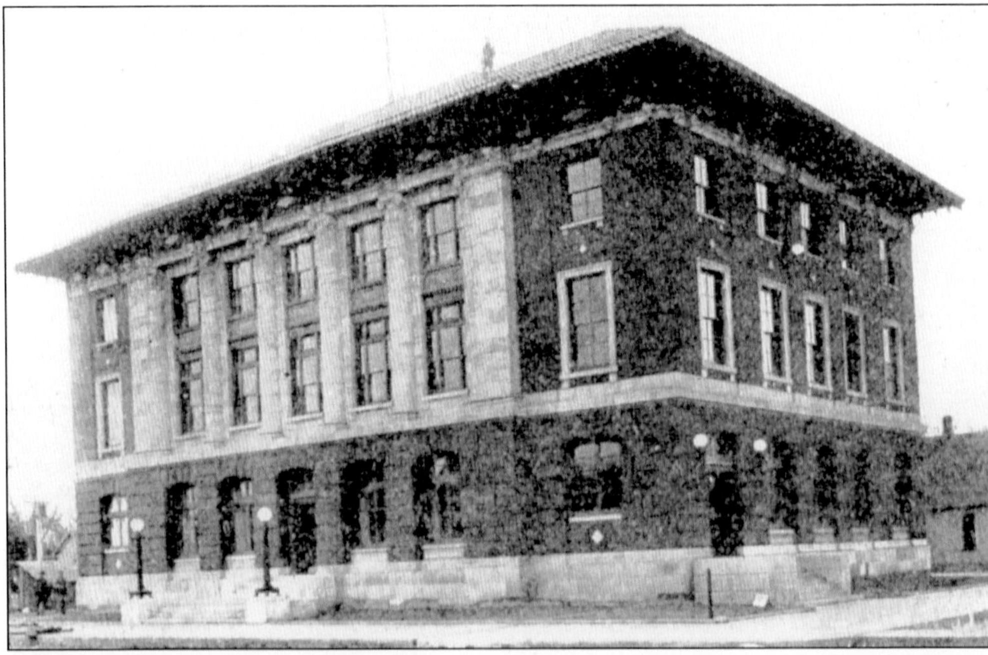

Built in 1913, at a total cost of $110,000, the U.S. Federal Building sat between Fourth and Fifth Streets on North Locust (Jeffers).

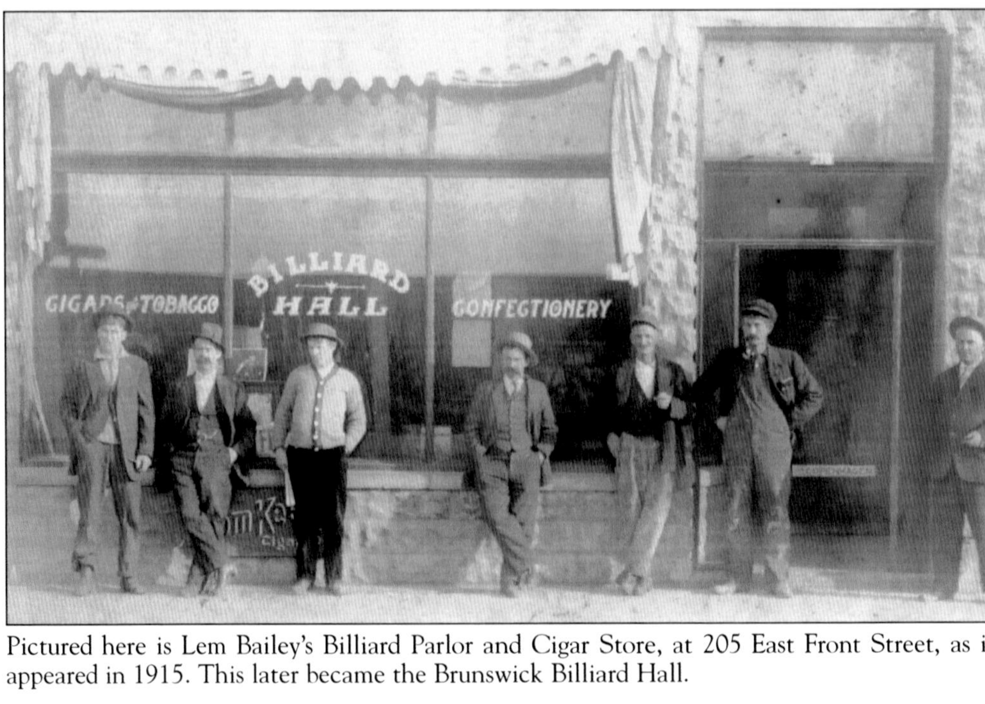

Pictured here is Lem Bailey's Billiard Parlor and Cigar Store, at 205 East Front Street, as it appeared in 1915. This later became the Brunswick Billiard Hall.

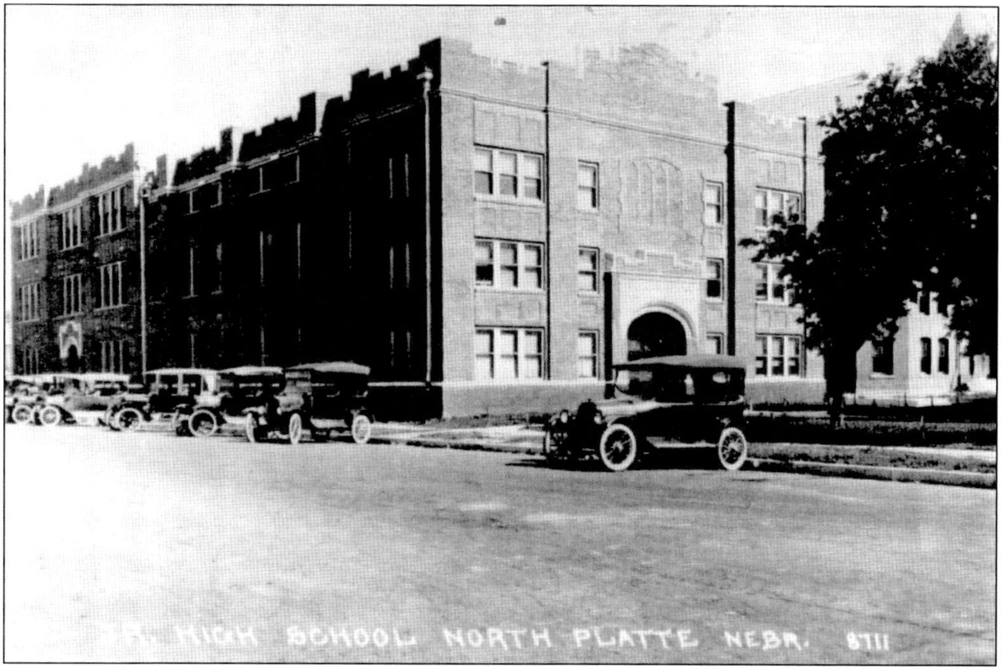

The Franklin Junior High School, pictured here, was built in 1917 at Fourth and Dewey Streets.

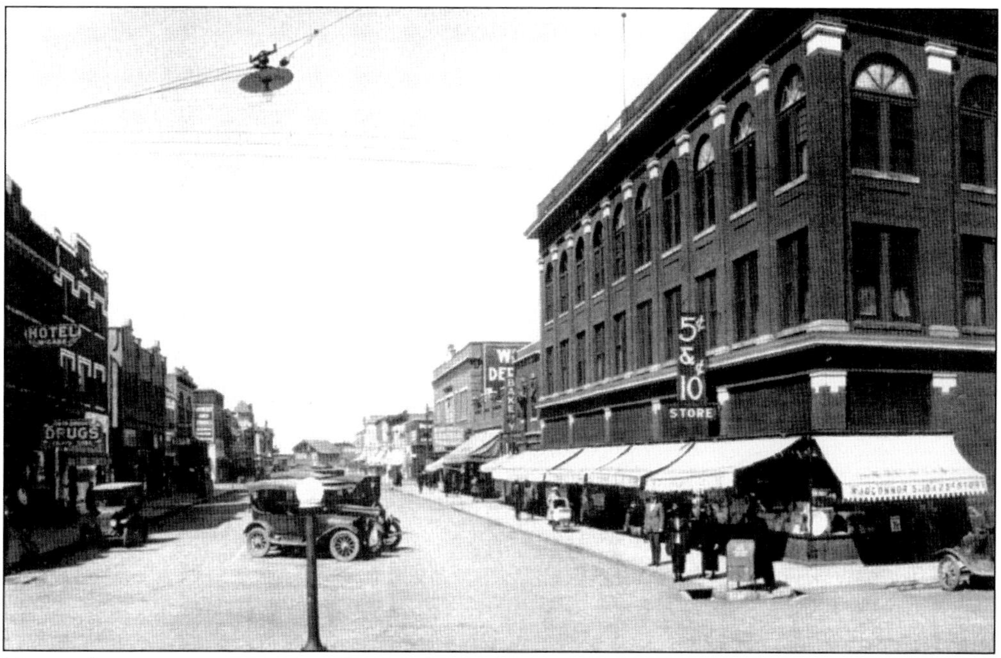

Various businesses operated on Dewey Street, near East Fourth. They include the O'Connor Five and Dime Store at 401 North Dewey; the Hendy-Ogier Auto Company at 402 North Dewey; the Nyal Drug Store, managed by Charles Tighe; The Hotel McCabe, managed by C.O. Weingard; the Model Bakery, managed by C.H. Stamp; W.R. Maloney, undertaker; the Keith Theatre, managed by R.A. Garman; the Wilcox Department Store, managed by J.Q. Wilcox, and the Platte Valley Bank, where F.C. Pielsticker served as President.

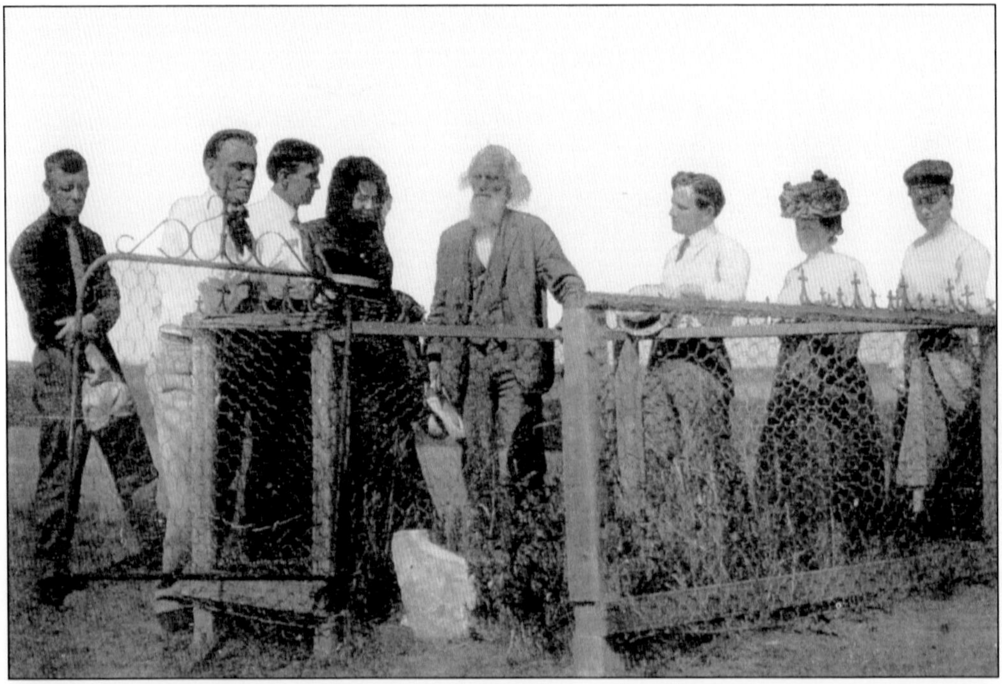

This photograph, taken in 1910, captures Ezra Meeker as he addresses a group at a lone grave on the Oregon Trail. He traveled the Oregon Trail with a team of oxen and a dog. The dog was named Jim and the oxen were Dave and Dandy.

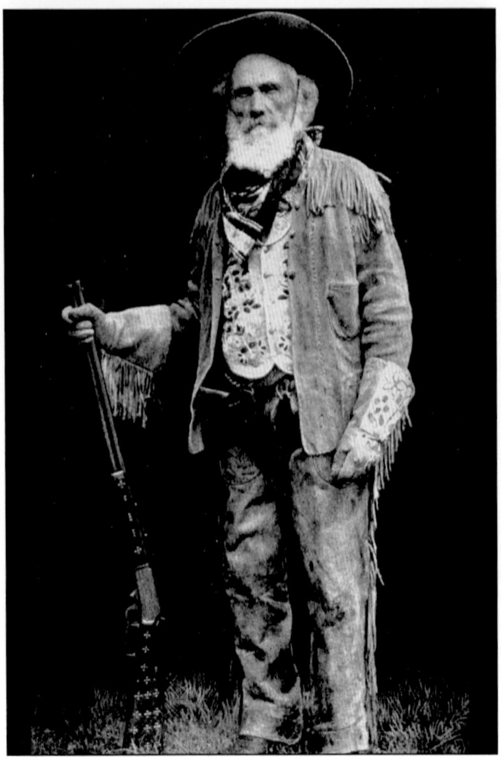

This photograph of Ezra Meeker in 1910 was taken south of North Platte on the Oregon Trail. He followed the Oregon Trail from Missouri to Oregon starting in 1906.

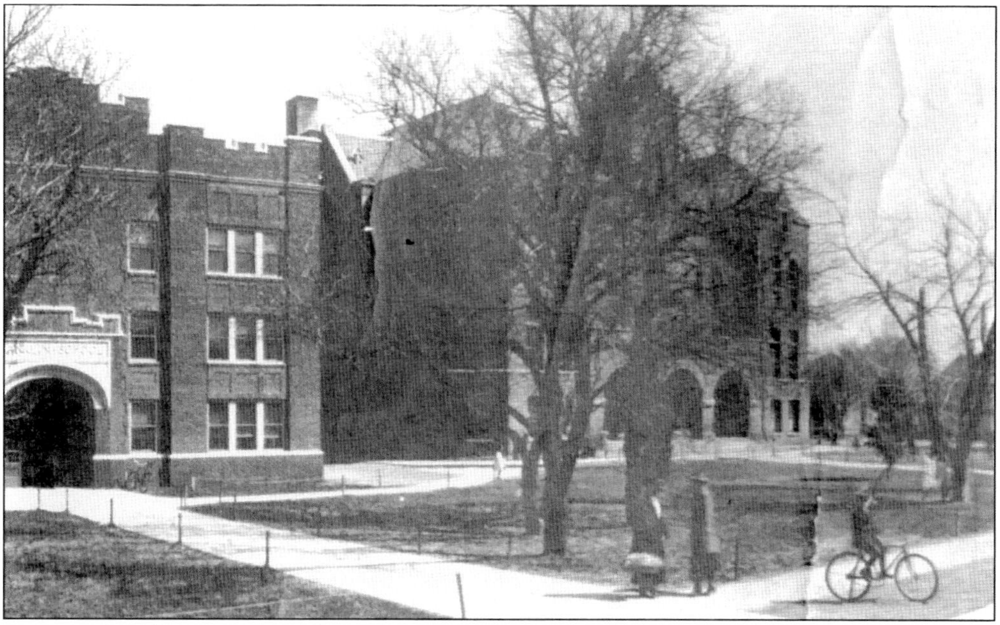

Here are Franklin Junior High and North Platte Senior High as they appeared in 1917. Both schools were located between Third and Fourth Streets on North Dewey.

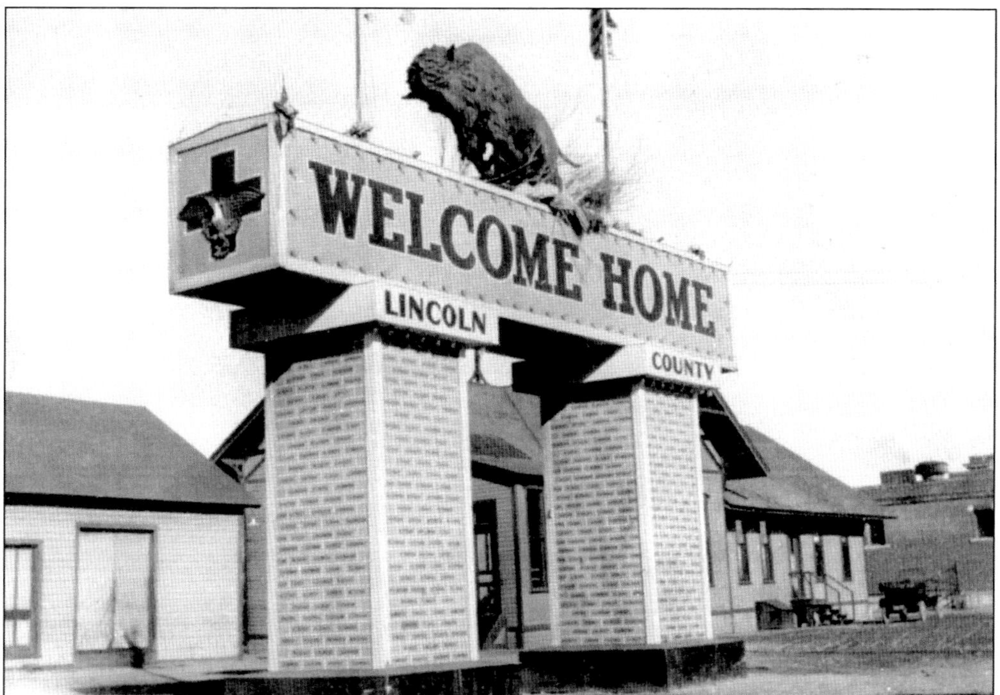

This picture, dated January 21, 1919, was taken just east of the new depot, which was built in 1917. The welcome home sign, between the 300 and 400 blocks of East Front Street, was for soldiers returning from World War I. A new park was installed here after the buildings were removed.

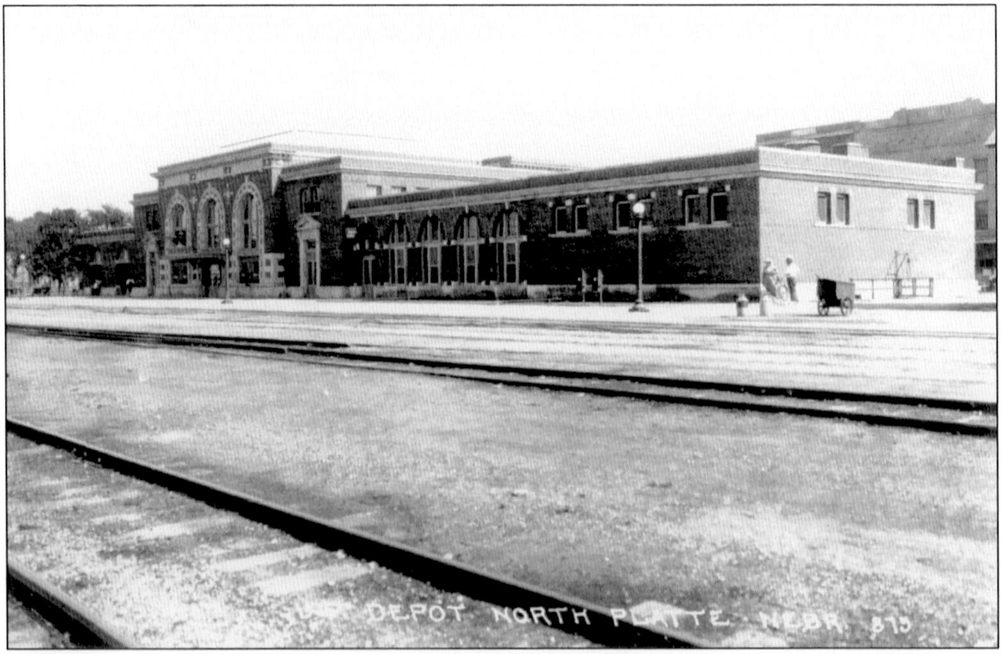

Pictured here is the north side of the new Union Pacific Depot, as it appeared in 1920.

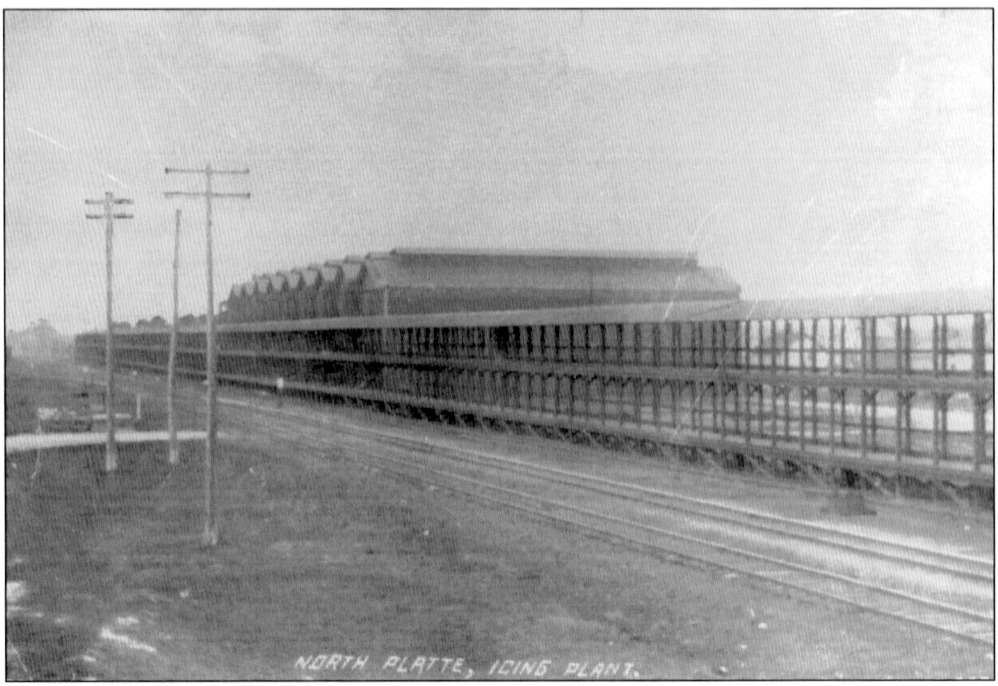

Ice was shipped in and stored at the Union Pacific icing plant, just west of Willow Street, to ice-down refrigerator cars.

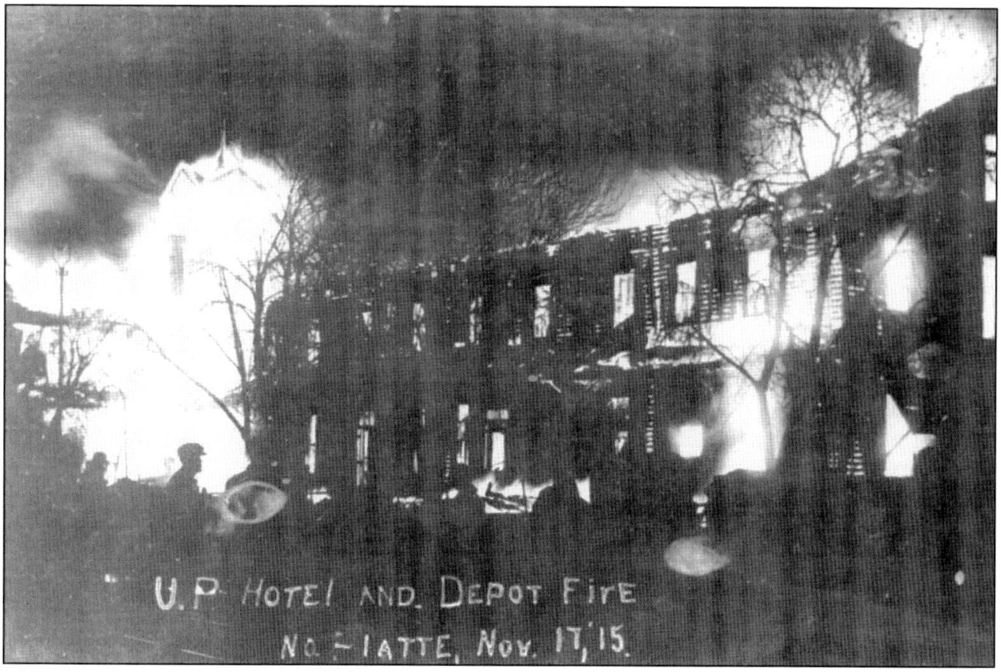

The Union Pacific Depot and Hotel, built in 1869, burned to the ground on November 17, 1915.

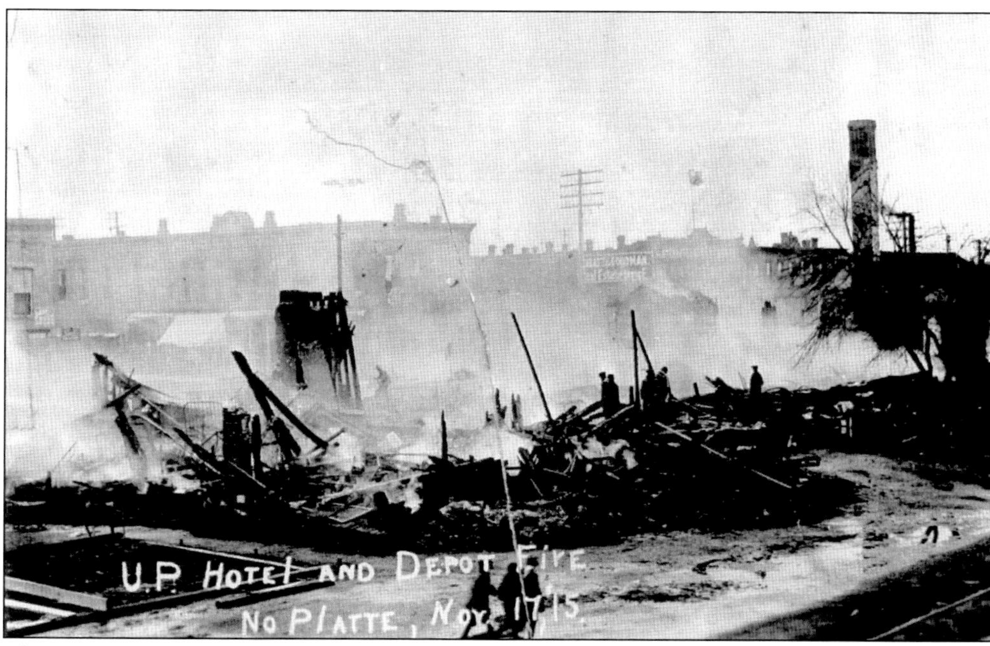

The Union Pacific Depot and Hotel was completely destroyed by the fire of 1915.

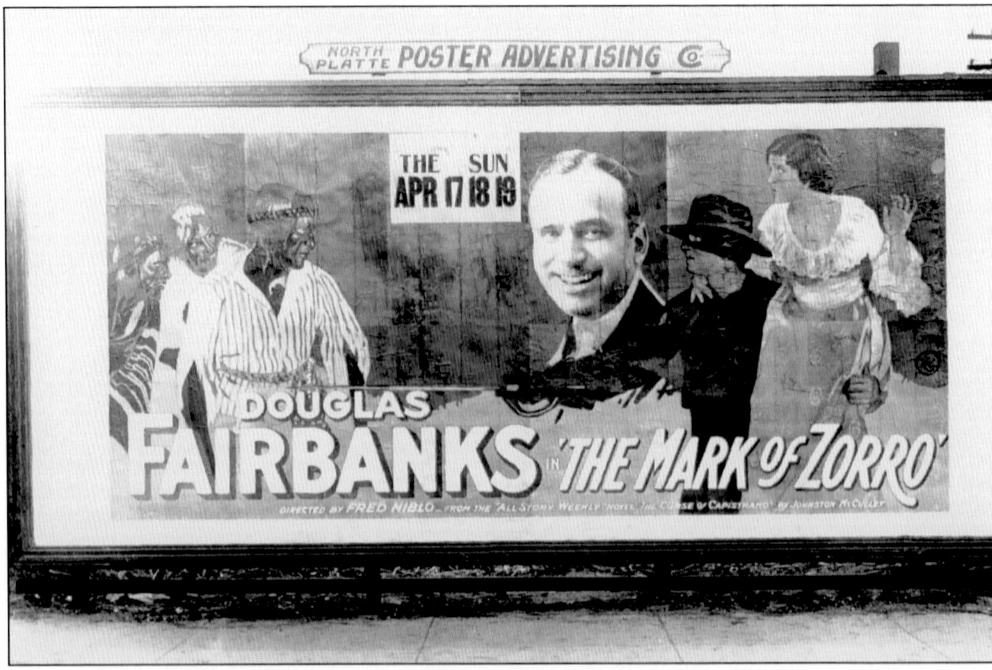

Pictured here is the southeast corner of Fifth and Vine Streets, as it appeared in 1920. It is now the parking lot of the Safeway store.

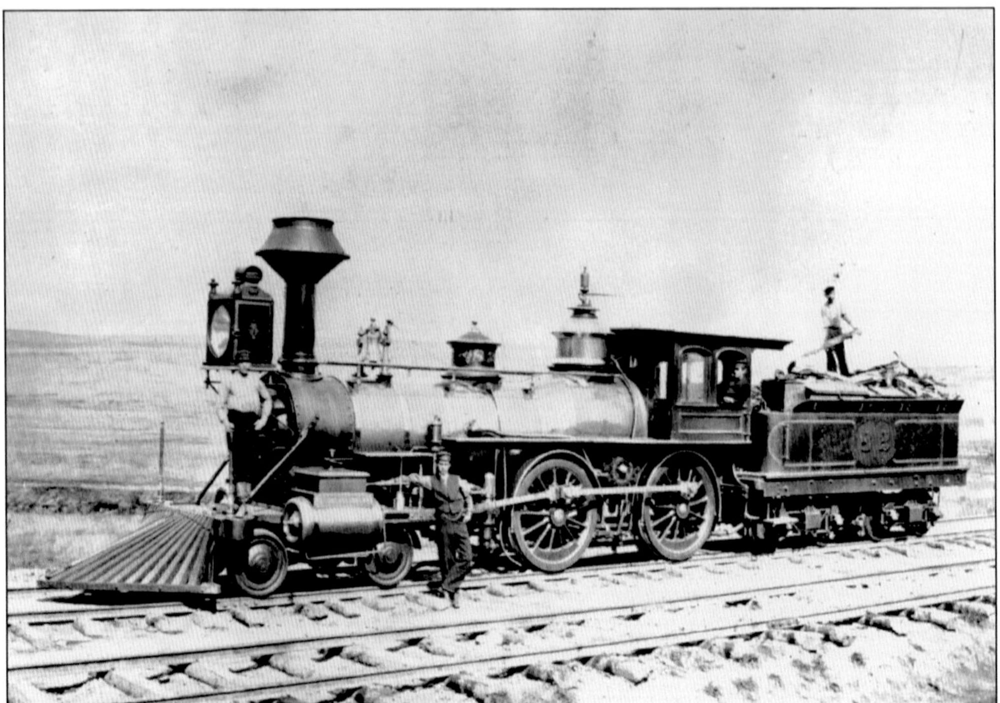

Engine #82 was built by Hinkley and Williams in 1868. The engine, which weighed only 54,000 pounds, was sold for scrap in 1903.

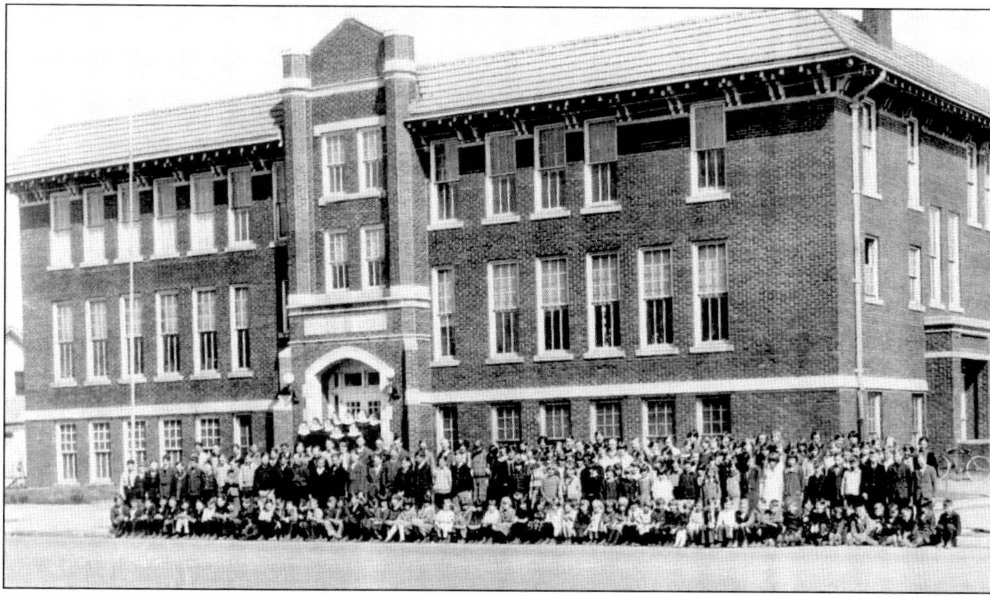

St. Patrick's School, which was located at 419 East Fourth Street, educated both grade school and high school students.

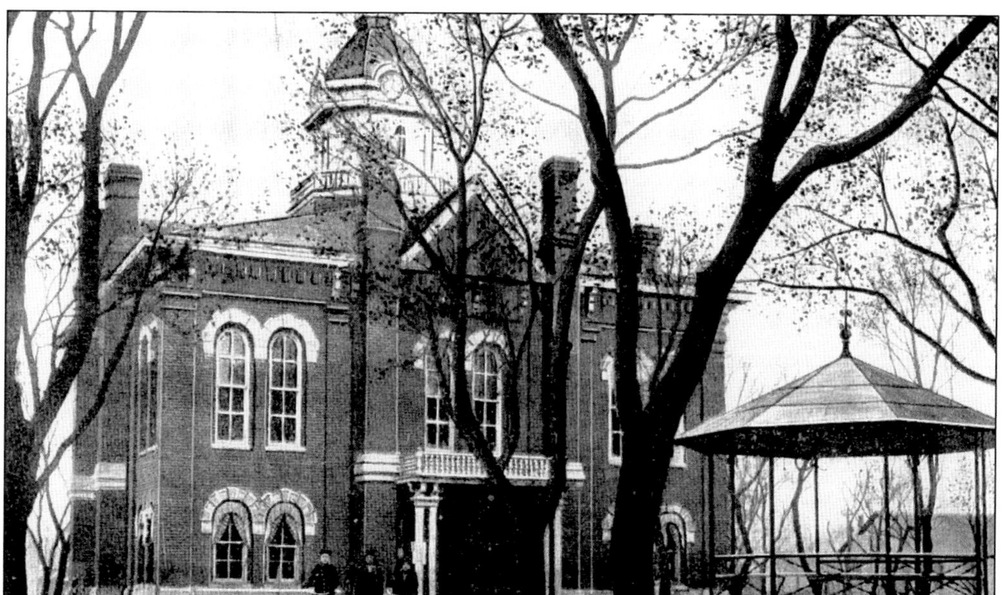

The Lincoln County Courthouse was built in 1876 and destroyed by fire in 1923. The gazebo in the front was moved to Cody park and used as a monkey cage. It has since disappeared. This photo was taken in 1920, just a few years before the courthouse burned down.

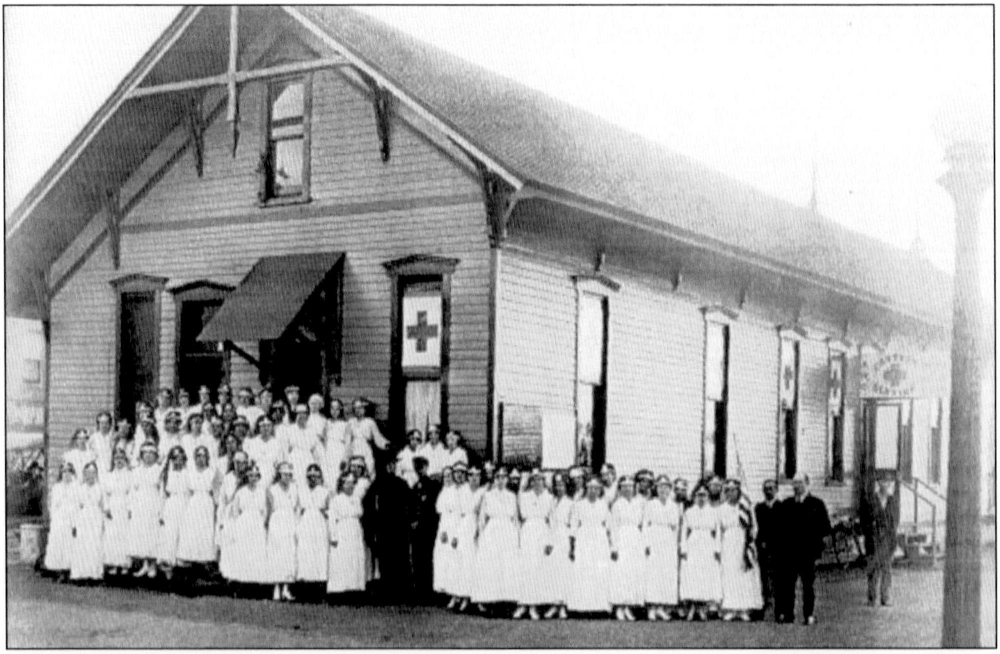

This photograph of the North Platte station and World War I Canteen was taken in 1919.

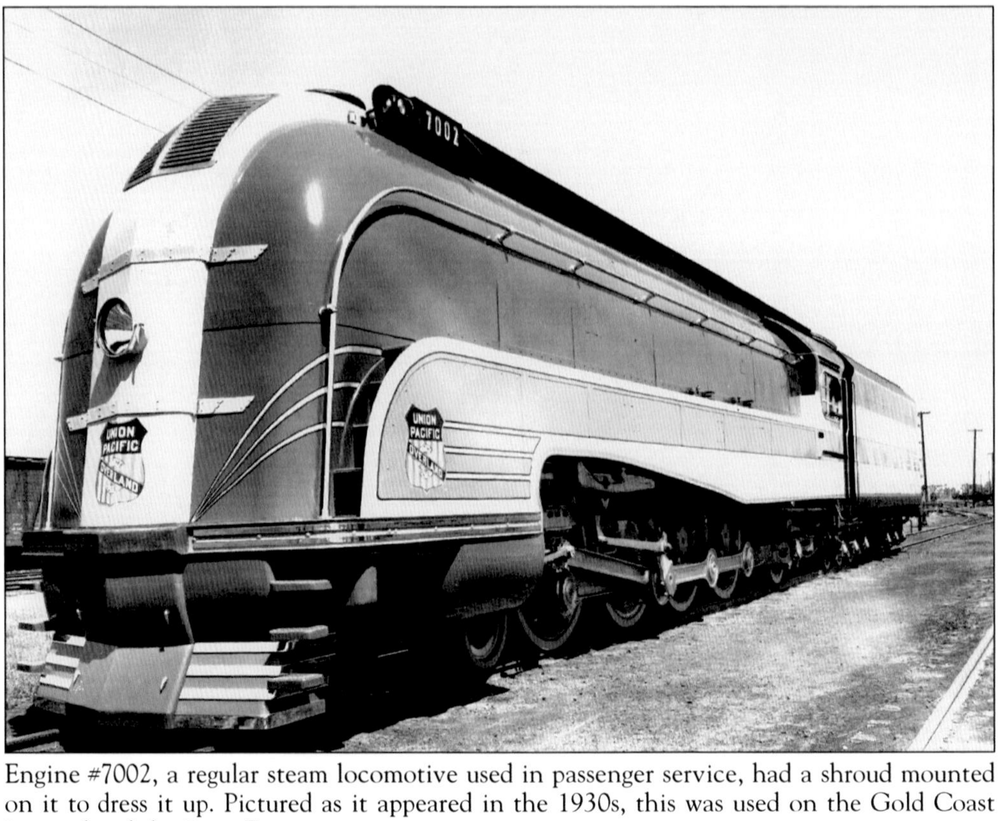

Engine #7002, a regular steam locomotive used in passenger service, had a shroud mounted on it to dress it up. Pictured as it appeared in the 1930s, this was used on the Gold Coast Limited and the Pony Express trains.

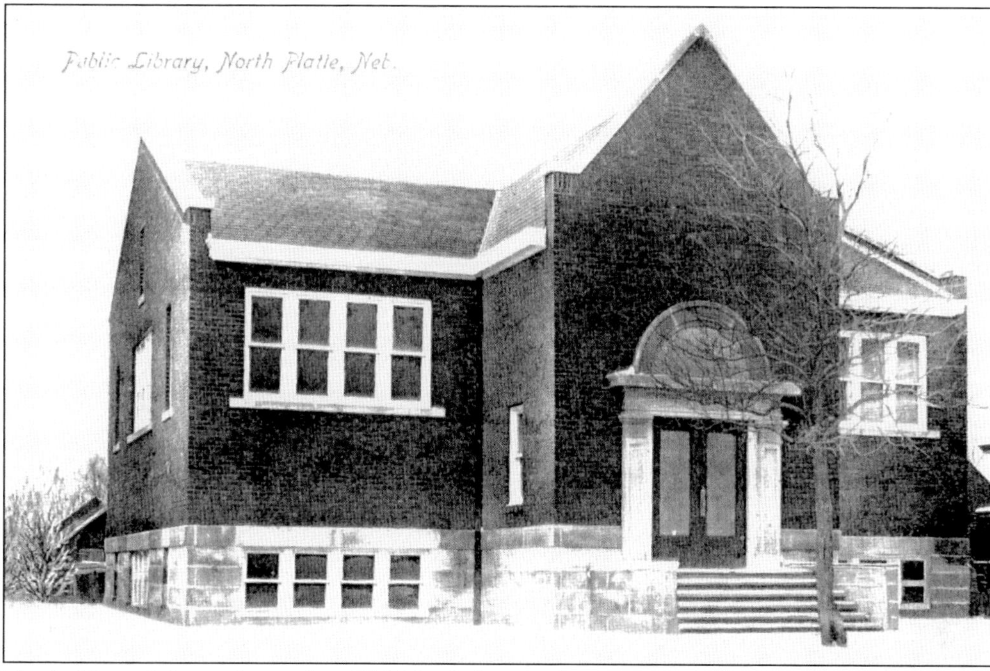

North Platte Library, located at 314 North Locust Street, is seen here as it appeared in the 1920s. The construction costs, which totaled $8,676.60, were donated by Andrew Carnegie. It was dedicated on April 4, 1912.

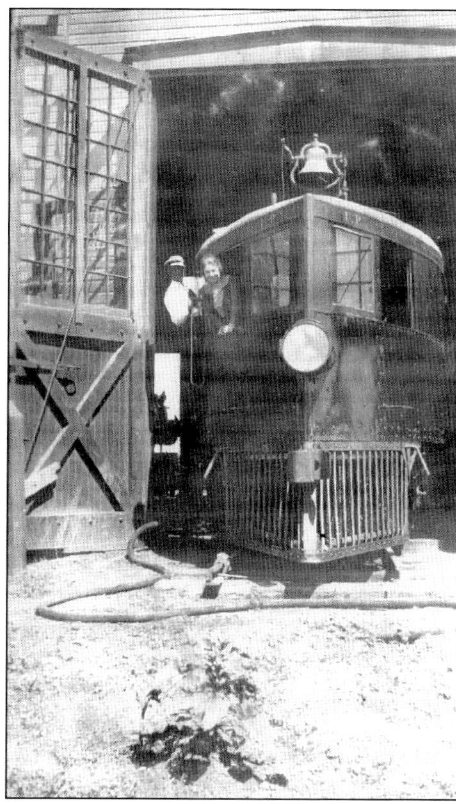

One of the early McKeon motor cars, purchased by the U.P. for service on branch lines, transported both passengers and freight. This photograph was taken in 1916.

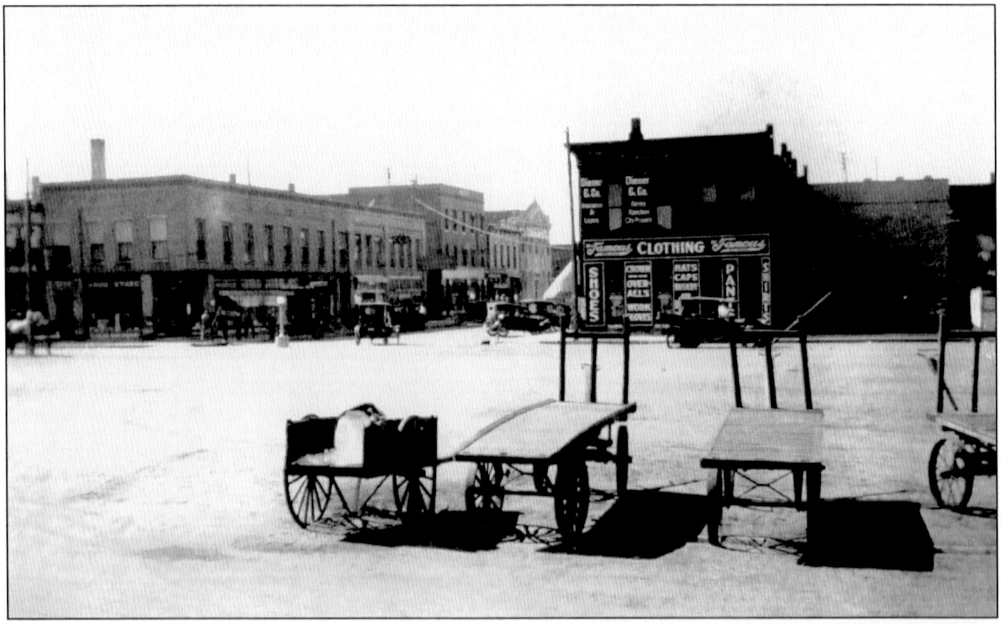

This is a glimpse of Dewey Street in 1921, as viewed from the U.P. parking lot on Front Street. The area thrived with local businesses, including the following: The Famous Clothing Store, at 622 North Dewey, run by Edmund and Dorothy Norton; the Fraters Drug Store, at the corner of Front and Dewey, run by George and Birdie Frater; Landgraf and Cantlin, barbers; the Rebhausen Barber Shop, owned by Mathias S. Rebhausen; the Silver Front Cigar Store, operated by Christ and Mary Paulson; the Edwards-Reynolds Clothing Store; the Western Union Telegraph and Telephone Company; the Carson Barber Shop, owned by Perry and Mary Carson; John Den Cigar and Sporting Goods, owned by John and Helen Den; and the First National Bank, where E.F. Seeberger served as President, and Ray Langford and Keith Neville served as Vice-Presidents.

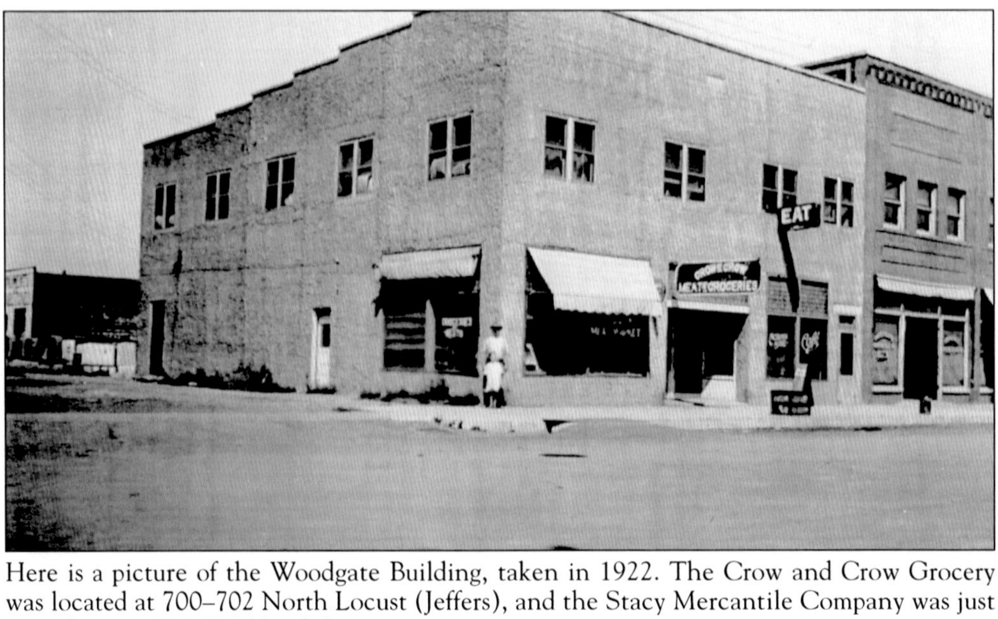

Here is a picture of the Woodgate Building, taken in 1922. The Crow and Crow Grocery was located at 700–702 North Locust (Jeffers), and the Stacy Mercantile Company was just next door, at 704–708 North Locust.

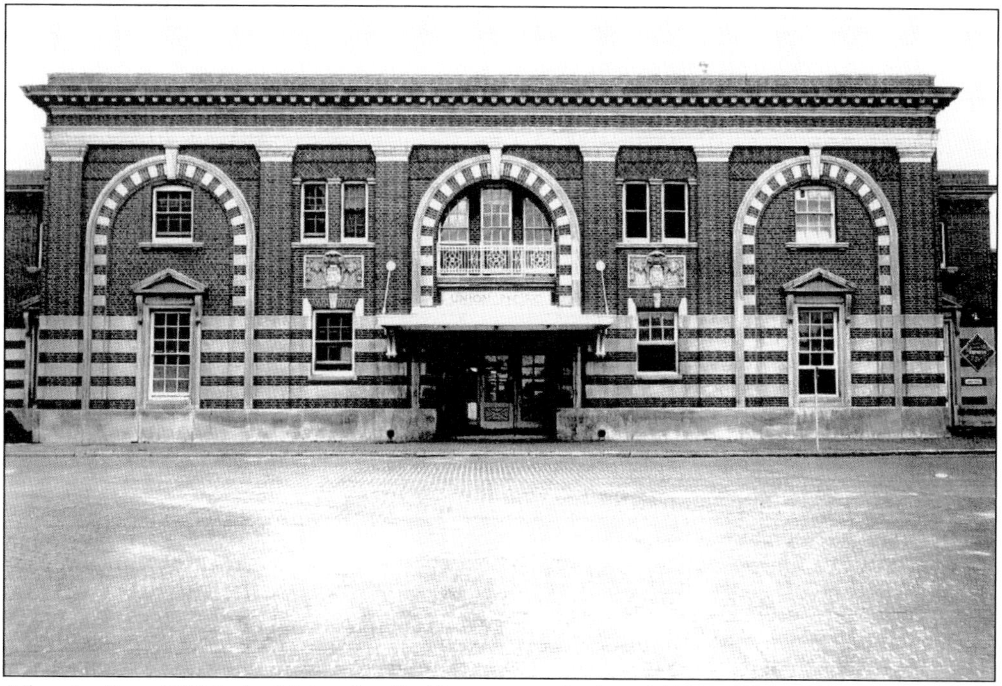

After the fire of 1915, the Union Pacific Depot was rebuilt at 300 East Front Street. This is how it appeared shortly after its construction, in 1917.

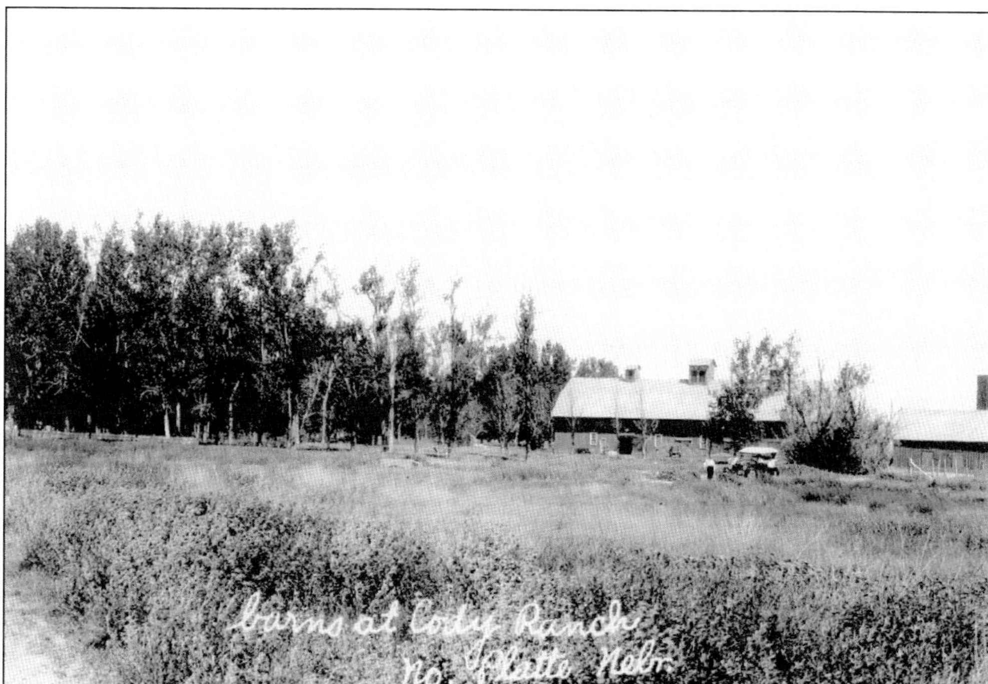

This is a view of the stock barn and the old T-barn at Scouts Rest Ranch. The T-barn burned down sometime in the late-1920s.

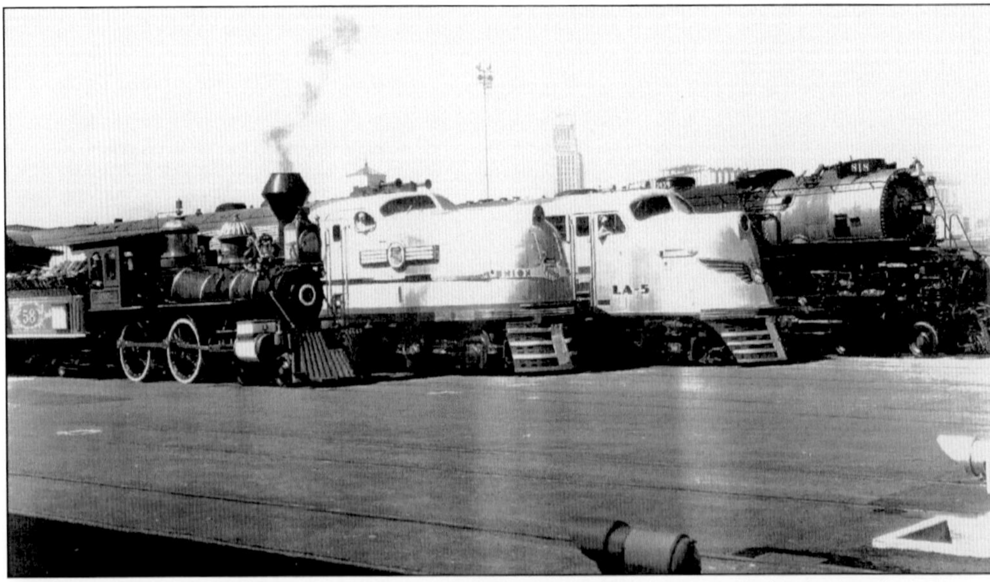

From the left is U.P. #58 (ex. Virginia and Truckee #18), originally built for the Central Pacific Railroad as its Dayton (original name), G.E. built steam turbine-electric #1 and #2, EMD E3 A/B LA 5 and LA 6, early Challenger 3939. Only the little 4-4-0 is now preserved at Carson City, Nevada. *c.* 1940.

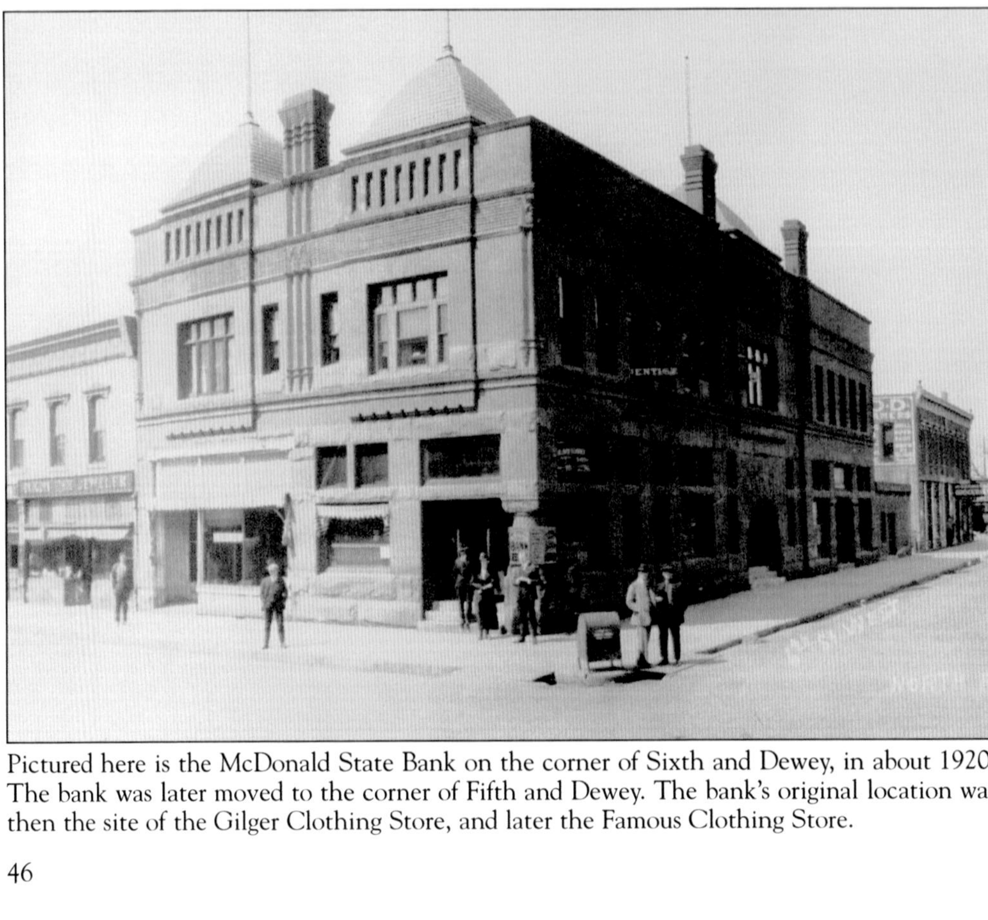

Pictured here is the McDonald State Bank on the corner of Sixth and Dewey, in about 1920. The bank was later moved to the corner of Fifth and Dewey. The bank's original location was then the site of the Gilger Clothing Store, and later the Famous Clothing Store.

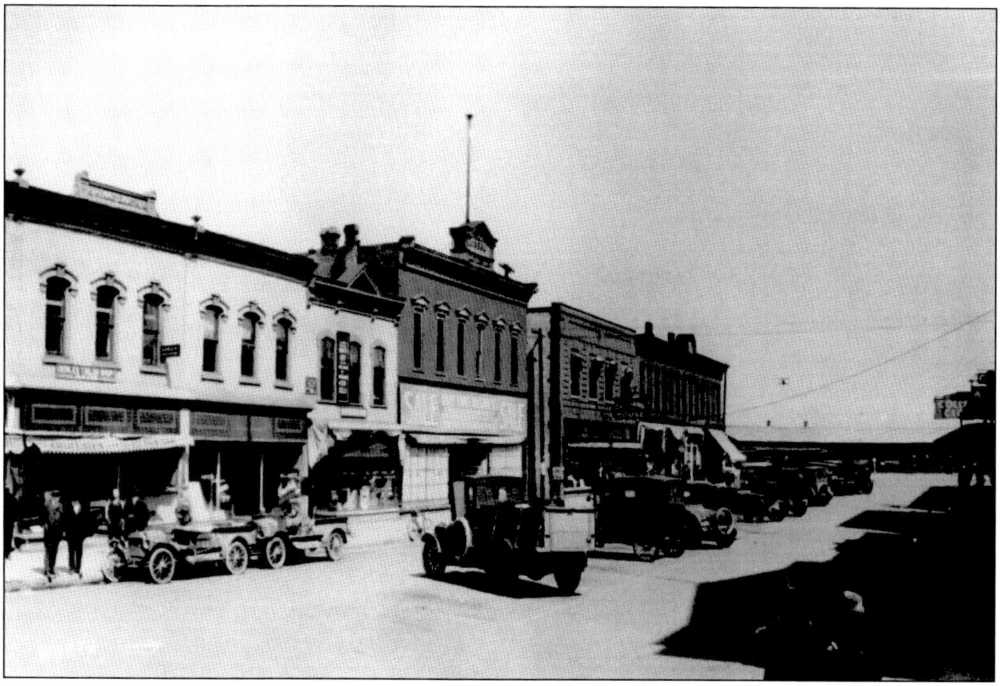

From the west side of 600 block of North Dewey, the Waltemath Building is in left foreground. This photograph was taken in 1920.

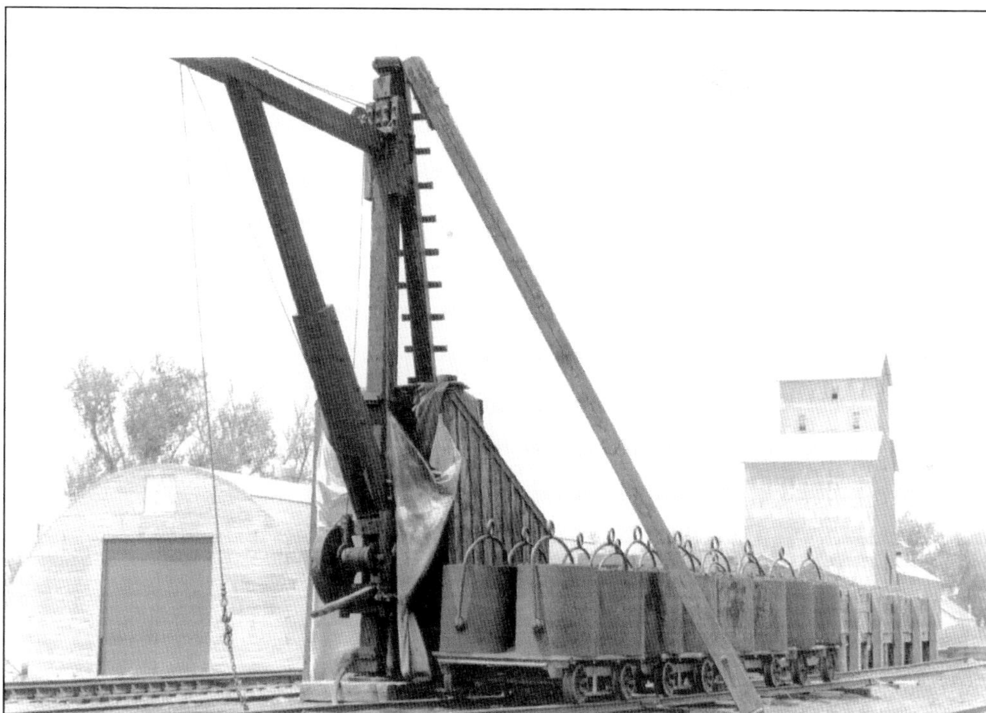

Taken in Lewellan, Nebraska, on May 19, 1956, this photo depicts a steam engine coal loading station. An air hose was hooked to the engine and air was used to lift the coal buckets.

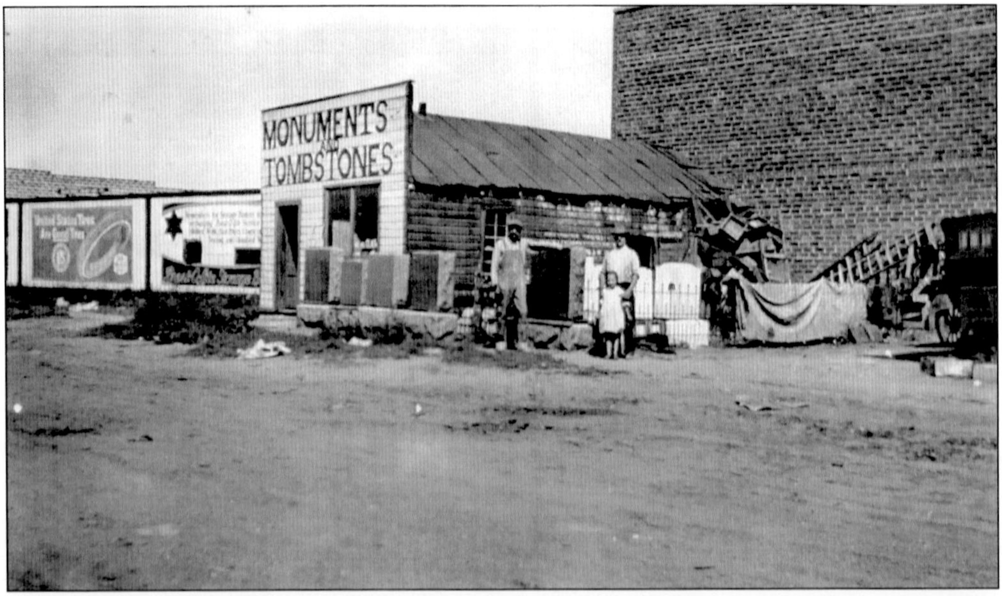

This picture of Woodgate and Abernathy Monuments and Tombstones, located at 111 West Seventh Street, was taken in 1922.

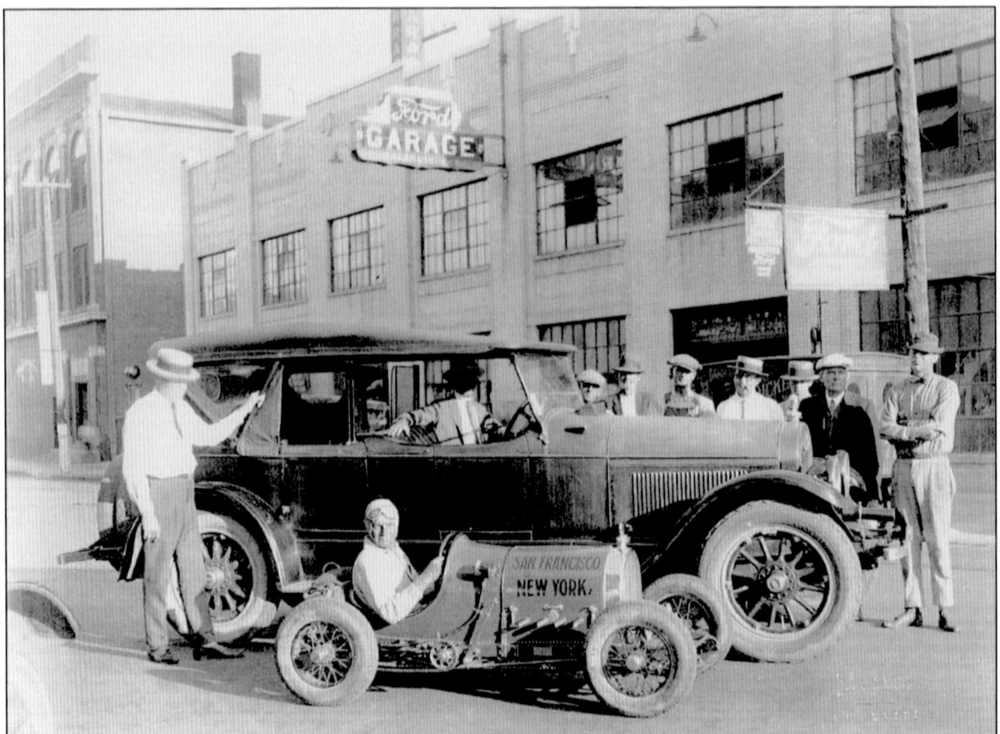

William Hendy sat in his new Lincoln in front of the Ford garage on the 200 block of East Fourth Street, in about 1924.

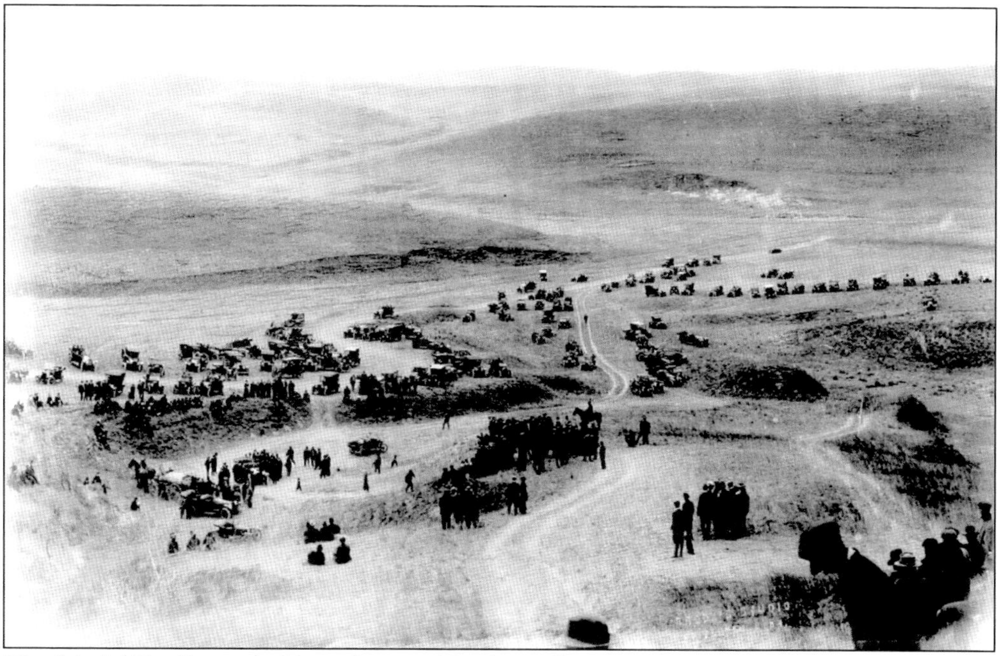

This Model T rally was held southwest of Dodge Hill, or southwest of the State Experimental Station, in about 1925.

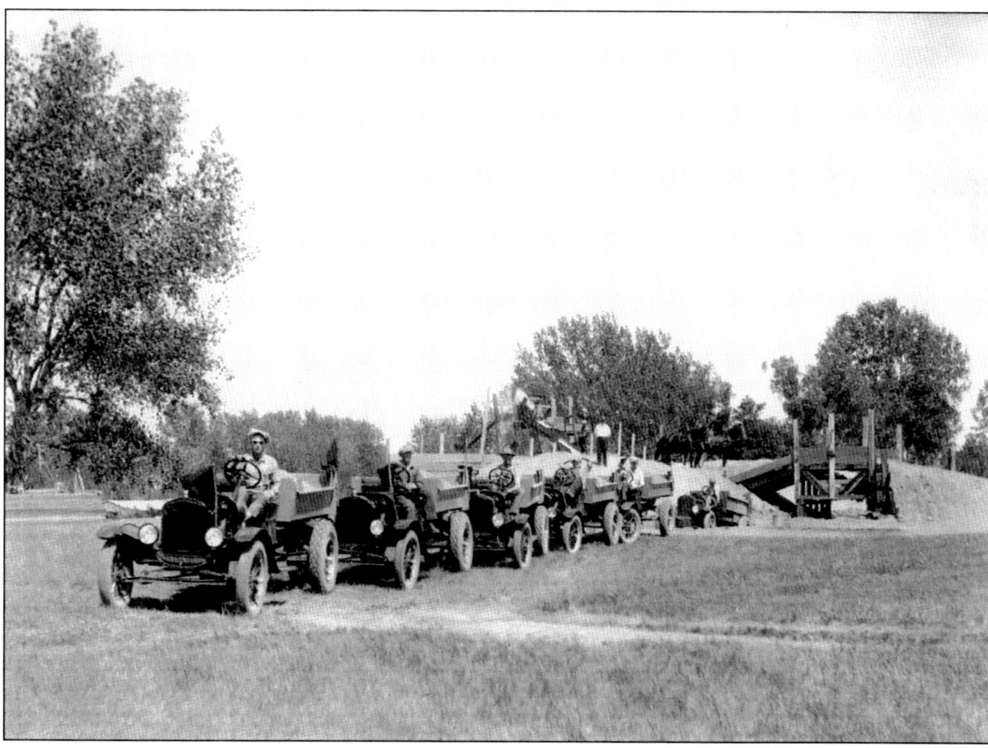

In 1926, the Edward Walker Construction Company was located at 1503 East Fifth Street.

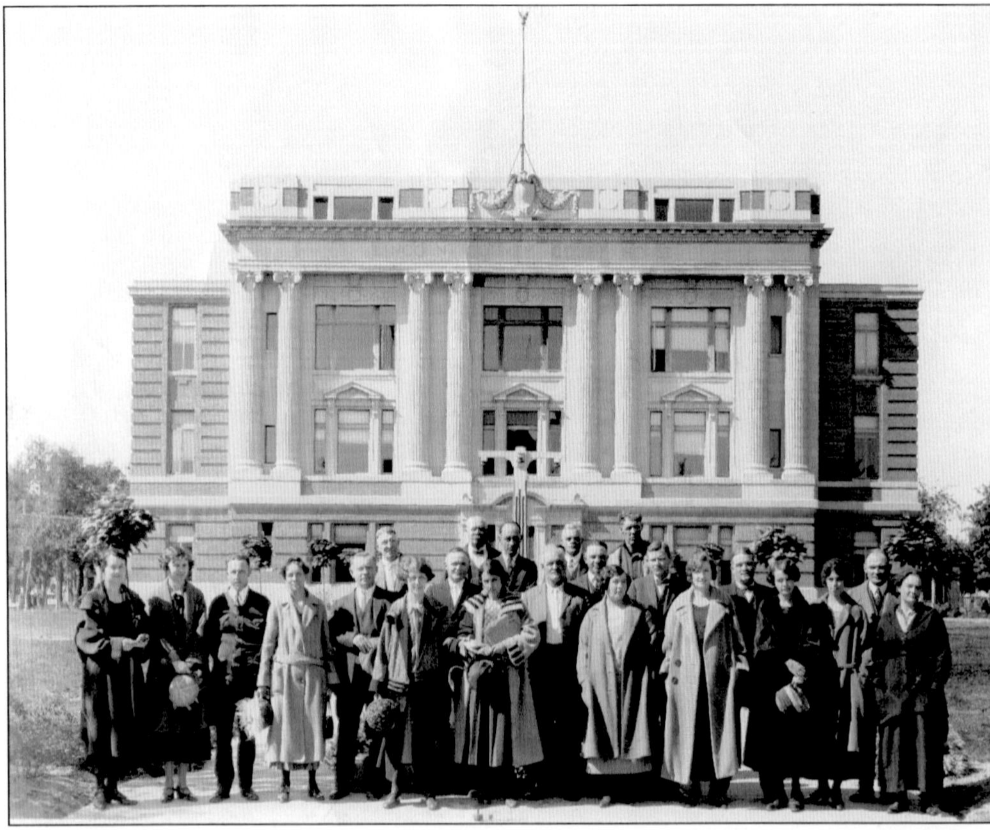

Although most of the people pictured here are not identified, we do know that this photograph of the east side of the new courthouse was taken in 1926.

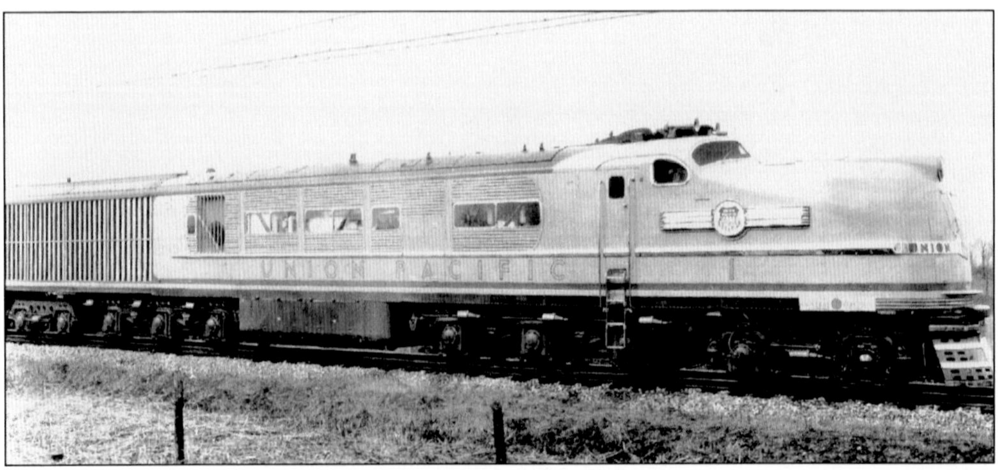

This is a 1939 picture of the steam turbine electric locomotive #1. Movie stars Barbara Stanwyck and Joel McCrae were aboard when the engine was used to pull a special train to North Platte for the premiere of the movie "Union Pacific." The engine itself was not successful and was subsequently returned to the manufacturer.

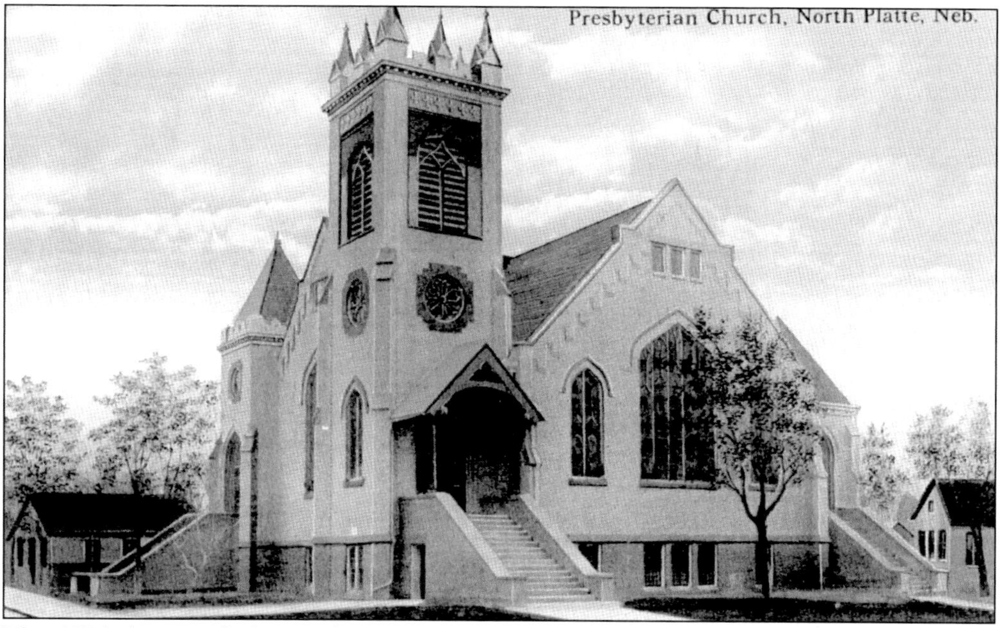

This 1926 photograph depicts the new Presbyterian Church at 321 West Fourth Street.

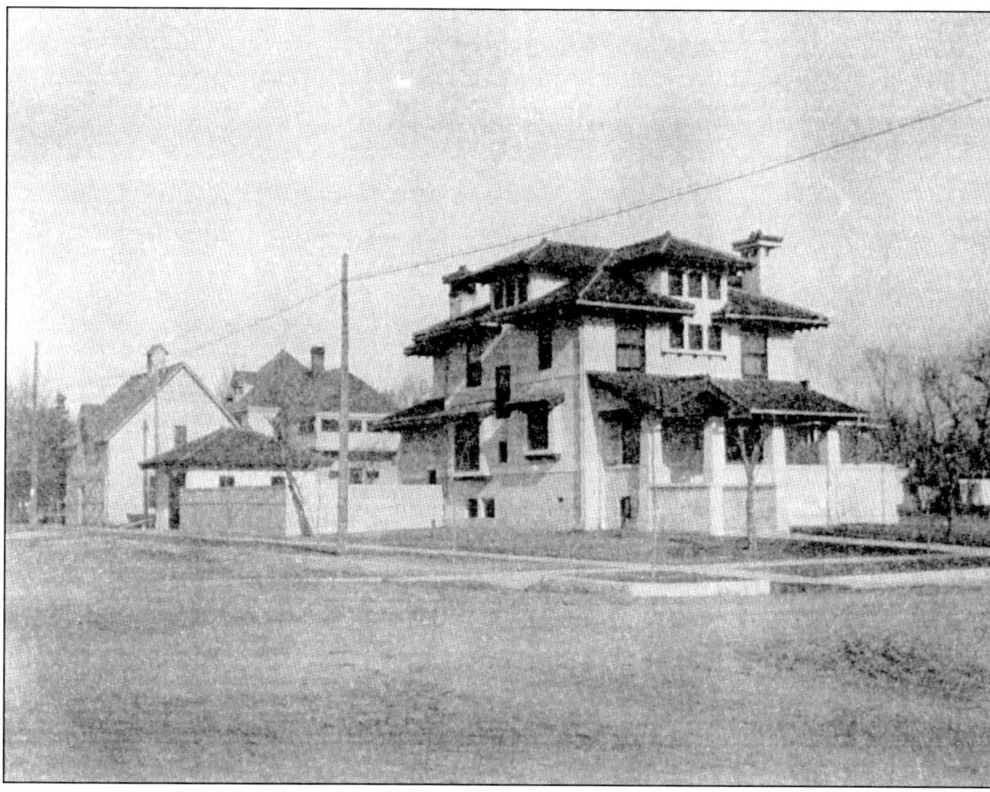

Governor Keith Neville's home at 421 West Fourth Street is now the site of the Adams and Swanson Funeral Home. The photograph is dated 1926.

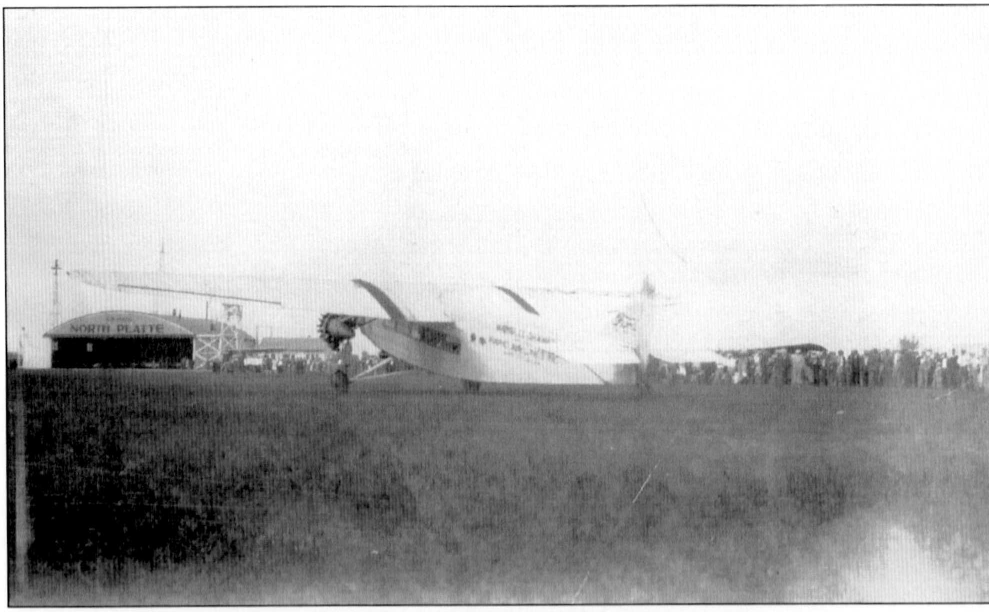

At the time this photograph was taken, in 1928, the North Platte Airport was located two miles east of North Platte. Charles A. Slieder served as airport manager. The airport was served by the U.S. Air Mail Boeing Air Transport Company. Pictured is a Ford Tri-Motor.

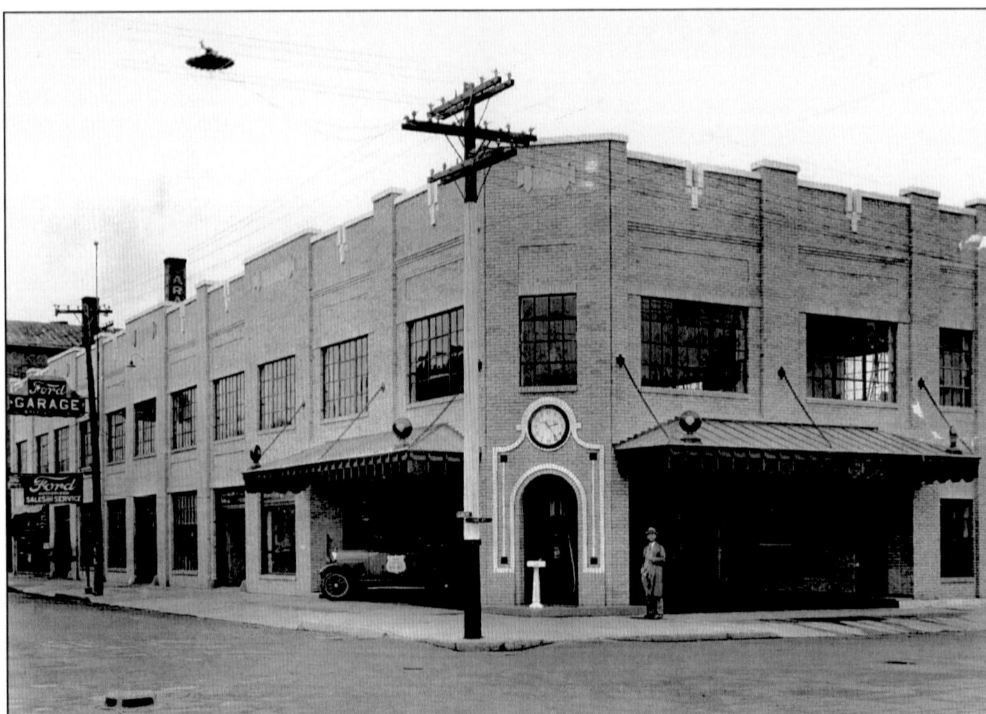

In 1928, the Hendy-Ogier Ford Agency was located on the corner of East Fourth and Pine Streets. William Hendy stood on the corner. It is now the site of the Whittaker Furniture Company.

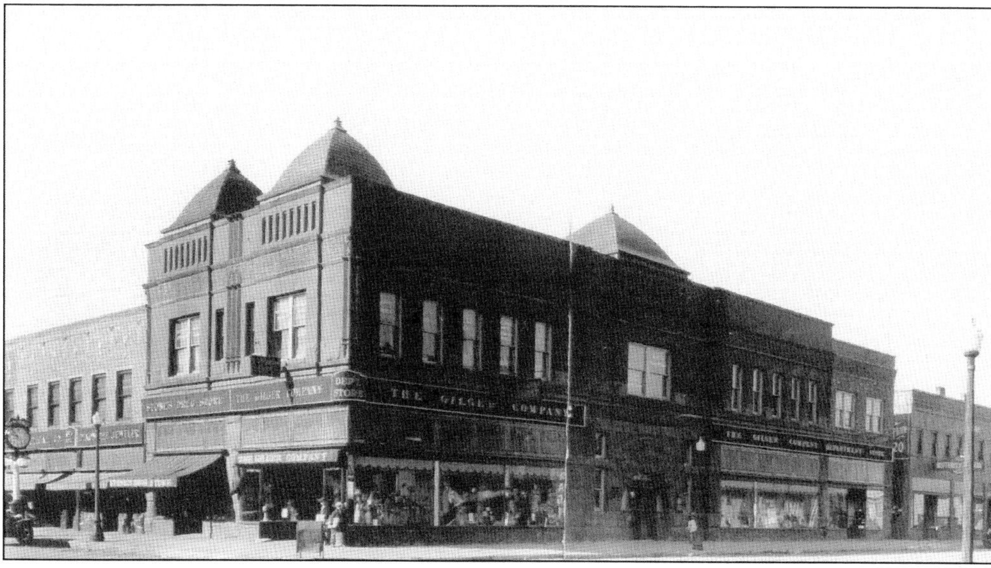

The Gilger Company at 622 North Dewey, pictured here in 1929, was owned and operated by Harry C. and Amy V. Gilger. Before housing the Gilgers' store, this was the site of the McDonald State Bank. After the Gilgers' store closed, it became The Famous Clothing Store. It is now Morgan's Sew and Vac.

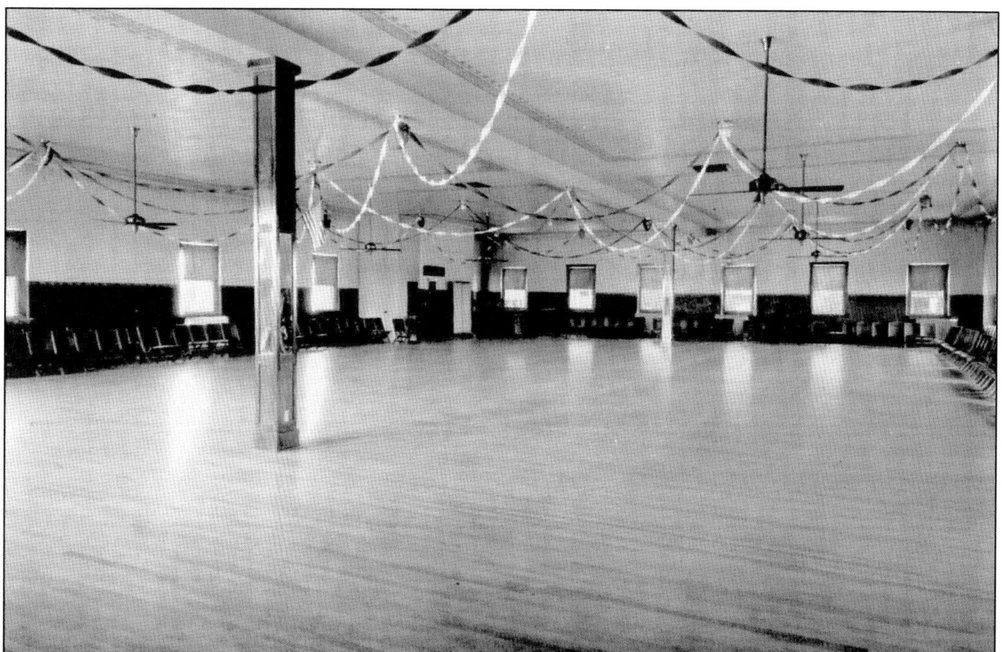

Dickey's Dreamland Ballroom, at 116 1/2 West Sixth Street, was managed by Robert R. Dickey. The location later housed the Recreation Bowling Lanes. This photograph was taken in 1929.

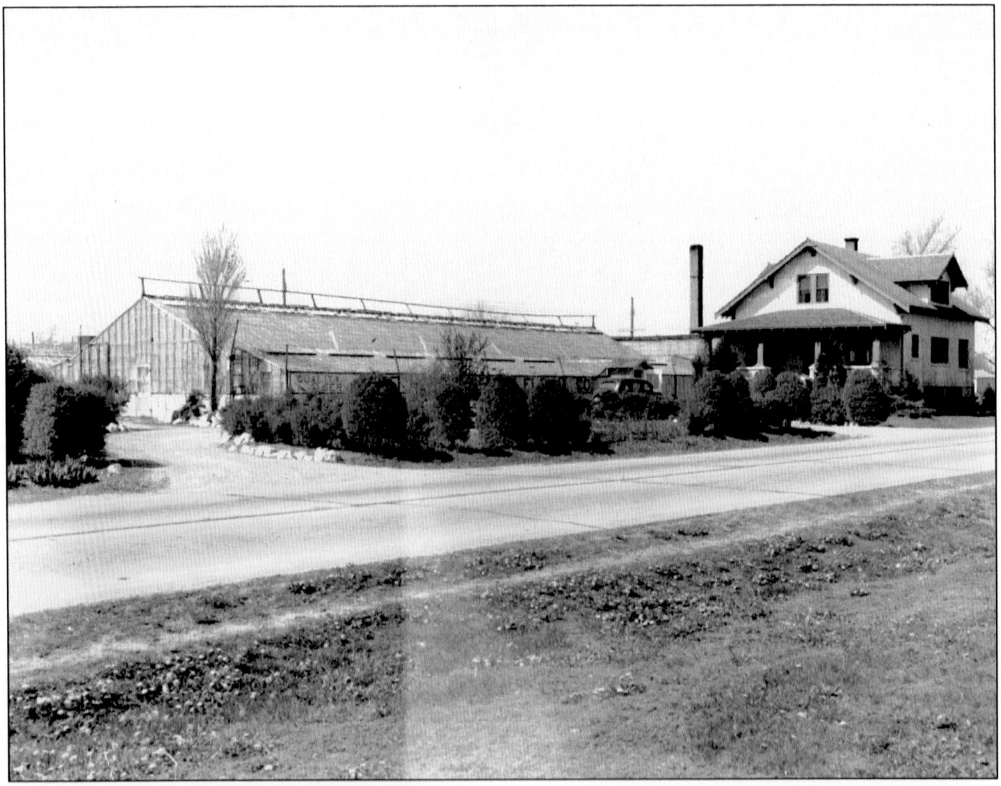

The North Platte Floral Company, pictured in this 1929 photograph at 1016 West Twelfth Street, was owned and operated by Emil and Helen Merscheid.

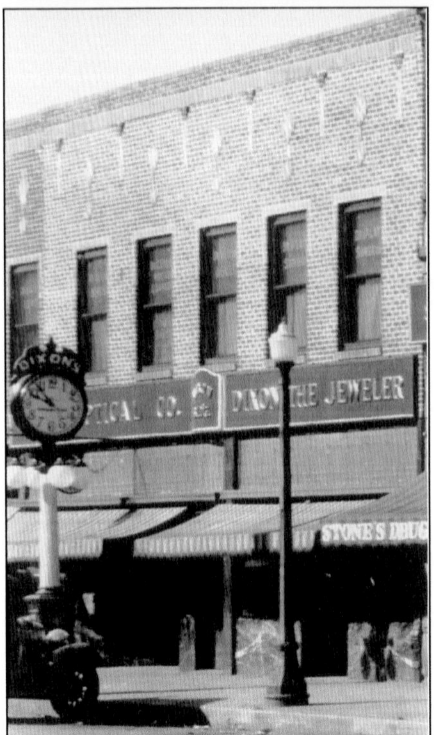

Harry and Clara Dixon ran the Dixon Jewelry Store, located at 518 North Dewey.

The North Platte Bakery, famous for its Butterfly bread, sat at 110 East Sixth Street. Tolle and Seiler were the bakery's proprietors. This photo was taken in 1929.

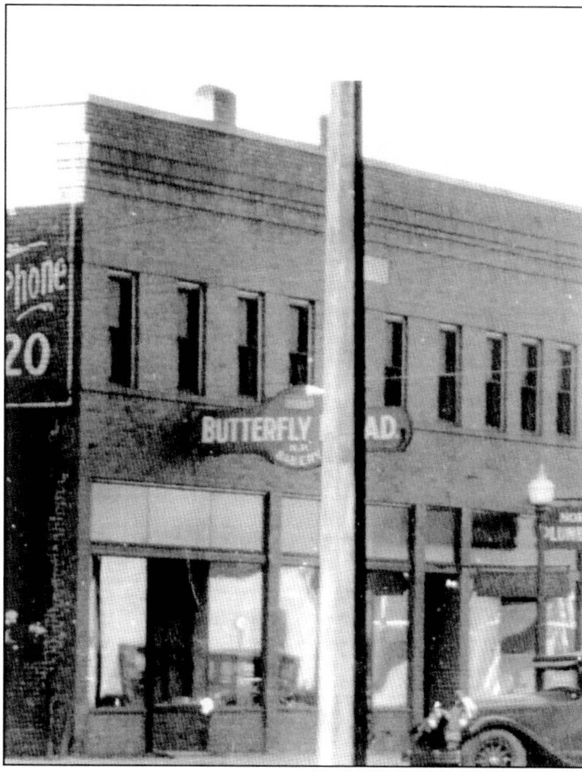

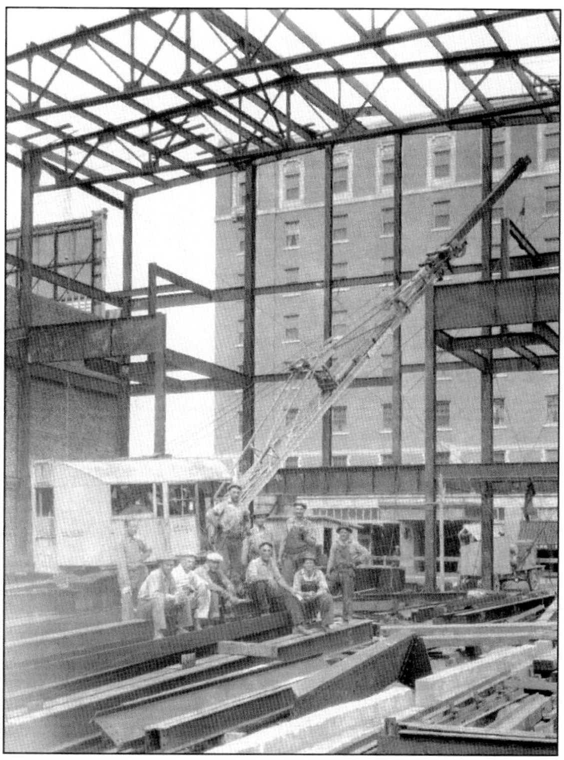

The Edward Walker Construction Company began building the Paramount Theatre in 1930. Notice the Yancy Hotel across the street, now named the Pawnee Hotel.

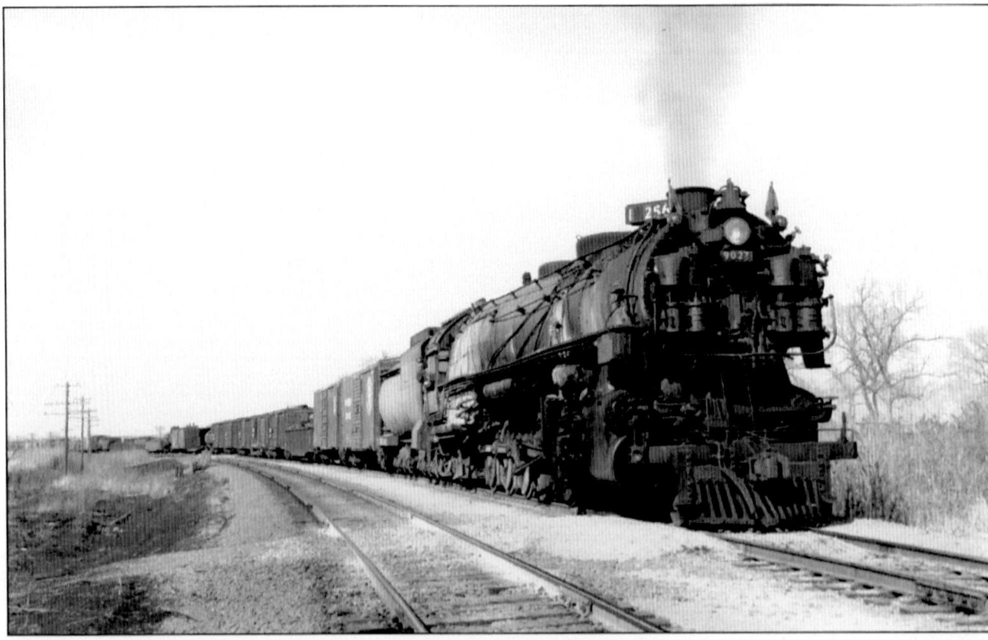

The U.P. #9027 steam locomotive, which featured a class 4-12-2 wheel arrangement, was a rare three-cylinder locomotive rated at 4500 HP. Union Pacific had hundreds of these; they served as the main workhorse for freight service. This picture was taken in 1926.

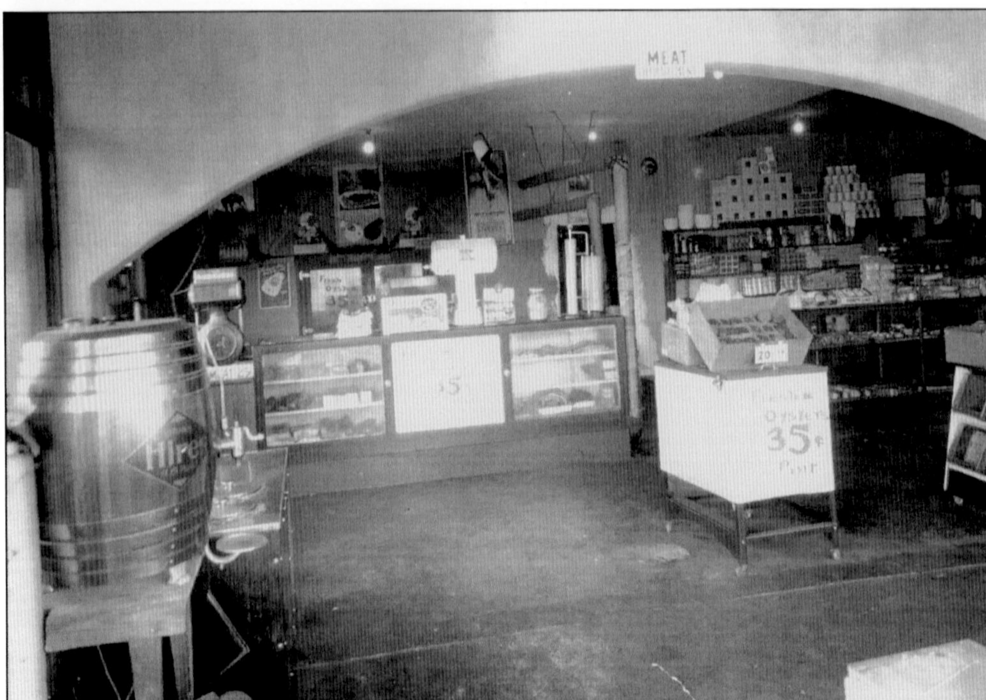

Gambles' Grocery, located at 823 North Locust (Jeffers), was owned by Edward A. and Loretta S. Gamble. This is how the store appeared in 1932. It later became Lyons' IGA, and it is now the City Discount Liquor.

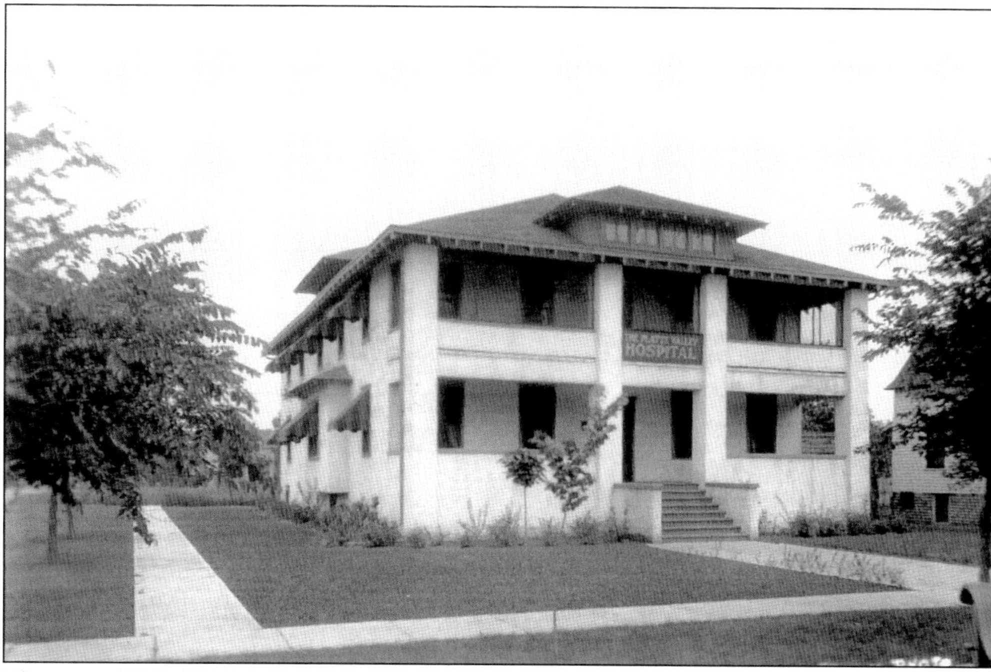

This is a 1930 photograph of the Platte Valley Hospital at 515 West Fifth Street. Otis R. Platte served as chief surgeon for many years. Later named the General Hospital, it closed on September 28, 1938. It is now the site of an apartment building.

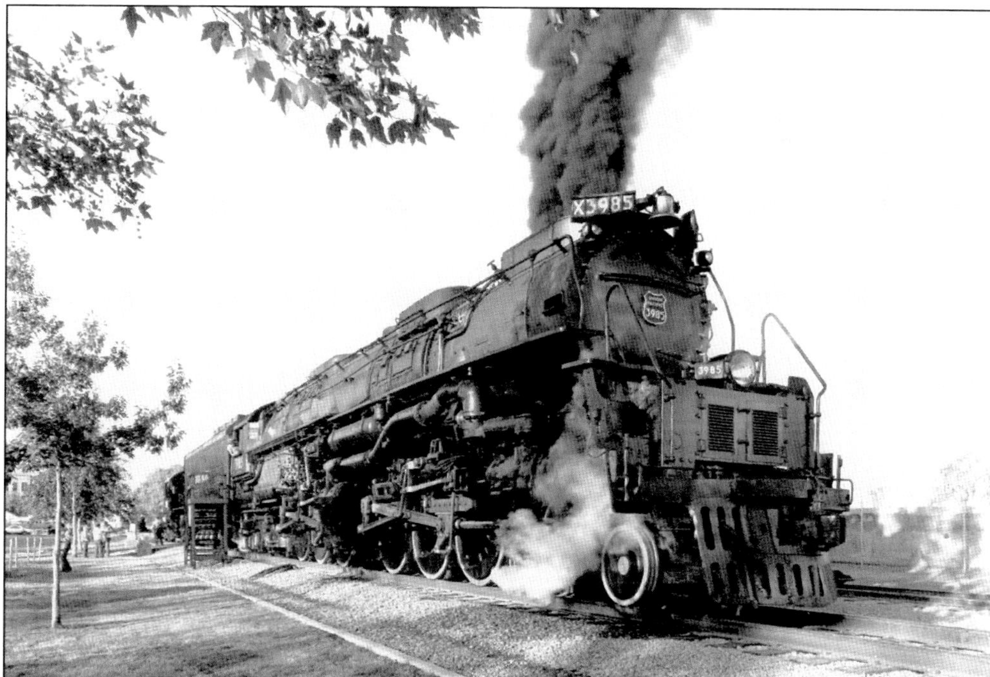

This is the Union Pacific Challenger #3985 steam locomotive, which had a 4-6-6-4 wheel arrangement. Built in 1936, it was the first articulated engine to move easily around tight curves.

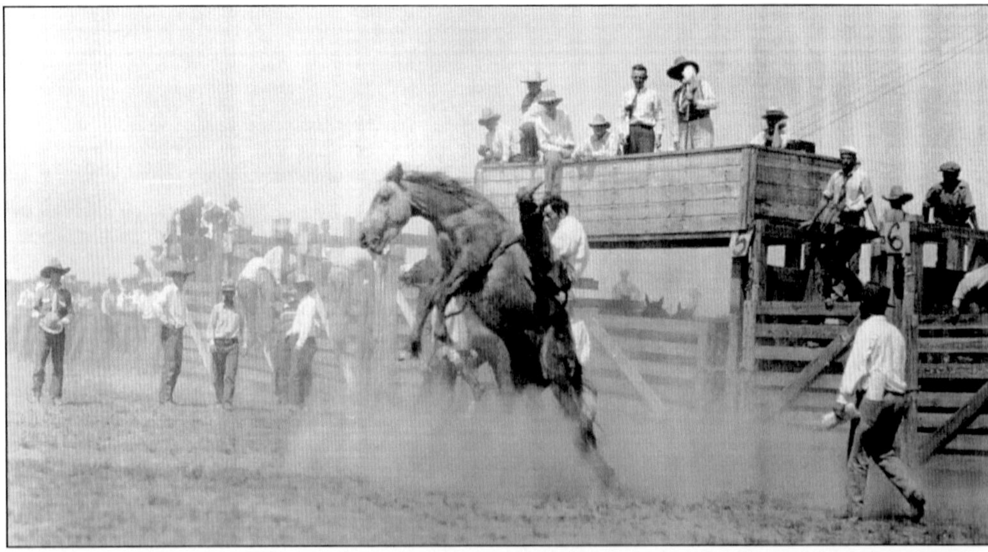

McCroy is making a bareback ride in the North Platte Roundup in this late-1920s photograph.

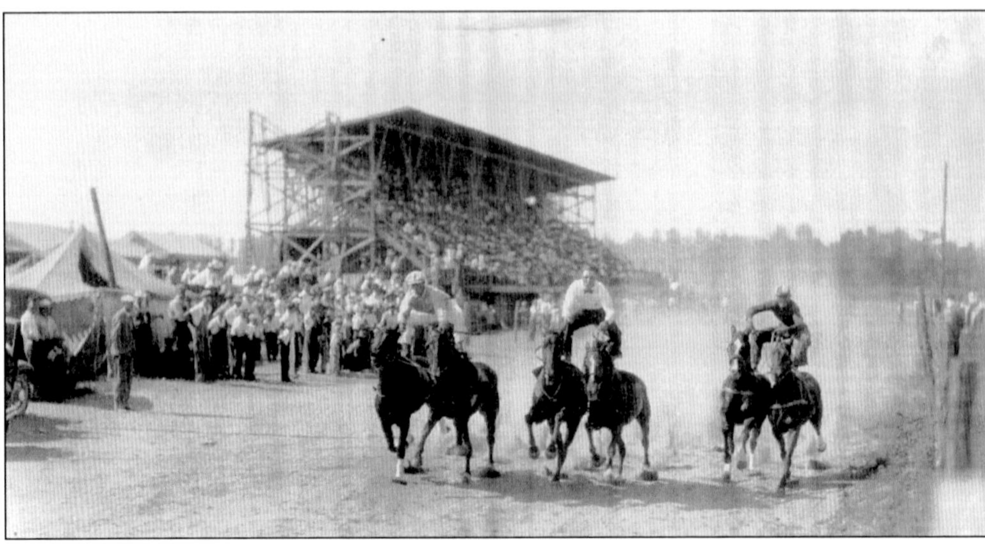

This 1926 photograph depicts a Roman standing race at the North Platte Roundup.

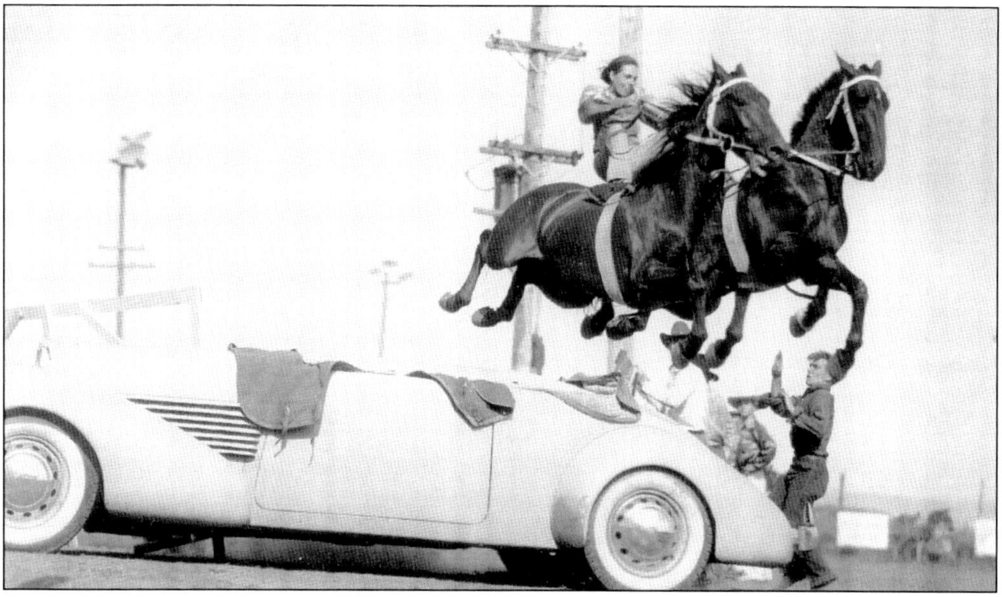

Here, Alice Sisty makes her famous auto Roman Jump at the North Platte Roundup. It looks like a Cord automobile.

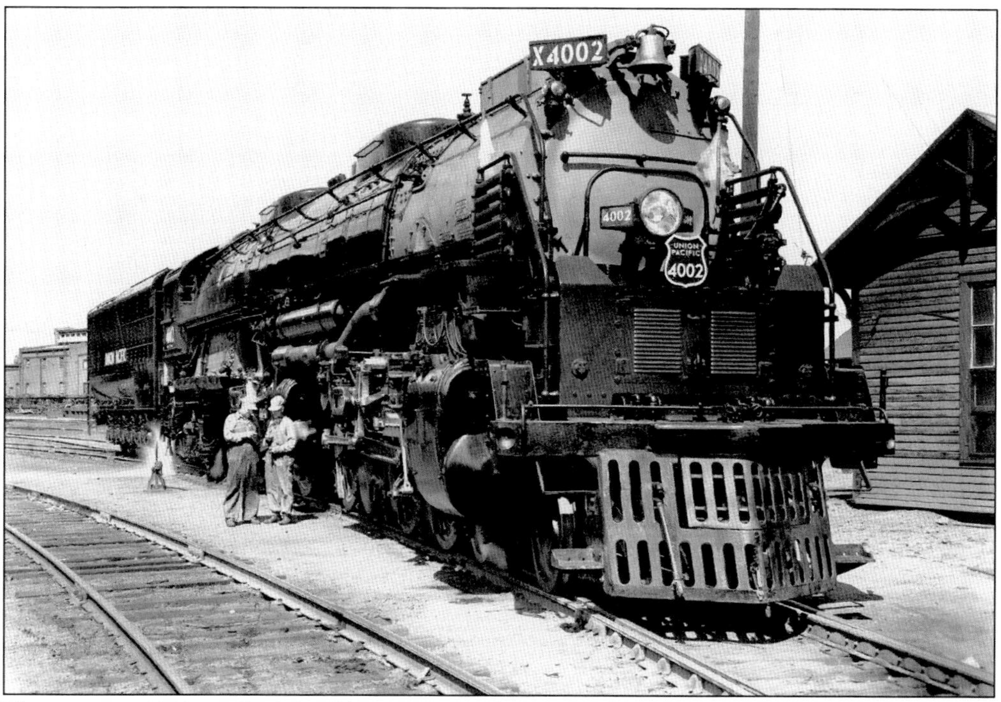

The engine #4002 was built by Alco in 1941. This engine had a 4-8-8-4 wheel arrangement and was also articulated. This was the "Big Boy": the largest steam locomotive ever built. Cylinders were 23 3/4 inches by 32 inches, drivers were 68 inches high, and the boiler pressure was 300 pounds. The engine and tender weighed 1,189,500 pounds The tender held 24,000 gallons of water, and accommodated 56,000 pounds of coal. Pictured in this 1948 photograph are Elston T. McConahay, a fireman (left), and August H. Tuenge, an engineer (right). This engine was scrapped in 1957.

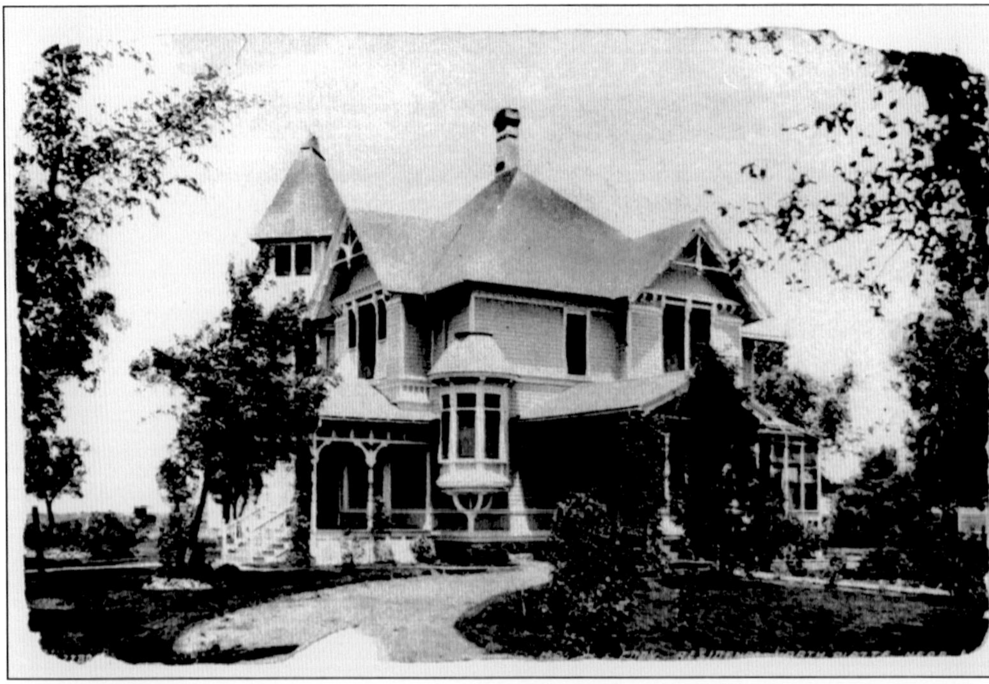

Buffalo Bill's Welcome Wigwam Town House was located at 1207 West Fourth Street, and it faced Washington Street. It was torn down in about 1934.

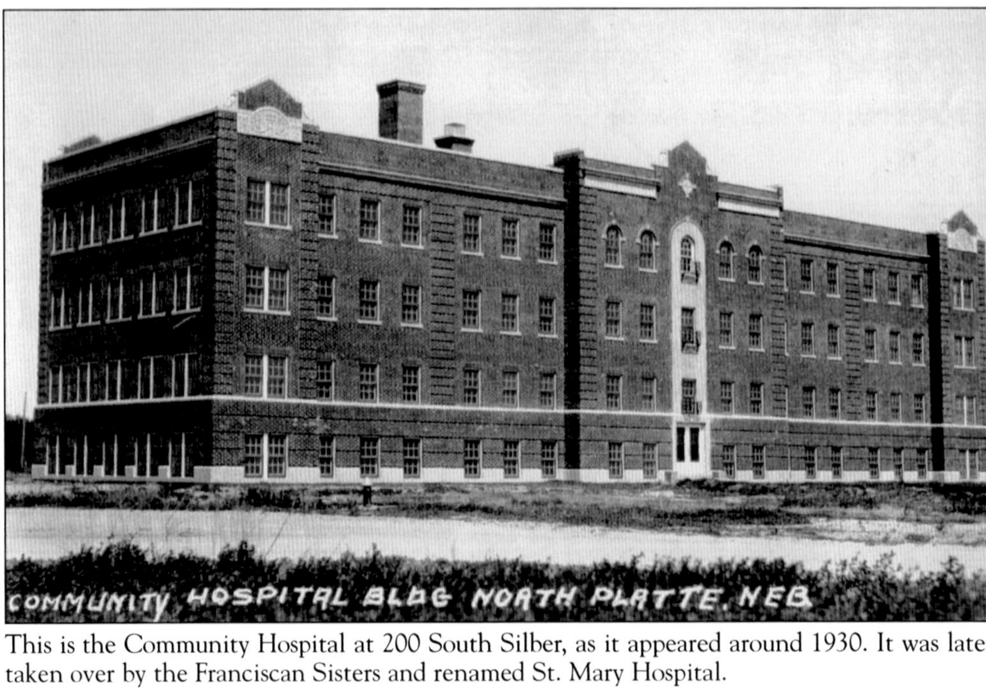

This is the Community Hospital at 200 South Silber, as it appeared around 1930. It was later taken over by the Franciscan Sisters and renamed St. Mary Hospital.

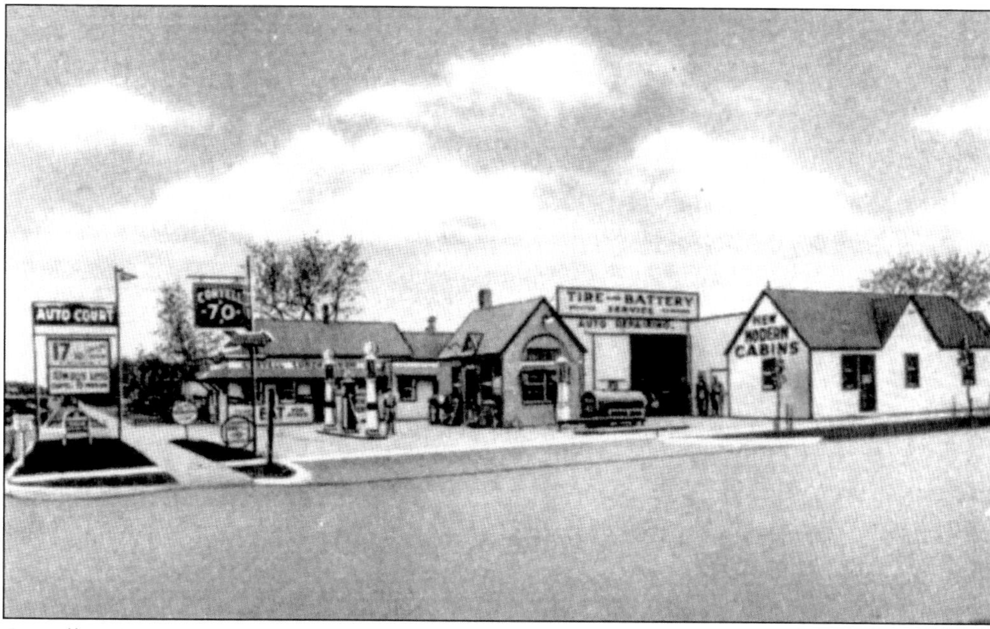

Coryell Cabins and Lunch Room was located on the corner of Fourth and North Chestnut. This picture was taken in 1931.

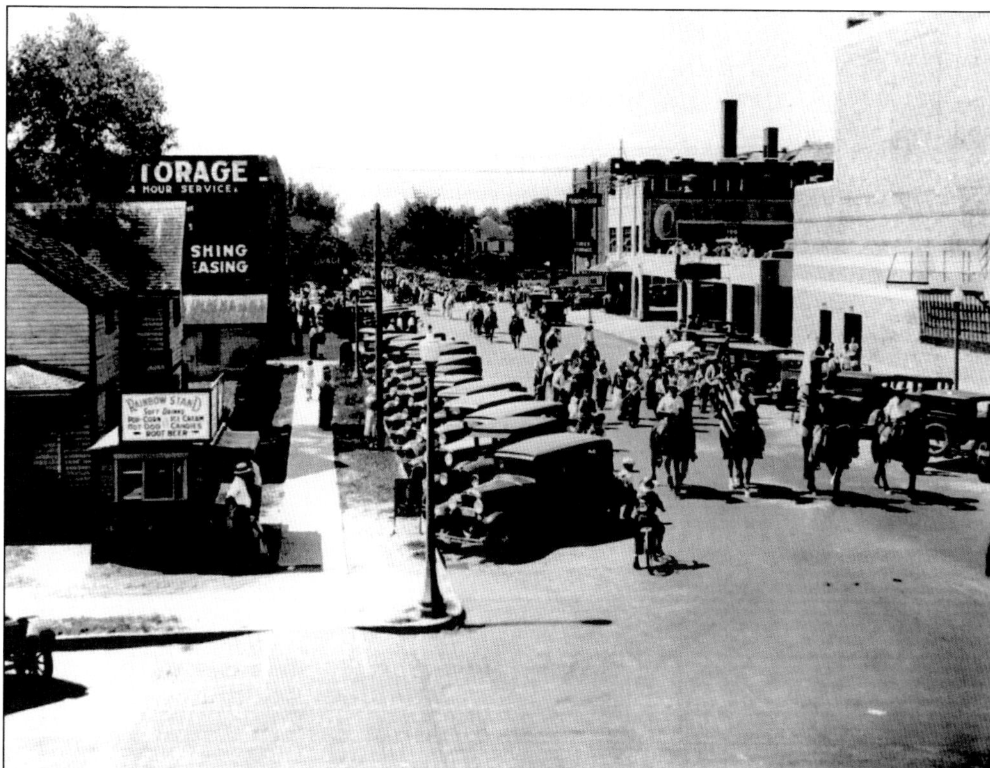

This is a view looking south of North Pine Street from Fifth Street in 1931. The popcorn stand is where the Sears Store now stands.

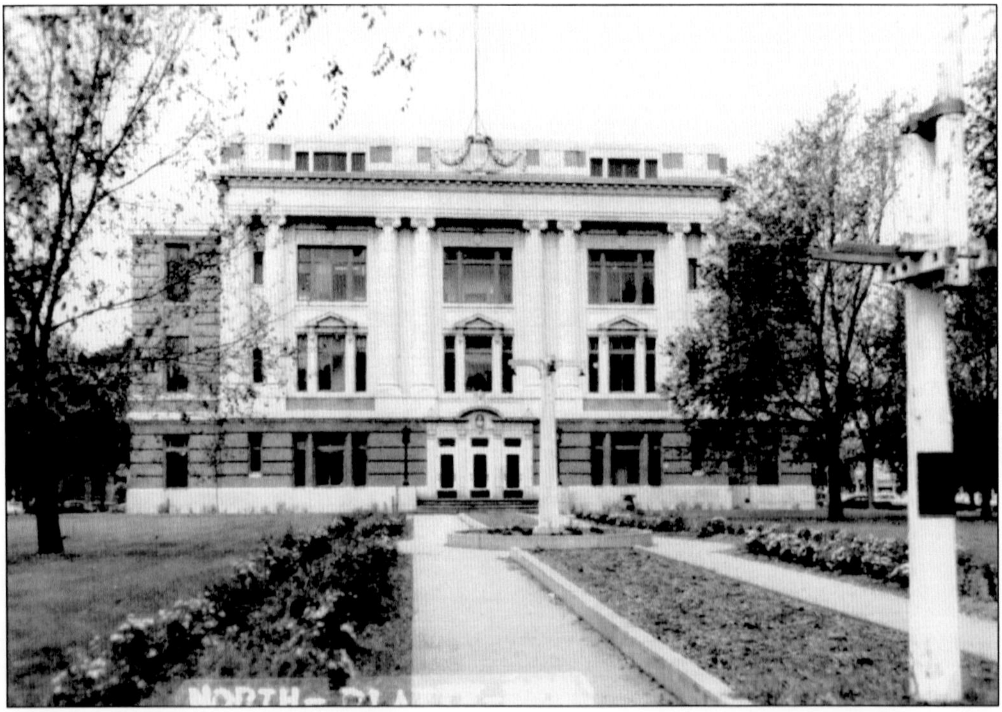

This photograph, taken in the 1930s, provides a glimpse of the Lincoln County Courthouse before the addition was built on the east end.

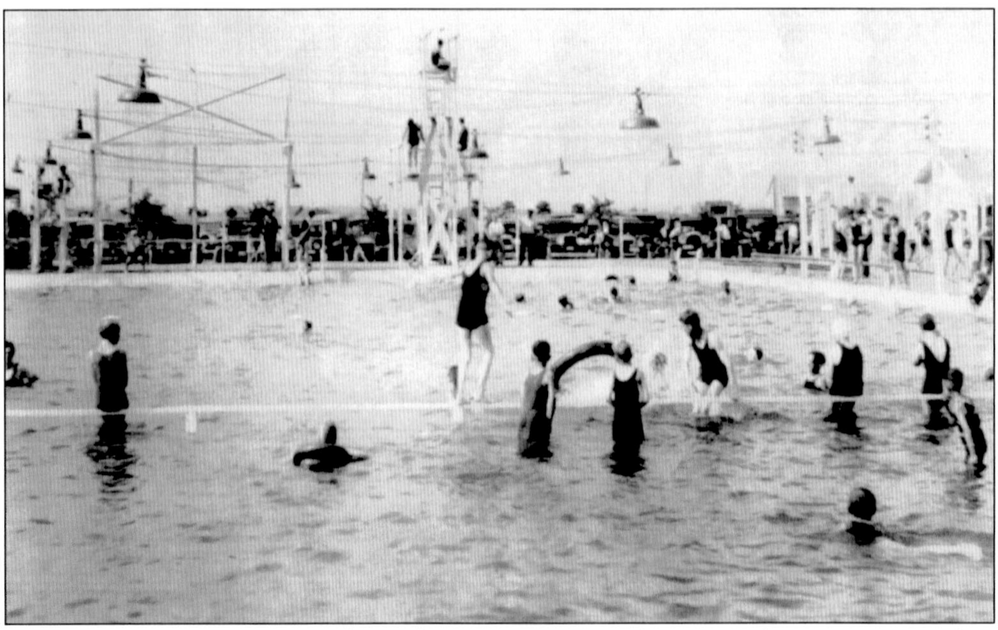

The Gerle swimming pool was located at 2000 West Ninth Street. This picture was taken in the early-1930s.

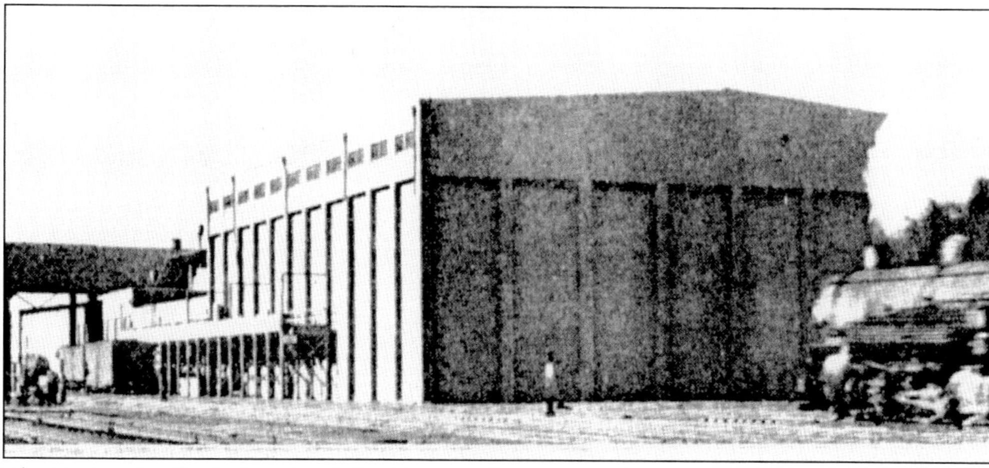

The Union Pacific Railroad and Pacific Fruit Express ice plant was located just north of Front Street and Buffalo Bill Avenue. The photo dates back to 1934.

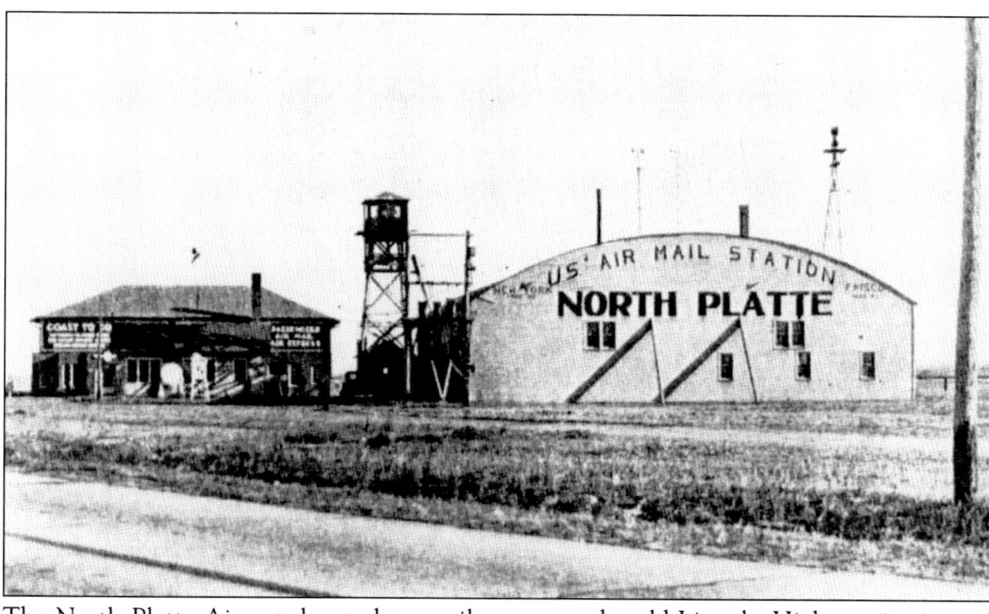

The North Platte Airport, located two miles east on the old Lincoln Highway, is pictured as it appeared in 1934.

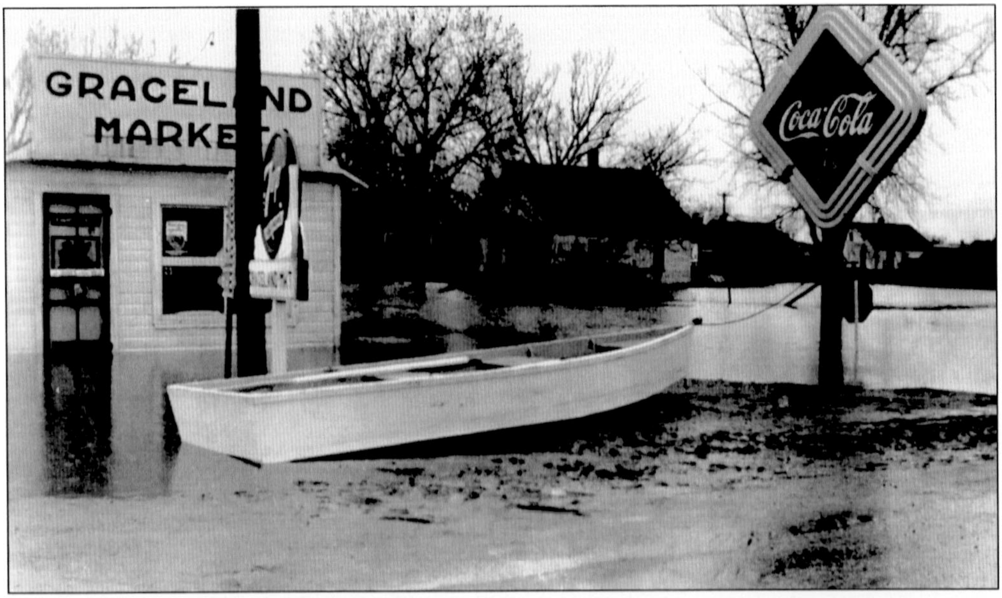

This photograph of Graceland Market was taken in 1935. The market was located at 1000 South Jeffers, on the northeast corner of South Jeffers and Williams. M. "Red" Merritt was the proprietor in the early years, a position handed over to Harold and Shirley Osterhoudt in the market's later years.

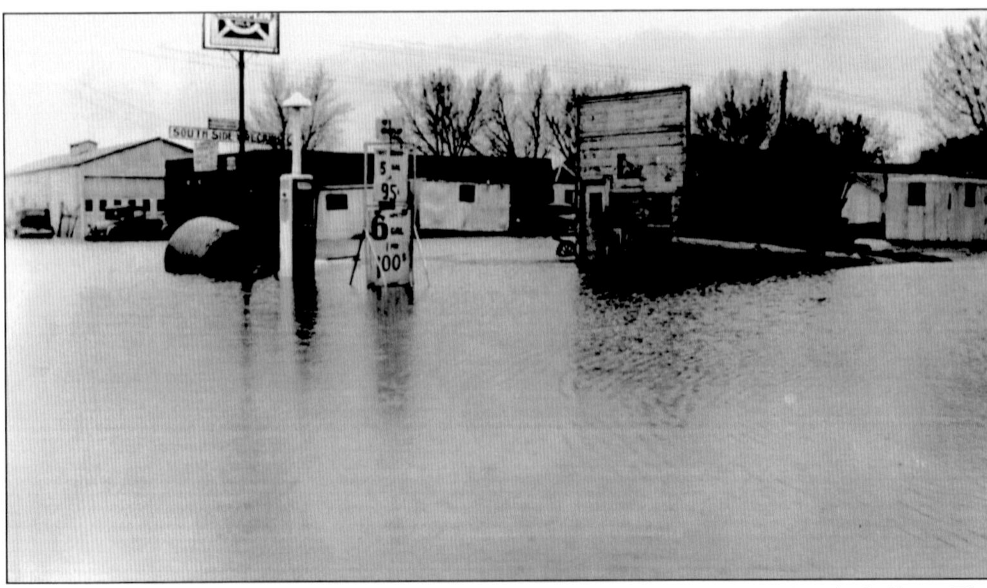

Edward V. Jennings managed the Jessen Service Station at 1008 South Jeffers. The Southside Wrecking Company, located at 1012 South Jeffers, was managed by Vilis G. Scott. This photo is dated 1935.

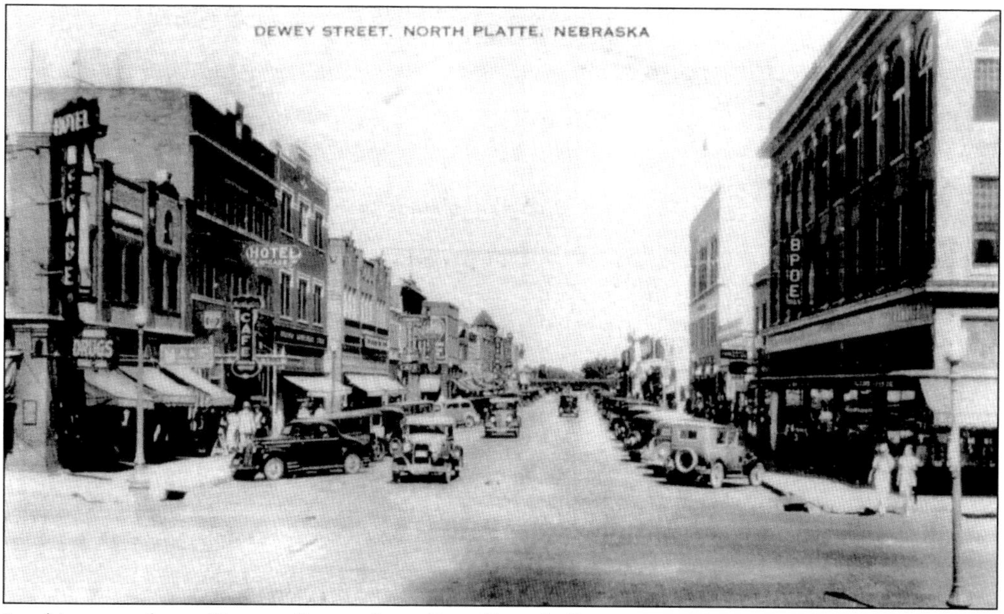

Looking north on Dewey Street from East Fourth Street in 1936, several local businesses are visible. On the corner is O'Connor Drugs, and then the Mars Shoppe, Schafer's Café, O'Connor Department Store, Brown's Studio, the Golden Rule Department Store, the Oasis Café, and the McDonald State Bank.

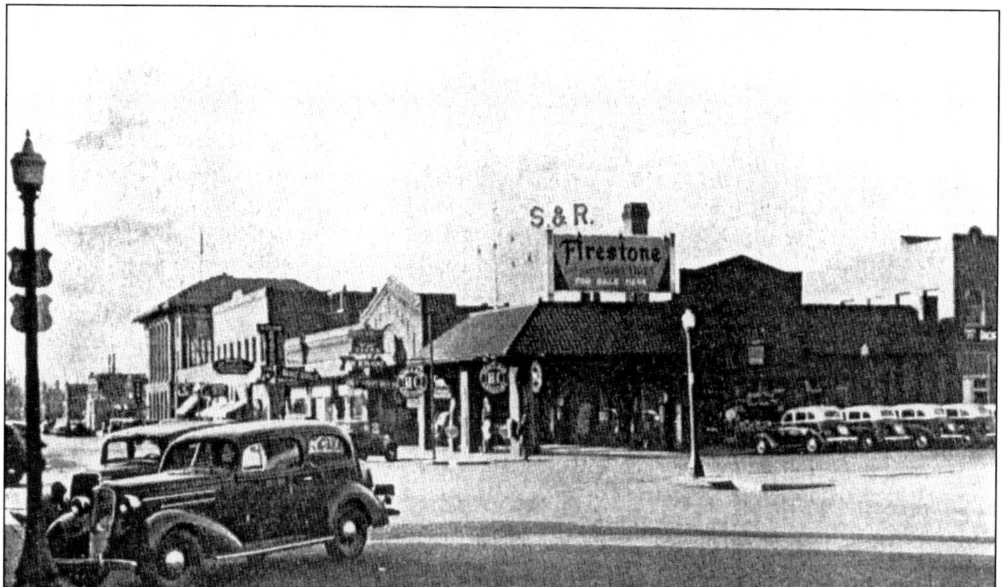

More local businesses are found on the 500 block of North Jeffers in this 1936 photograph. On the west side of the street, they are identified, from left to right, as the following: Reitan Service, Oscar's Clean Food, Gould Jewelry, United Finance Company, Valentine's Book Shop, Miles' Cleaners, Crawford Electric, the Hamburg Inn, and Firestone Service. The Austin Cab Company is in the background.

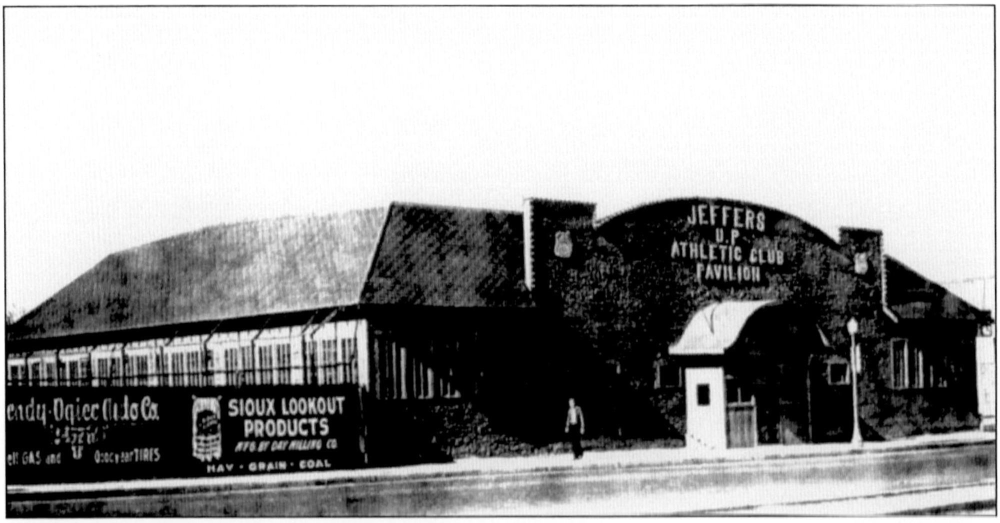

Some of the most memorable dances and musical performances were held at Jeffers Pavilion at 640 North Jeffers. Bands such as Tommy Dorsey, Jimmy Dorsey, Lawrence Welk, Benny Goodman, and countless others performed there, much to the delight of North Platte citizens. This great building burned down in the early-1960s.

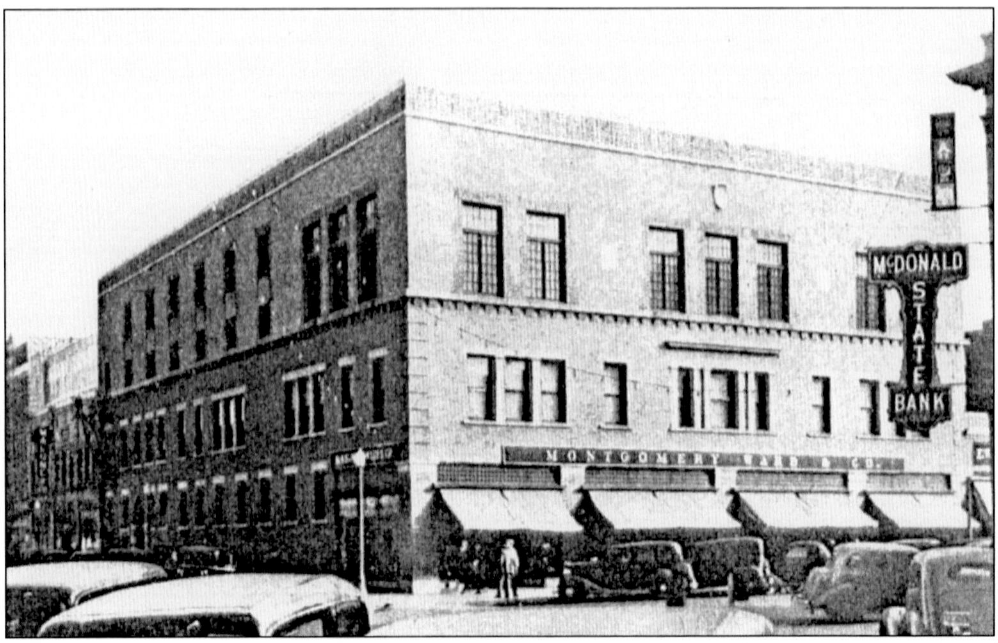

This is a picture of the northwest corner of Fifth and Dewey Streets taken in 1936. Just east of Montgomery Ward is the William Maloney Furniture and Undertaking Parlor, and beside it, the Paramount Theatre.

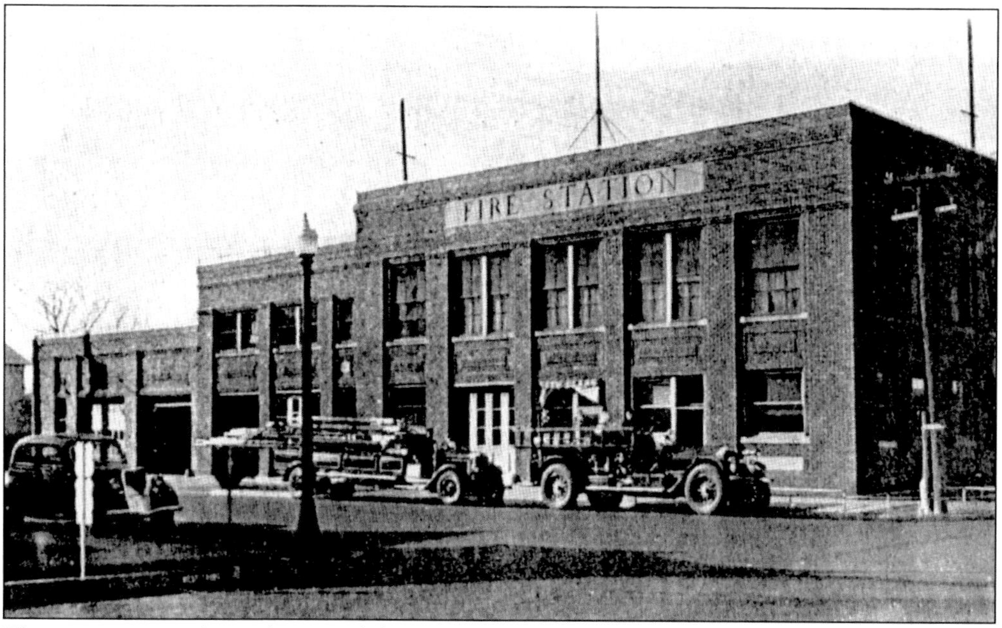

This picture provides a glimpse of the North Platte City Hall and Fire Station, as it appeared in 1936. The building has since been converted to apartments by Larry Steele.

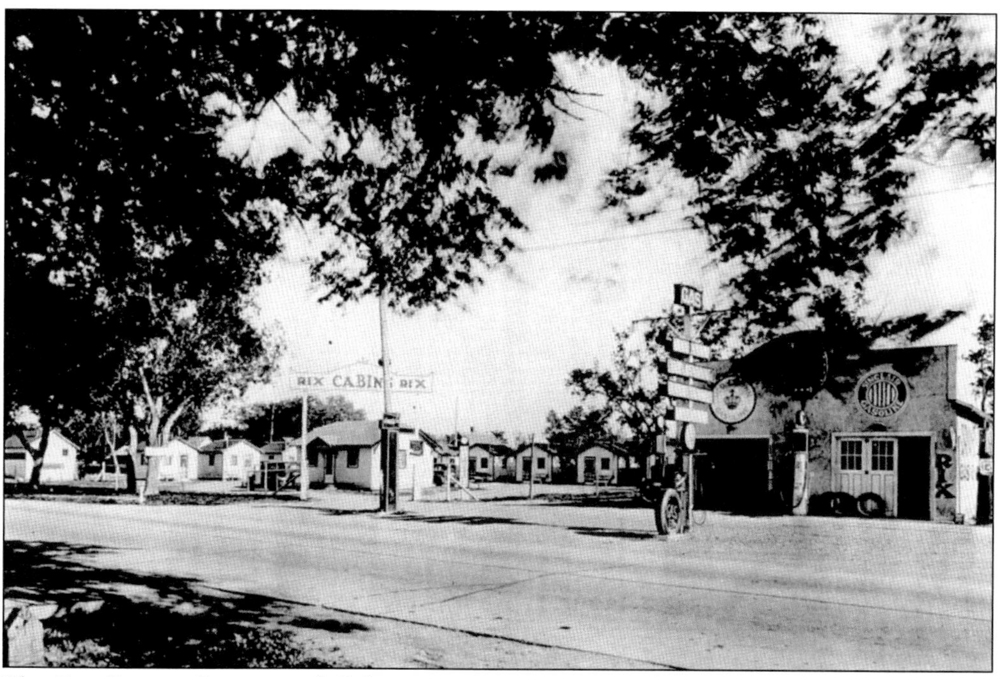

The Rix Service Station and Cabins sat at 320 West Twelfth Street. Harry Reger served as manager.

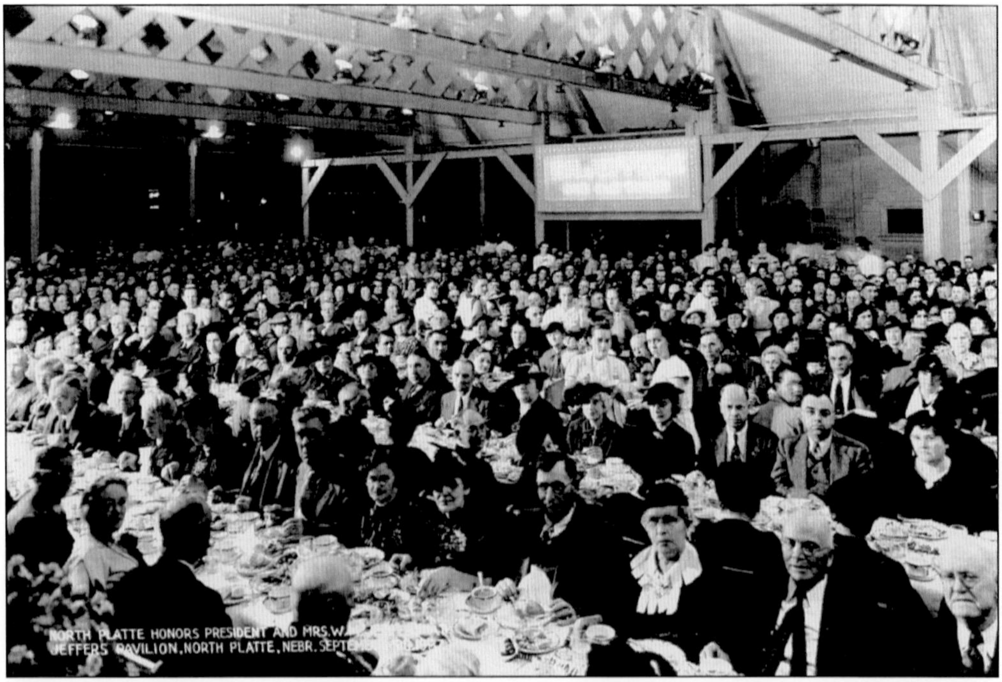

After William Jeffers was named President of the Union Pacific Railroad Company, this banquet was held at Jeffers Pavilion to honor him. The banquet was catered by the Union Pacific dining room that was then open in the Depot. This picture was taken September 30, 1937.

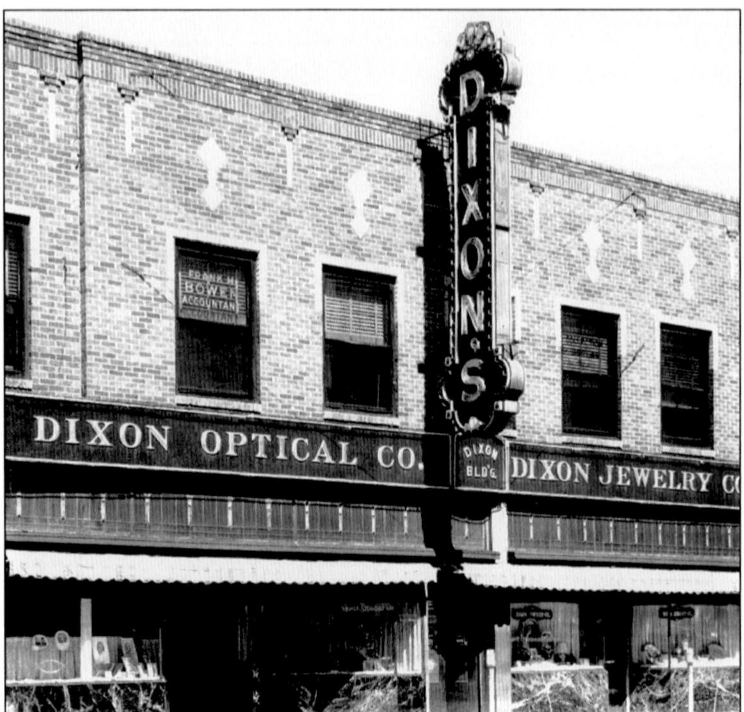

The Dixon Optical and Jewelry Store, pictured here, was located at 516–518 North Jeffers.

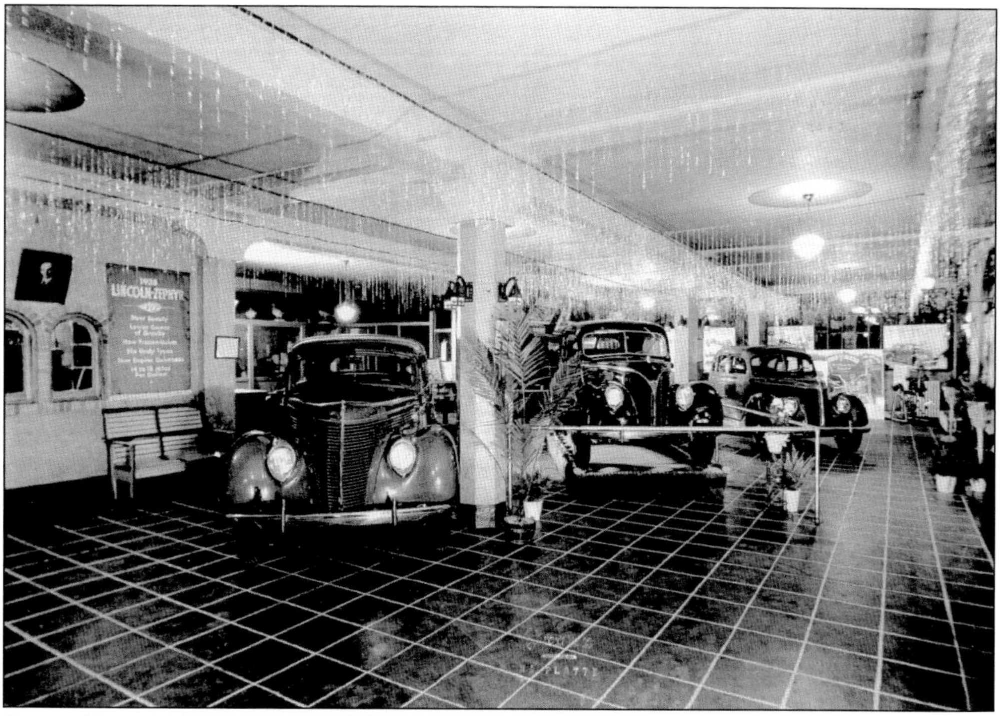

Pictured here is the showroom of the Hendy-Ogier Ford-Mercury-Lincoln dealership, in 1938, when the next year's models really meant something.

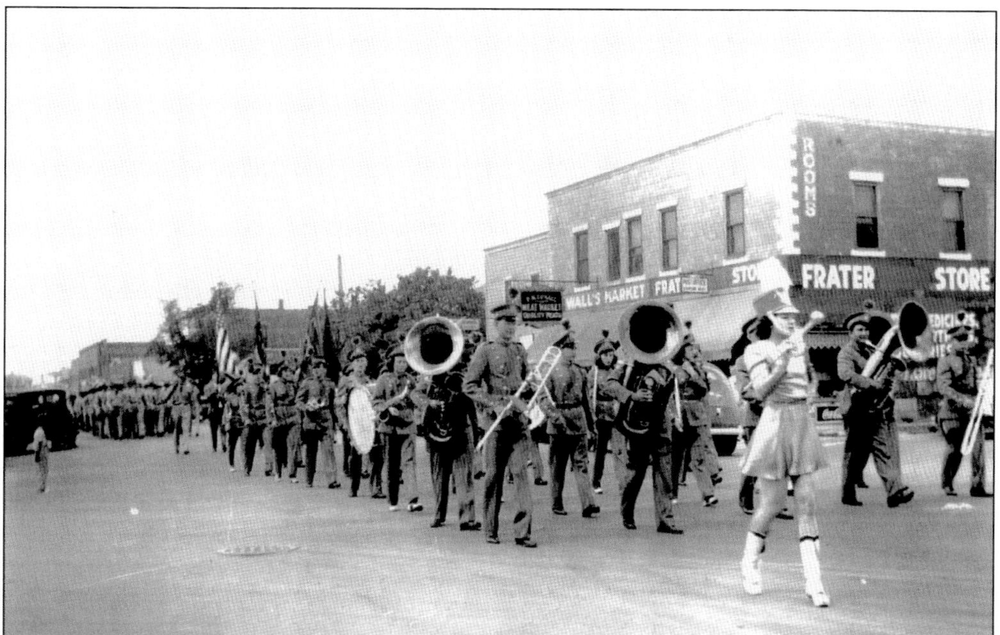

On November 11, 1938, a Veterans Day parade was held in North Platte. The parade is pictured here as it moves through the corner of Ninth and Jeffers. Twin sisters Jerry and Bunny Allison march as drum majorettes, though Bunny is out of the camera's frame.

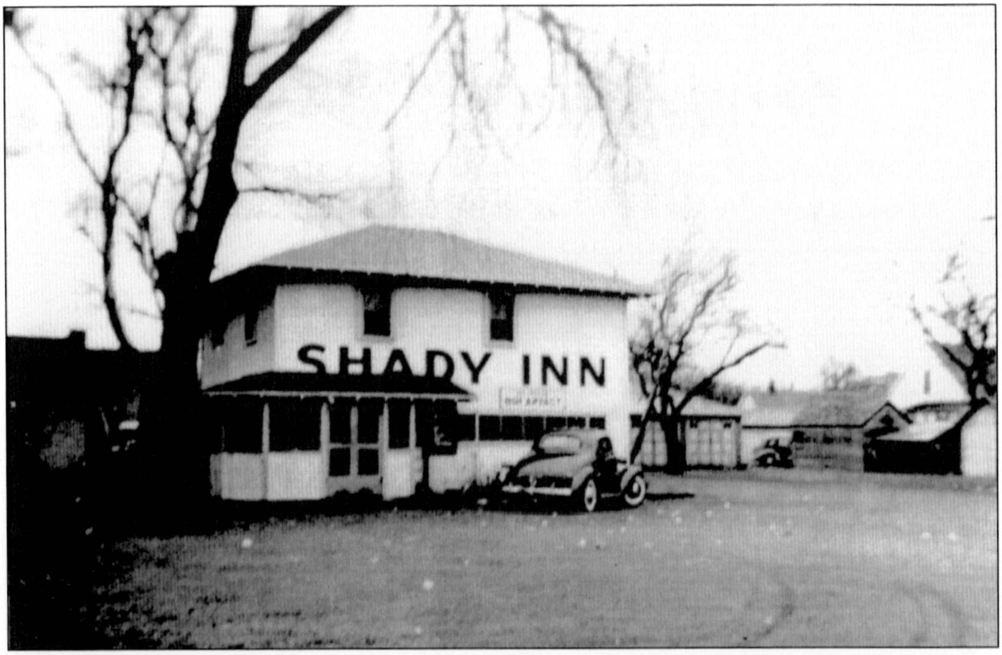

H.R. Heglin ran the Shady Inn Drive Inn, which was located at 104 North Jeffers Street. This picture is from 1938.

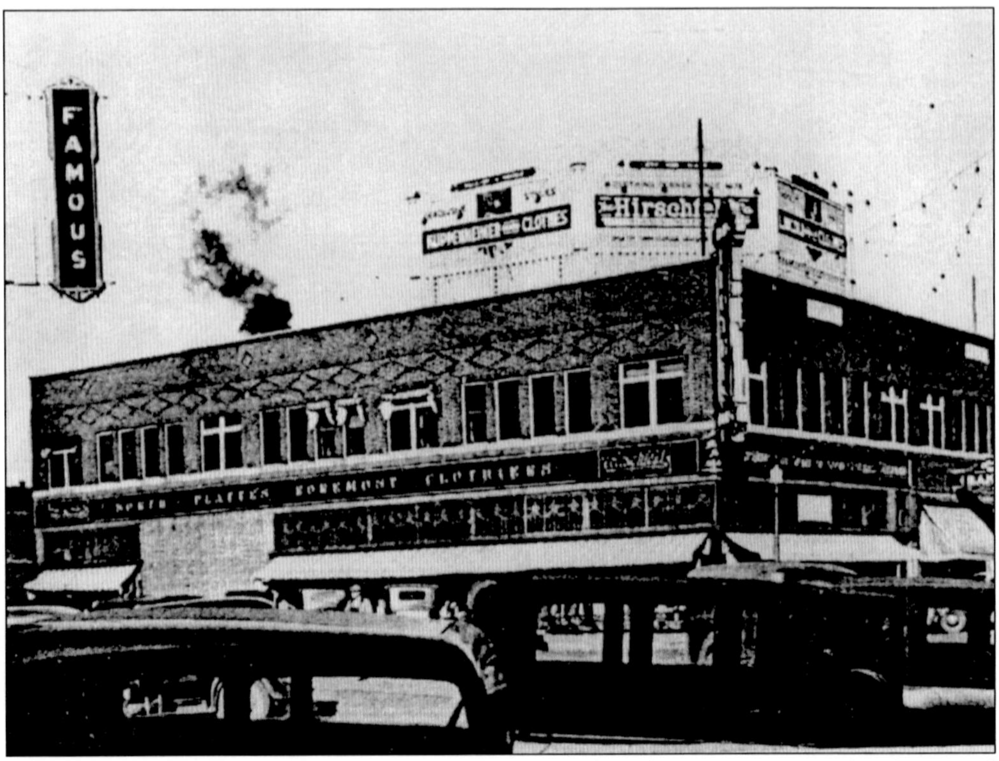

The Hirschfelt Building, on the northwest corner of Sixth and Dewey, was owned and operated by Joe and Hyman Hirschfelt. This picture was taken in 1938.

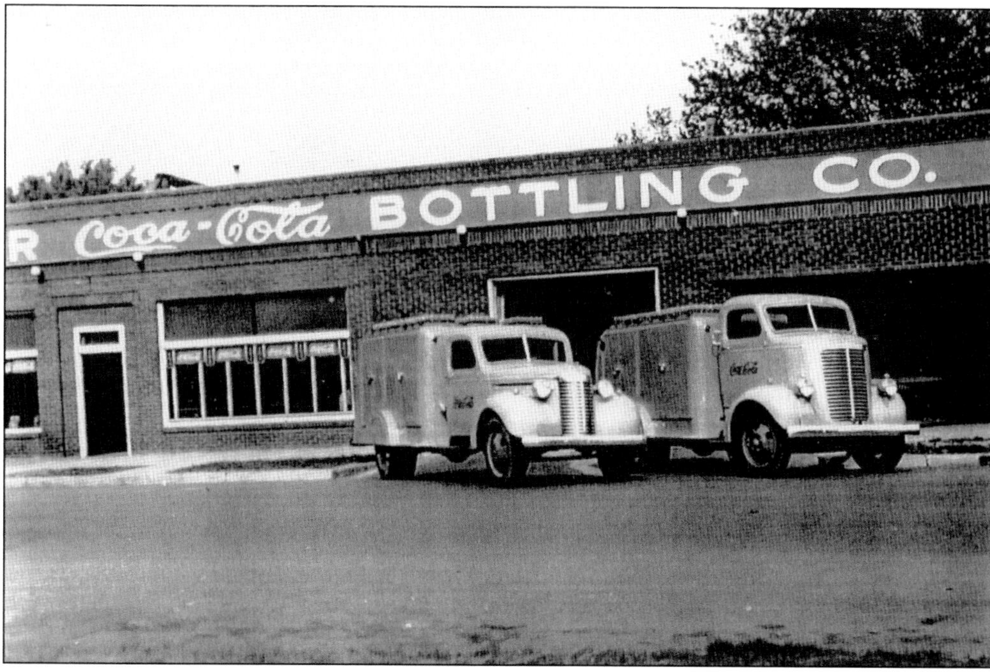

This photo of the Star Coca-Cola Bottling Company, at 203 North Dewey, was taken in 1940. J. Leroy and Katherine Keenan owned and operated the business for years.

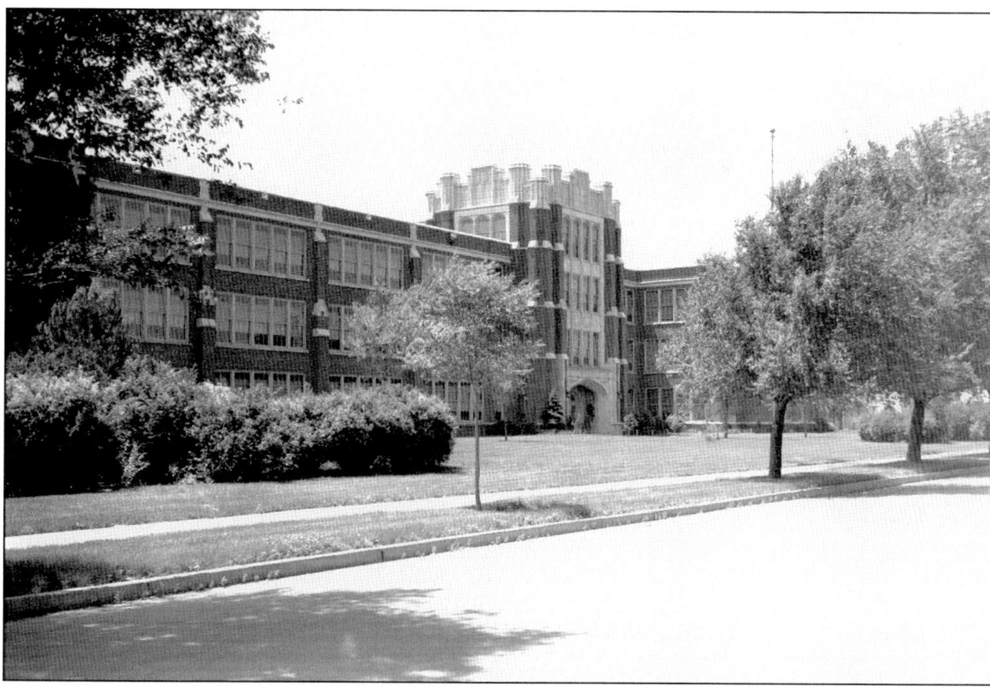

Pictured here is the North Platte Senior High School at 1000 West Second Street, as it appeared in 1942. At that time, the school was overseen by Principal L.W. Nelson. A new school is being built at the start of the 21st century, and the citizens have worked hard to save the old school building, built in the 1930s, and convert it into a new city library.

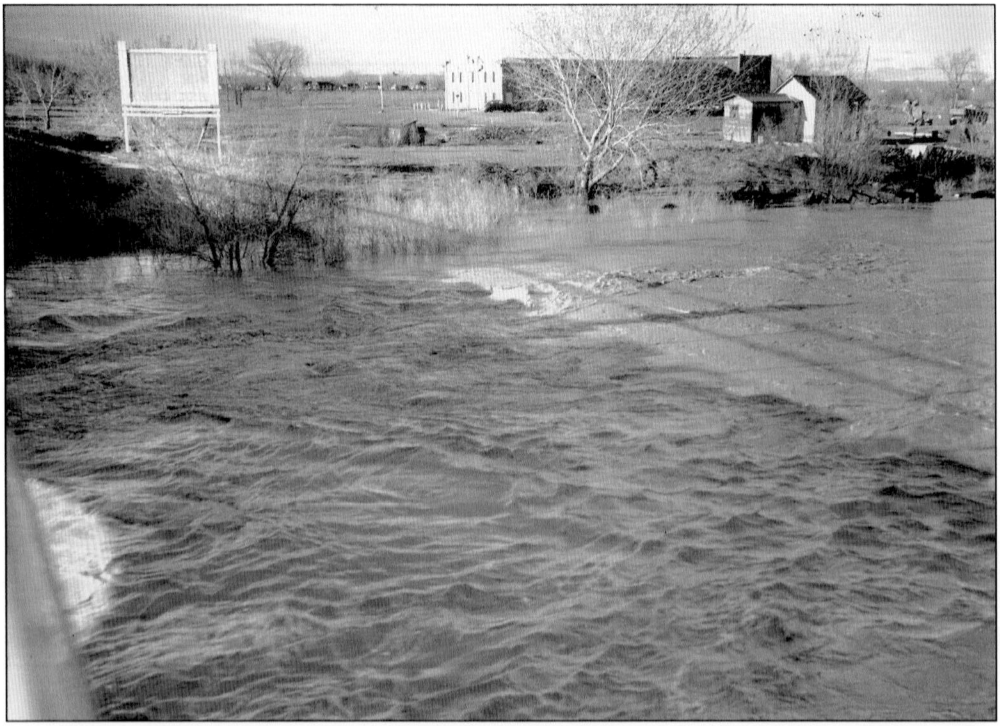

This photo of the American Legion Memorial Building, taken in 1942, reveals a very flooded South Platte River. The American Legion building was used for stage shows, and as a skating rink and dance hall. This building burned down and was replaced by a new one that has since been converted into a church. The small building close to the river is an old ice house used to store ice cut during the winter.

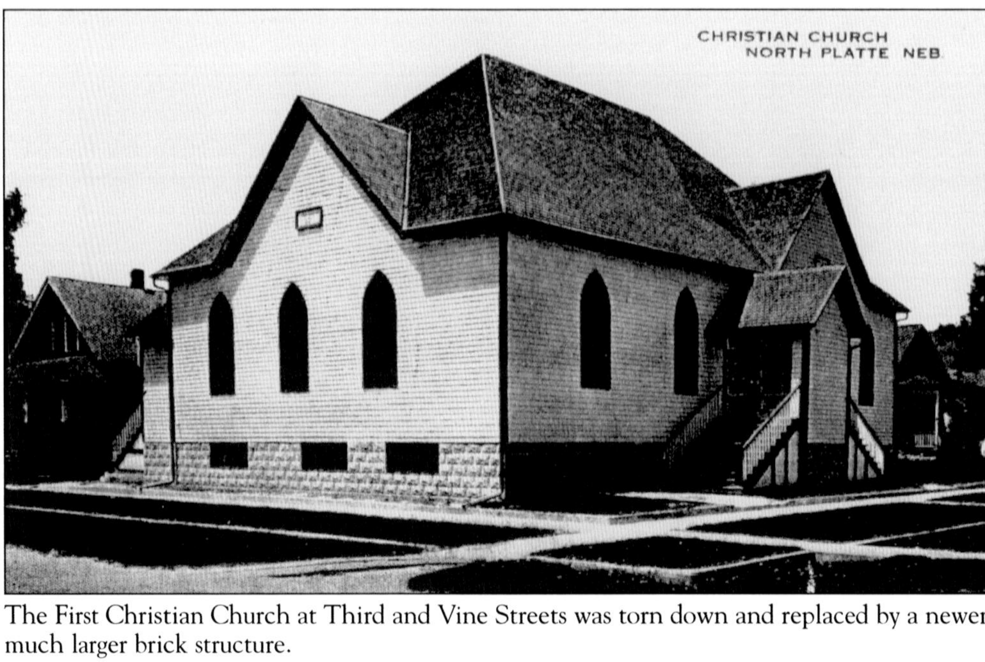

The First Christian Church at Third and Vine Streets was torn down and replaced by a newer, much larger brick structure.

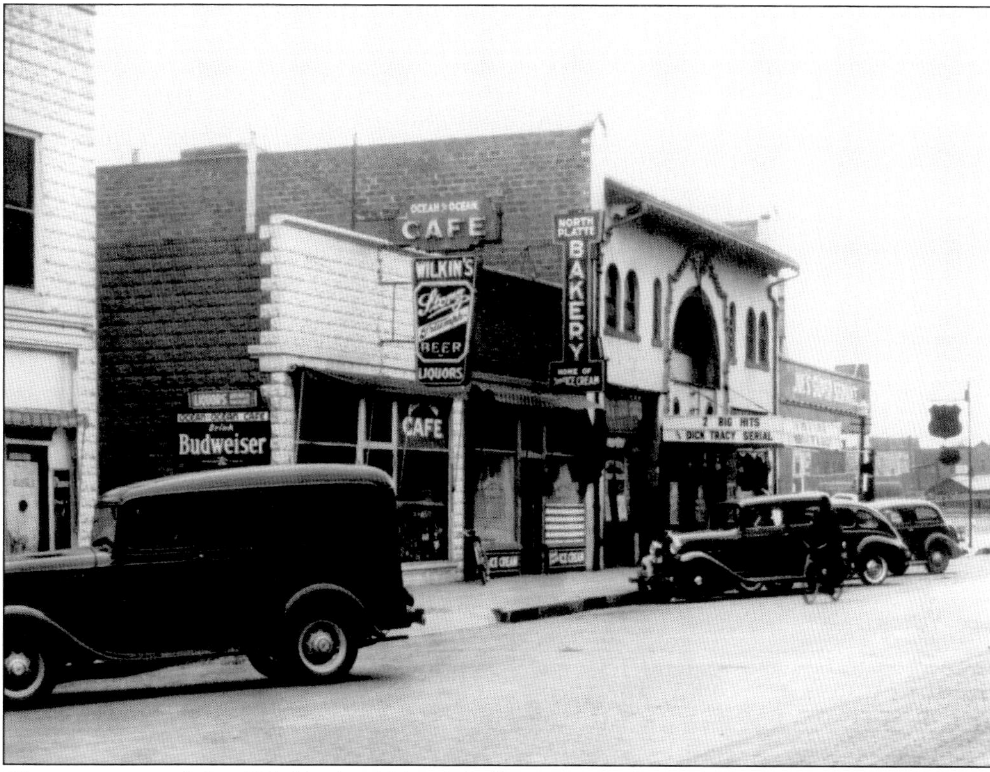

This is a view of the 700 block of North Jeffers, captured in 1939. Some of the businesses operating here at the time were the Ocean to Ocean Café, run by Harry and Maud Wilkens; the North Platte Bakery, owned by Emil and Evelyn Seiler; the State Theatre, run by George Allan; and Joe's Super Service, owned by Frank and Ethel McKain.

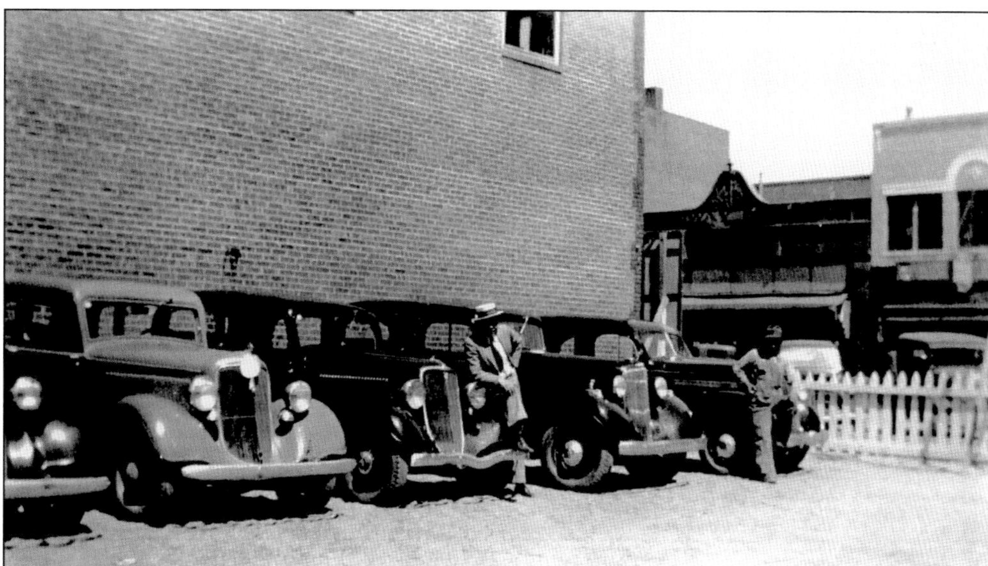

In 1938, the Foster Motor Company was located at 212 East Sixth Street, close to the brick building that housed the Model Cleaners and the Beauty Academy.

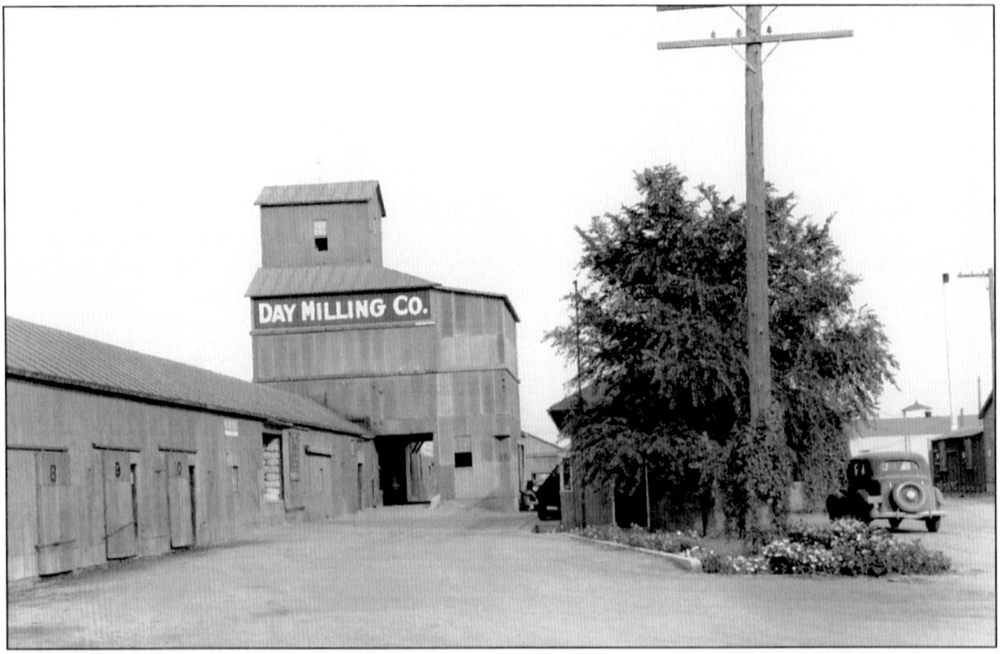

Harold E. Day owned the Day Milling Company at 801 East Front Street. This picture was taken in 1938.

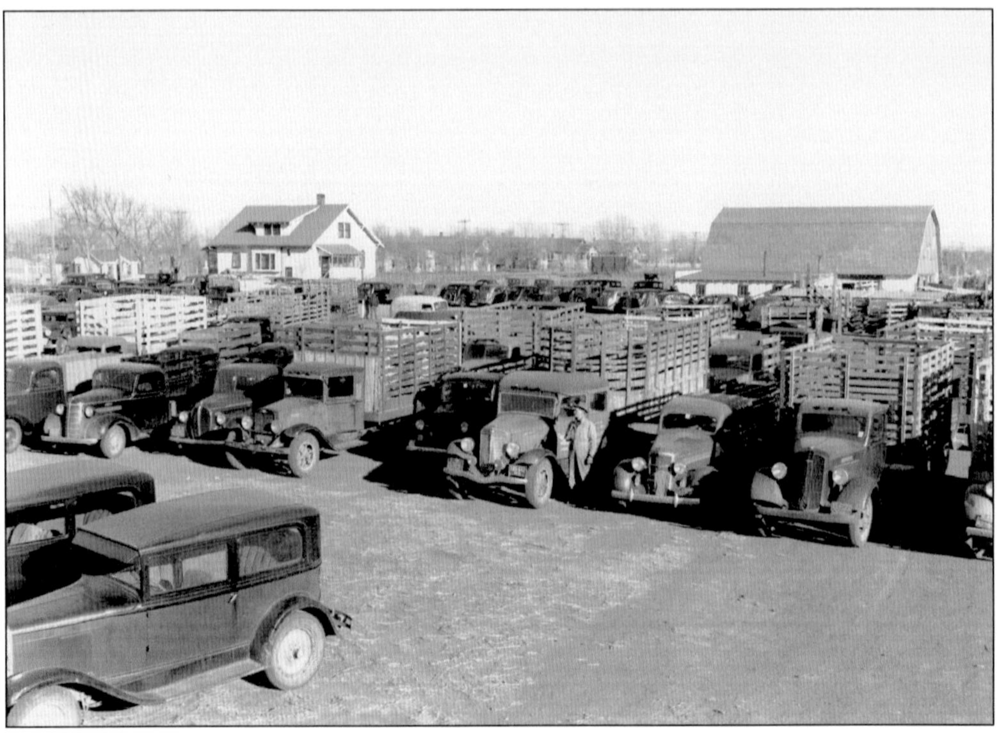

Now the home of the Isabell Furniture and Auction Company, this building at 2006 East Fourth Street was the site of the North Platte Auction Company in 1939. It was managed by Fred L. Burke.

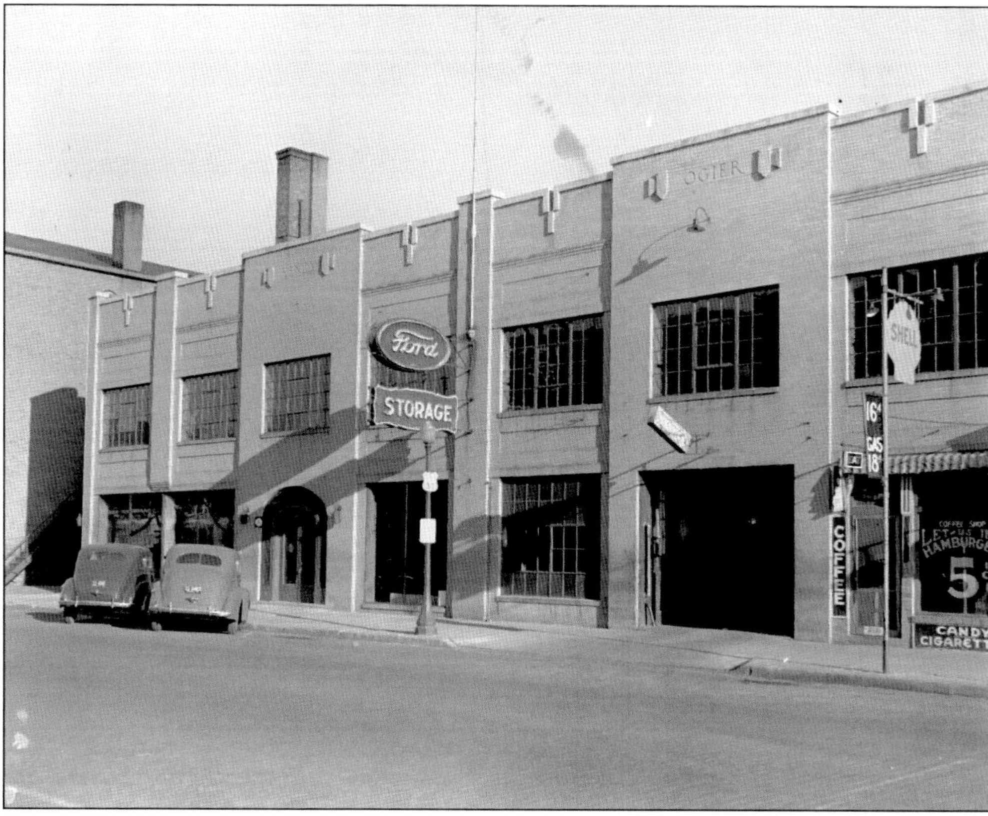

McGuire-Souder Motor Company is pictured here, at 209 East Fourth Street, in 1939. Notice the small Let-Us-Inn Cafe where many of the Franklin Junior High students had their lunch.

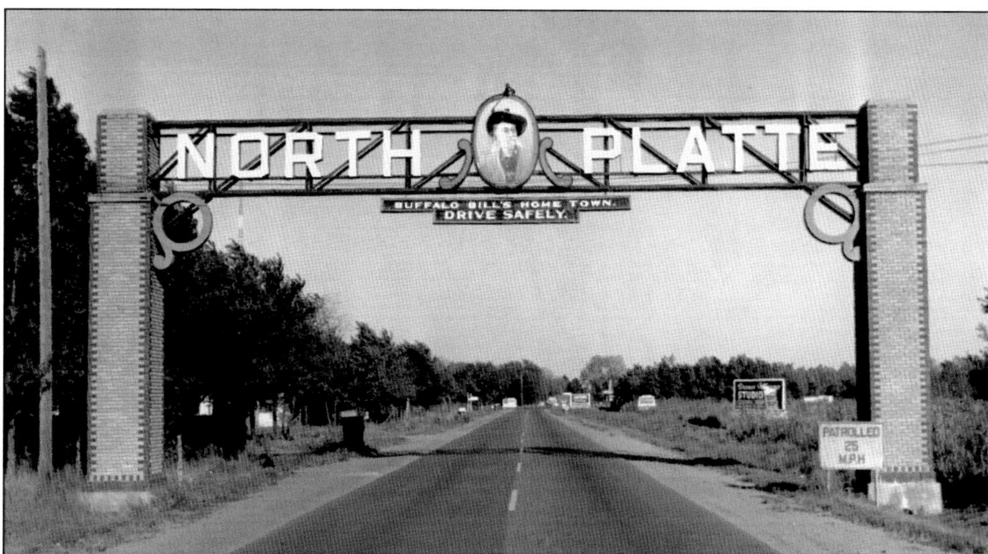

The North Platte Arch could be found at the western city limits on the old Lincoln Highway. This is a picture of it in 1939. Just a few feet west of this sign, the time zone changed from central to mountain. This sign was destroyed when the highway was widened.

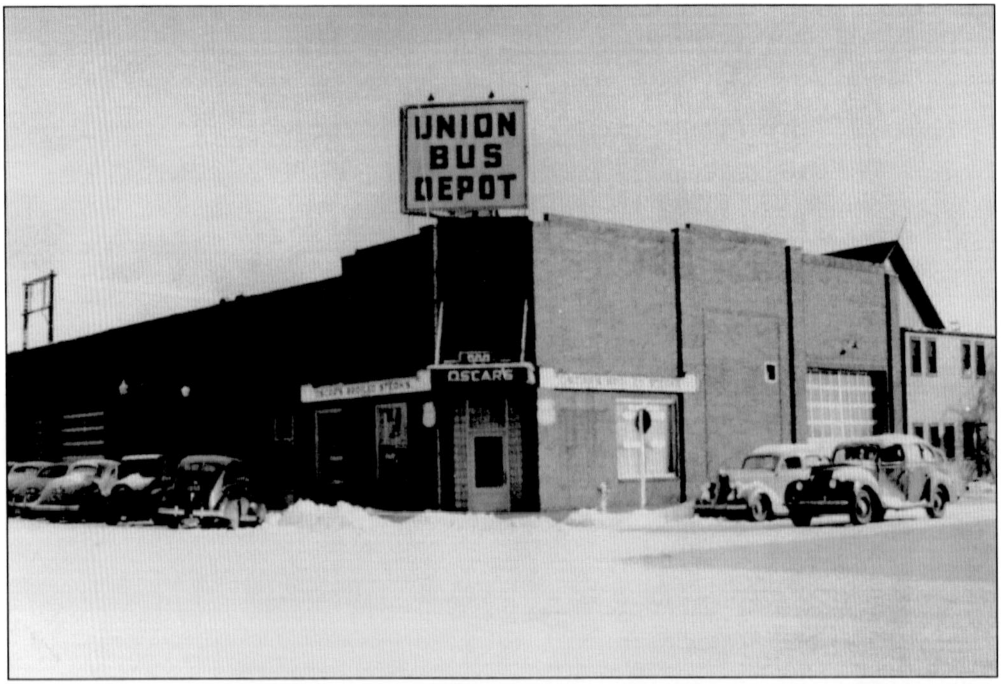

Oscar's Café was located within the Overland Greyhound Bus Depot on the northwest corner of Sixth and Pine Streets. Notice the old Langraff Hotel to the right.

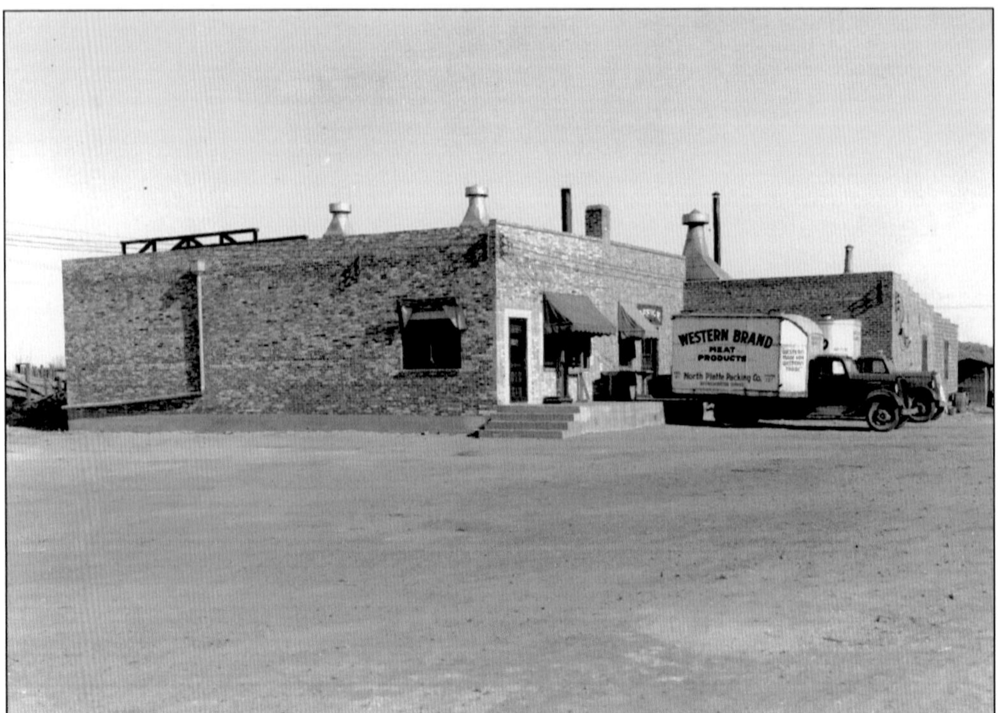

The North Platte Packing Company, at 2301 East Eighth Street, was overseen by Frank Jr. and Albert Interholzinger. This is how it looked in 1939.

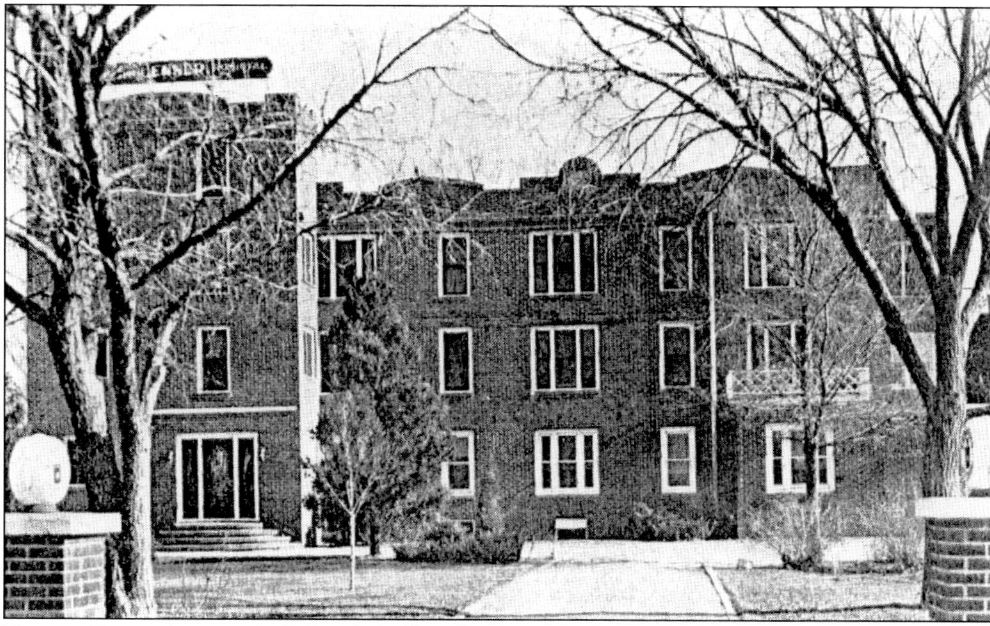

Fenner Hospital sat at 715 South Jeffers for many years. It was named after Dr. Harold A. Fenner. This picture was taken in 1940. It later became Memorial Hospital.

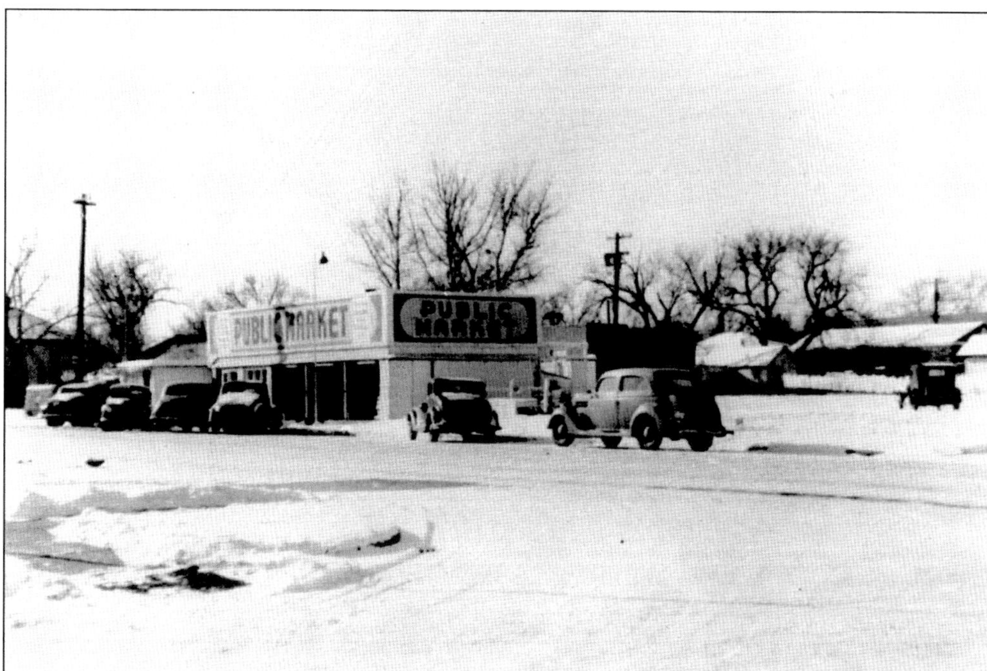

Austin S. and Blanche E. Gregg owned the Public Market at 112 North Jeffers. This picture was taken in 1939.

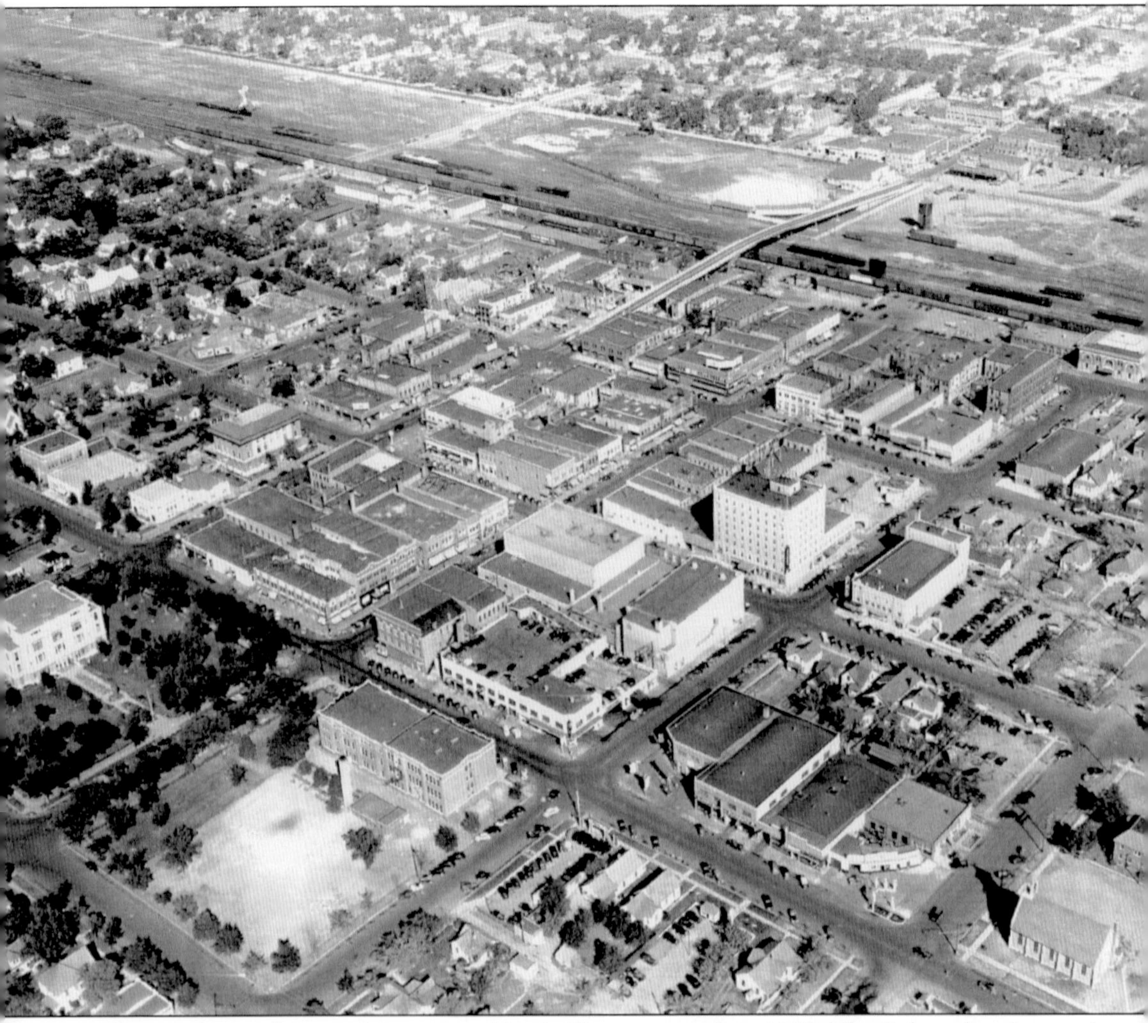

Here is an aerial view of downtown North Platte captured in 1940. The light-colored ground in the left foreground is where the old high school, built in the 1900s, stood before it was torn down.

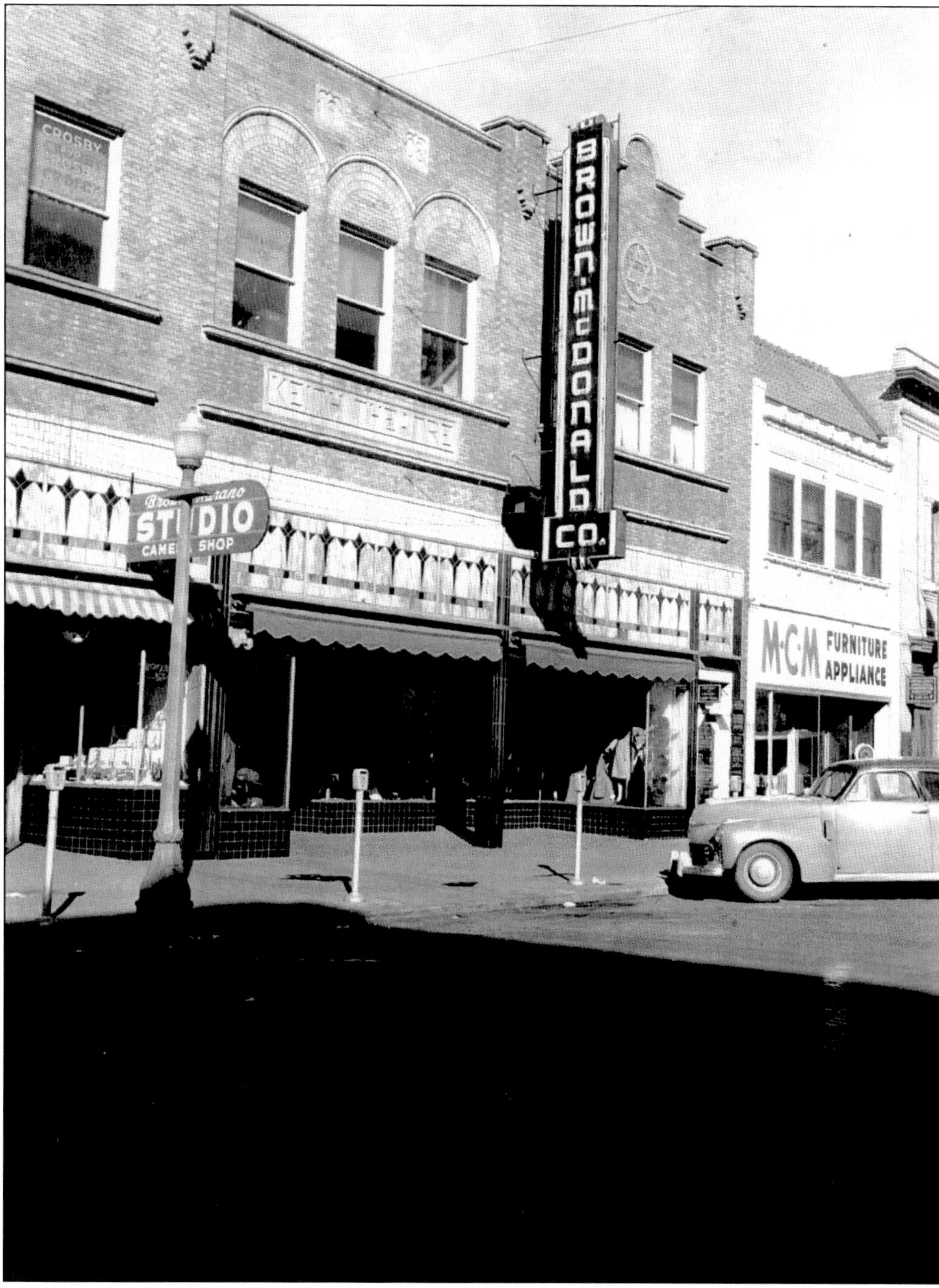

This 1942 picture provides a glimpse at the 400 block of North Dewey Street.

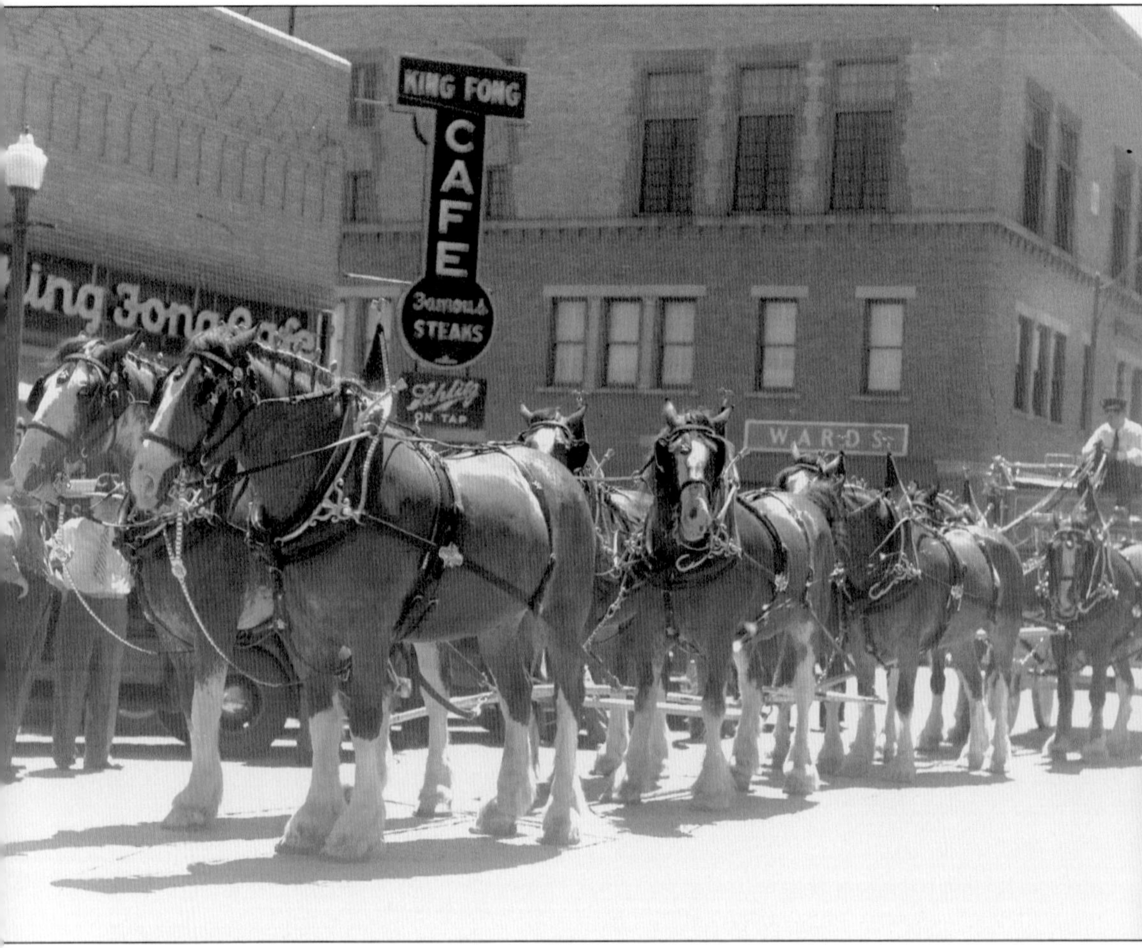

A Budweiser eight-horse hitch stands at the corner of Fifth and Dewey. Behind it is the King Fong Café, which was one of North Platte's finest restaurants. Established in 1921, the café was owned and operated by Harry and Henry Chinn for decades.

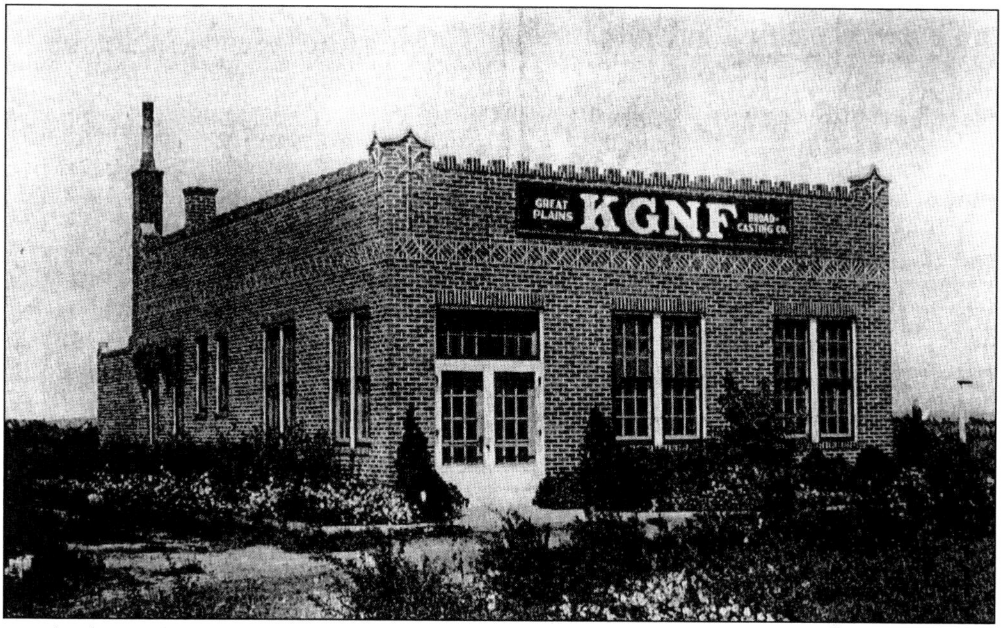

North Platte's first radio station, KGNF, was located at 1521 West Twelfth Street. KGNF first broadcasted on July 5, 1930, only to go off the air on December 11, 1943. On December 13, 1943 it came back on the air as KODY.

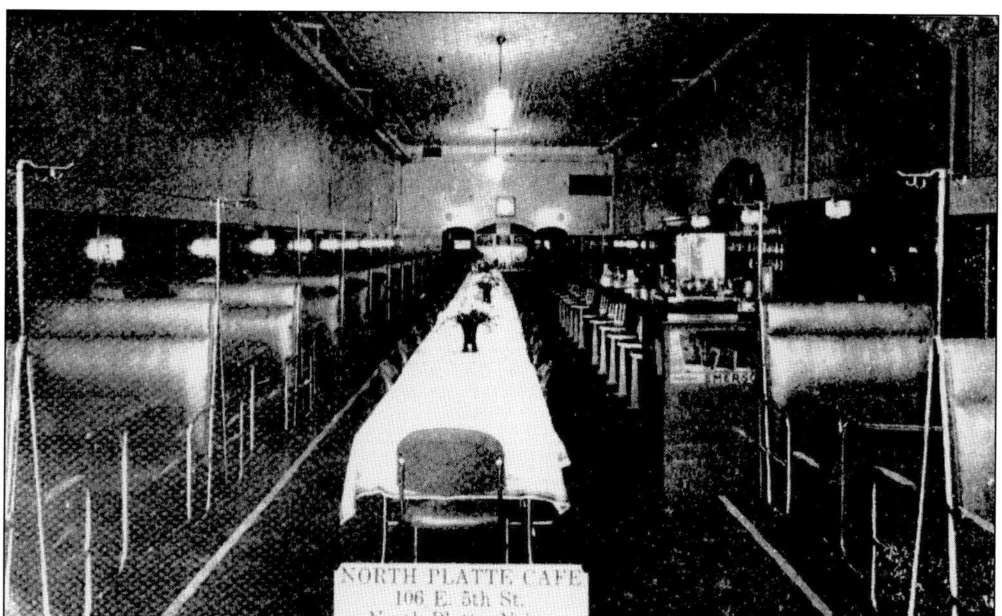

Here is a view of the North Platte Café as it looked in 1942. Located at 106 East Fifth Street, it was operated by Chin Wing for many years.

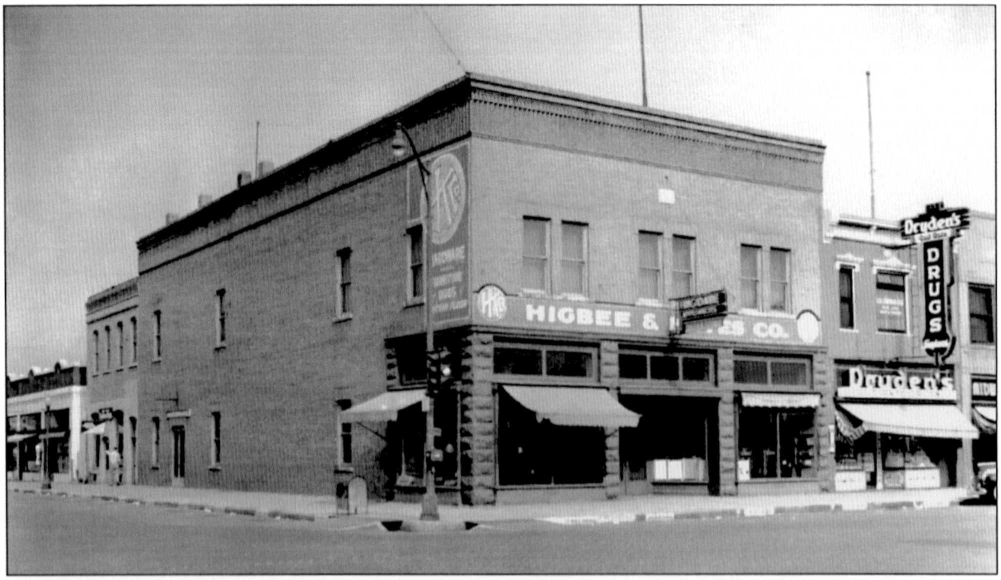

The Warner building, located on the corner of Fifth and Dewey, housed Higbee-Keyes, and then the J.C. Penney store, for many years. This photo dates back to 1942. The Warner building was the only structure on that block to be torn down during urban renewal. Afterwards, the building that now houses Brown Shoe Fit was erected.

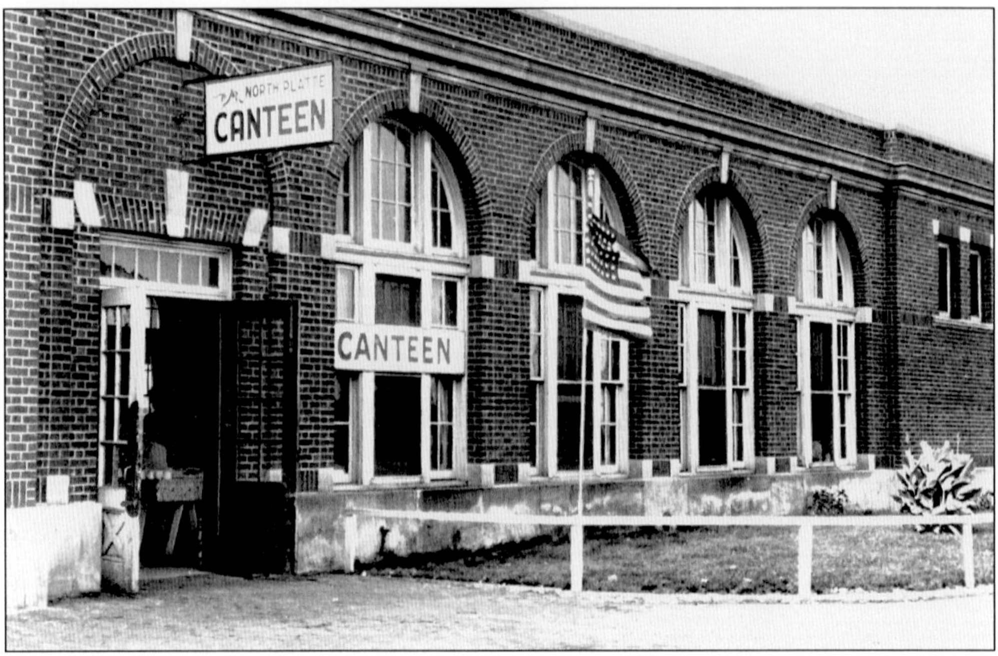

Here is the famous North Platte Canteen, as it appeared in 1944. Located on the west end of the Union Pacific Depot, the Canteen opened on December 25, 1941, and became a gathering place for over 6 million servicemen and women during the next 5 years. For those in the service, everything was free, including cigarettes, books, sandwiches, pie, and birthday cakes. The North Platte Canteen was supported by 125 communities in Nebraska and Colorado. It closed its doors forever on April 1, 1946.

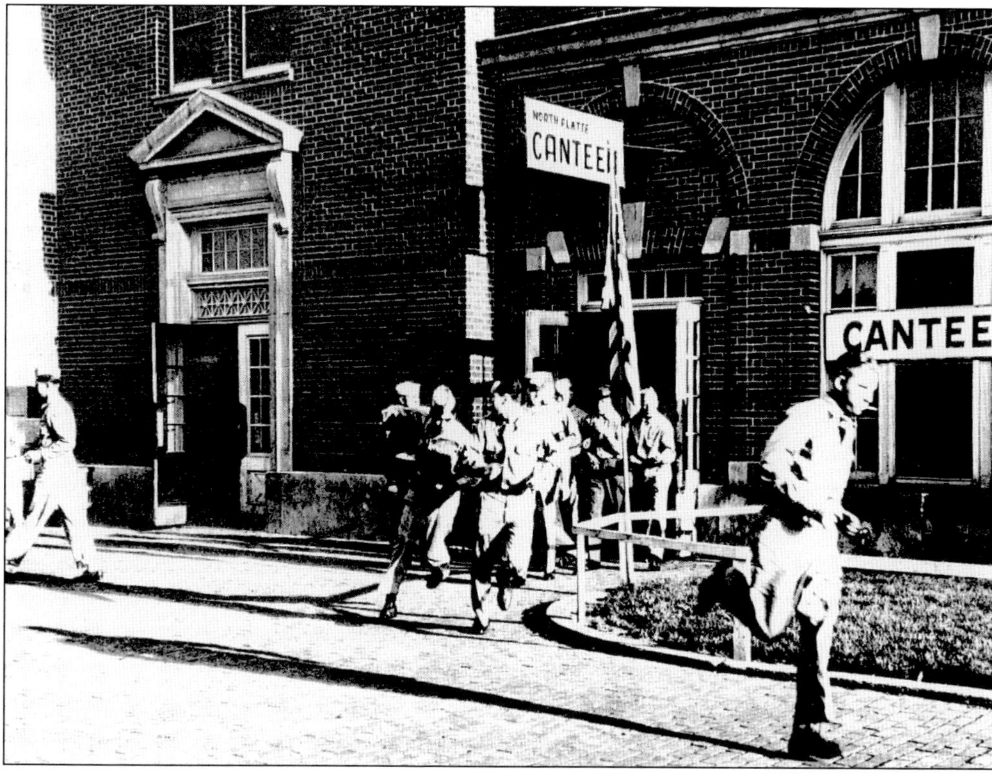

This is how the canteen appeared to those aboard a departing train.

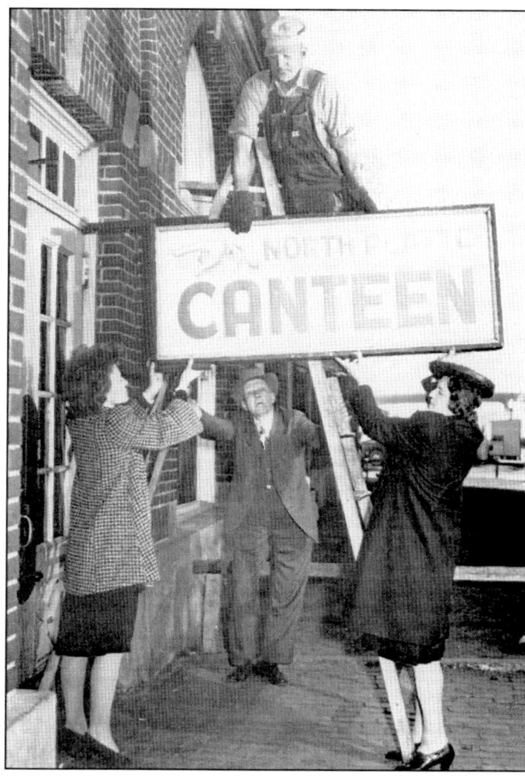

April 1, 1946, was the day the Canteen closed forever. It was a bittersweet experience for those in North Platte, for though the war was over, many important memories had been made.

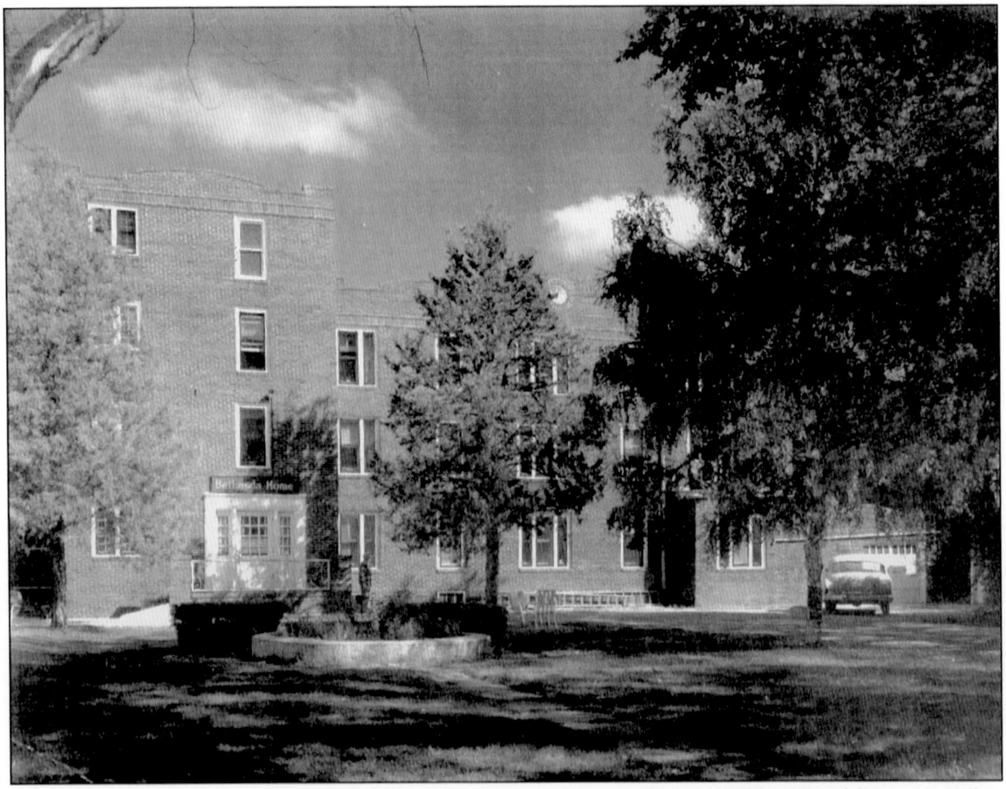

Bethesda Nursing Home was located at 715 South Jeffers and operated by Harold Fenner. This picture was taken in 1942.

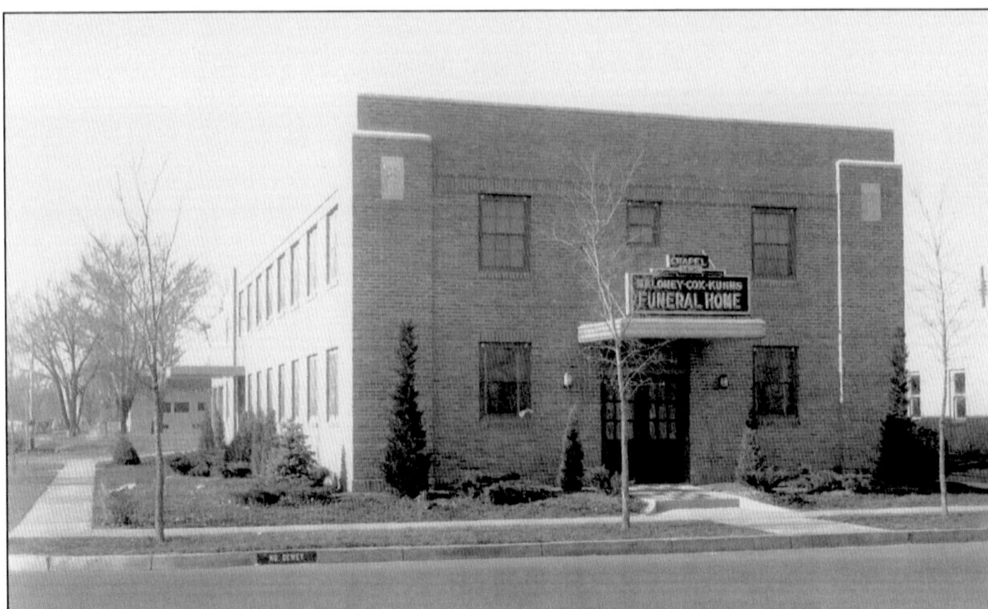

Maloney, Cox and Kuhn's Funeral Home, at 102 North Dewey, later became the site of American Family Insurance. This image dates back to 1942.

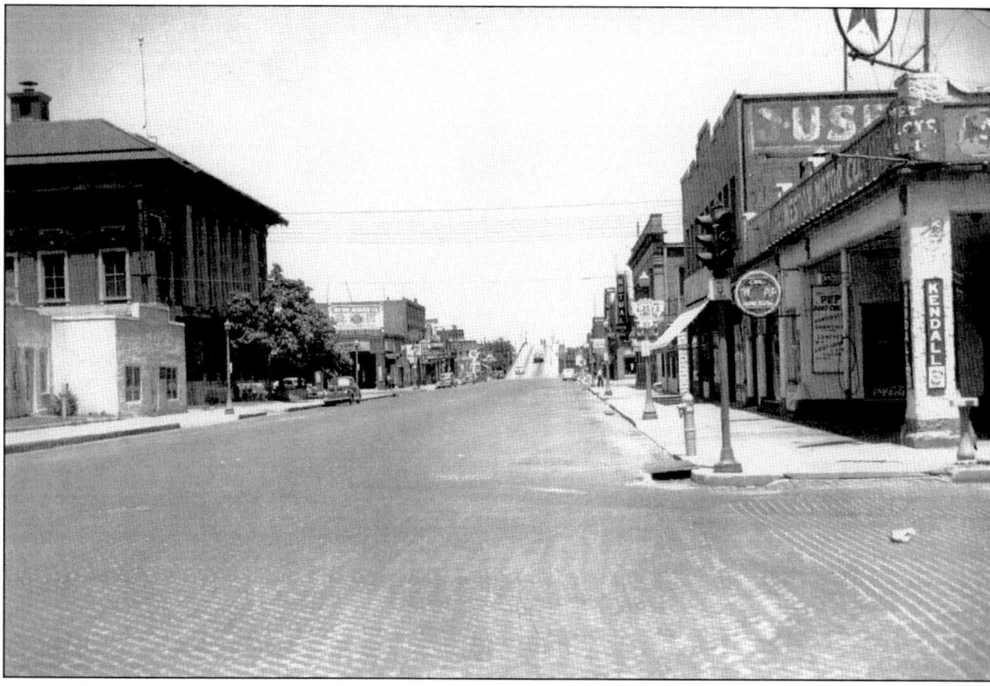

Pictured here is a glimpse of Jeffers Street from Fourth Street in 1942. Notice how nice the brick streets still look after frequent use since 1917.

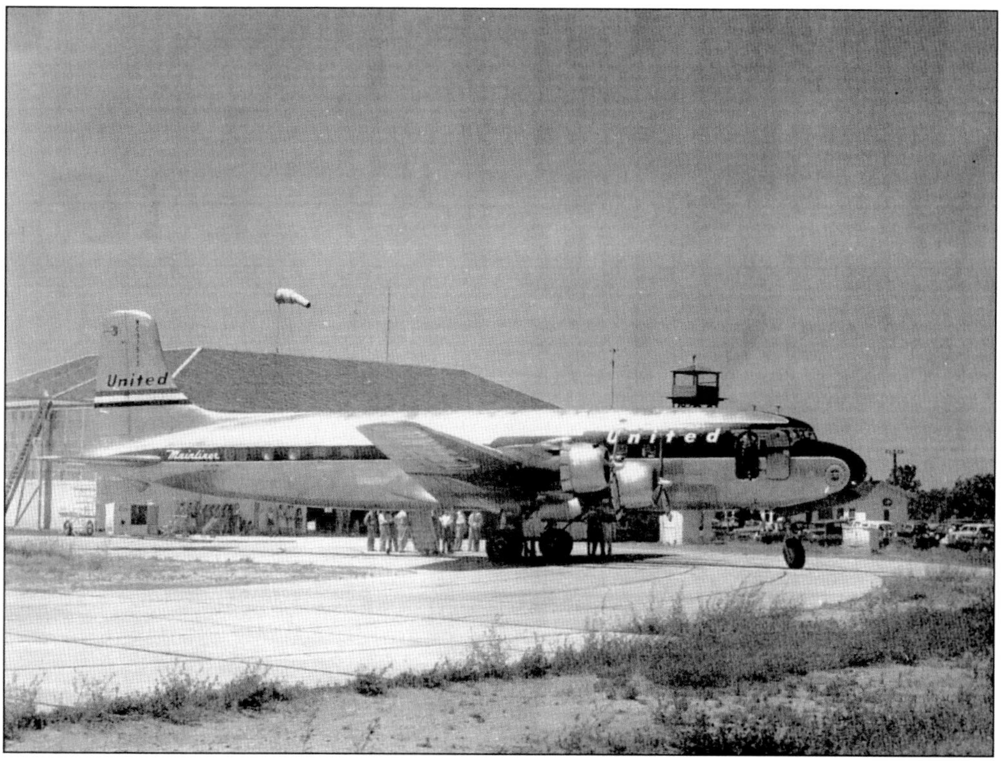

One of United Airlines' DC-3s is loading at the North Platte Municipal Airport.

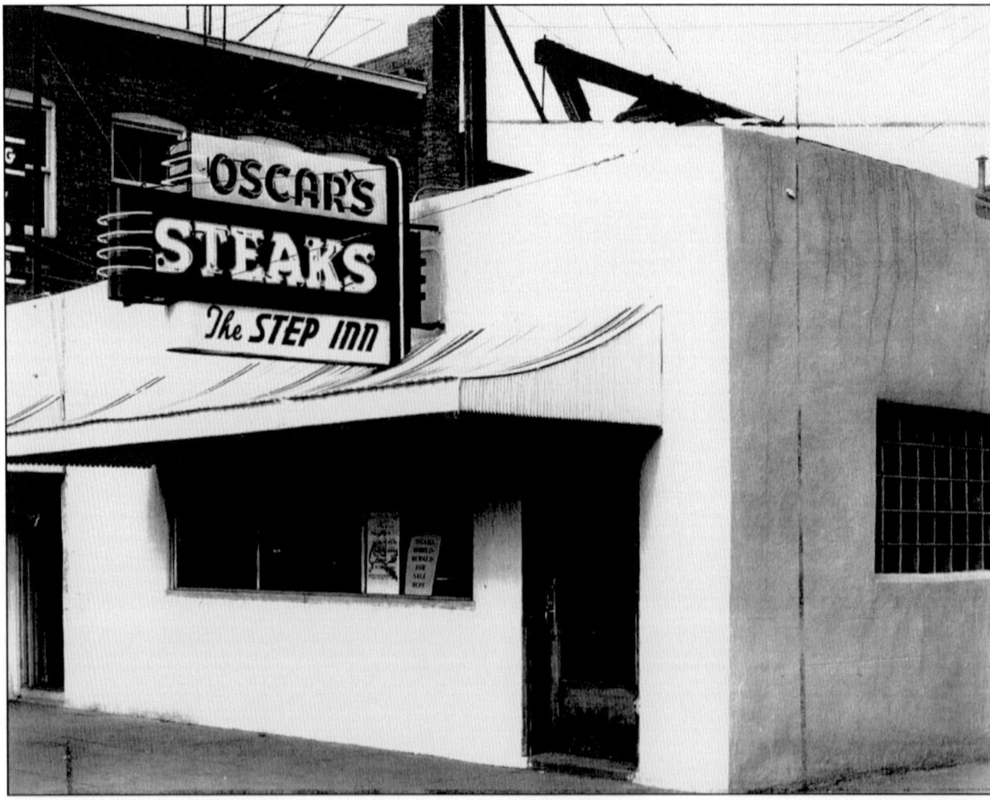

The Step Inn Chile Parlor was owned and operated by Oscar Henry at 413 North Jeffers. This photograph was taken in 1942.

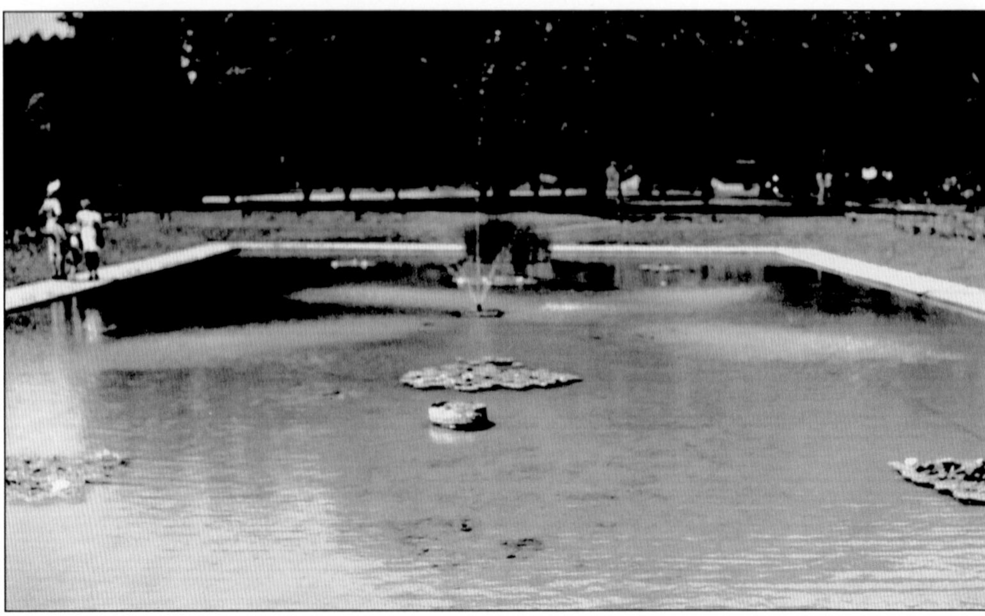
Pictured here is Fish Pond in Memorial Park, as it appeared in 1943. It was located between East Third and East Fourth Streets, near North Tabor and North Bryan.

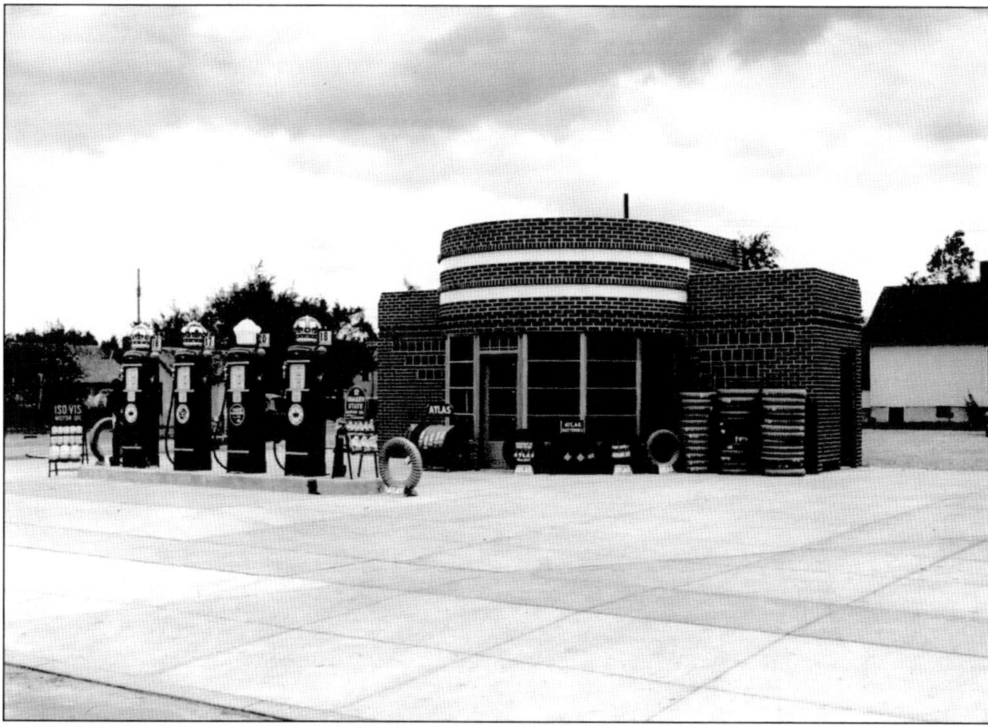

This is a 1943 picture of Hahler's Standard Service at 420 East Fourth Street.

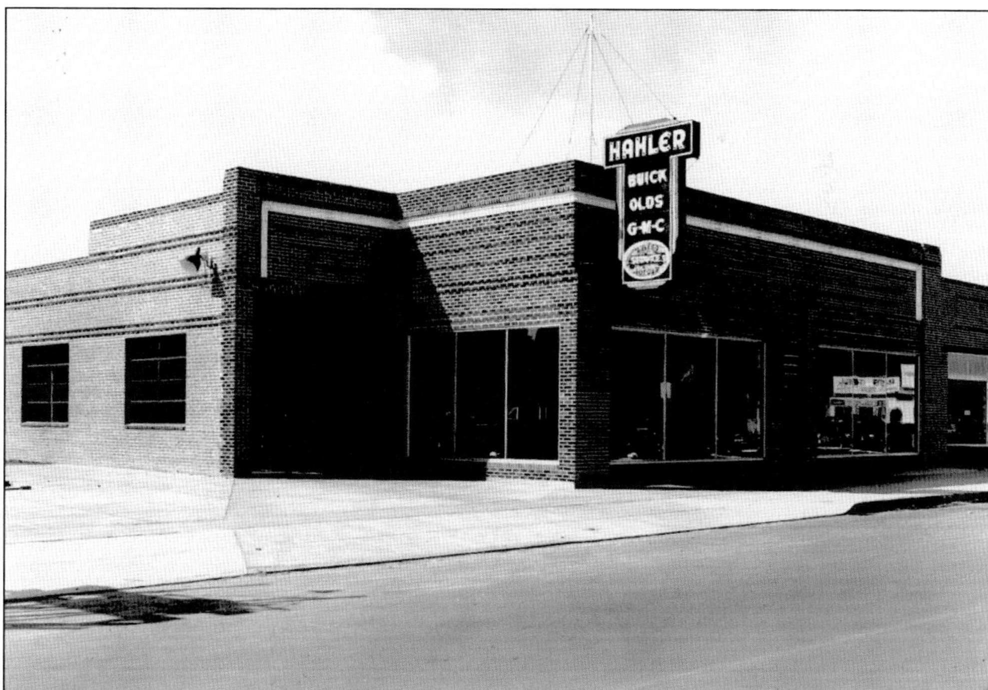

Now the home of Swan's Furniture Store, Hahler's Buick, Oldsmobile, and GMC dealership once sat at 414 East Fourth Street. This is how the agency looked in 1940.

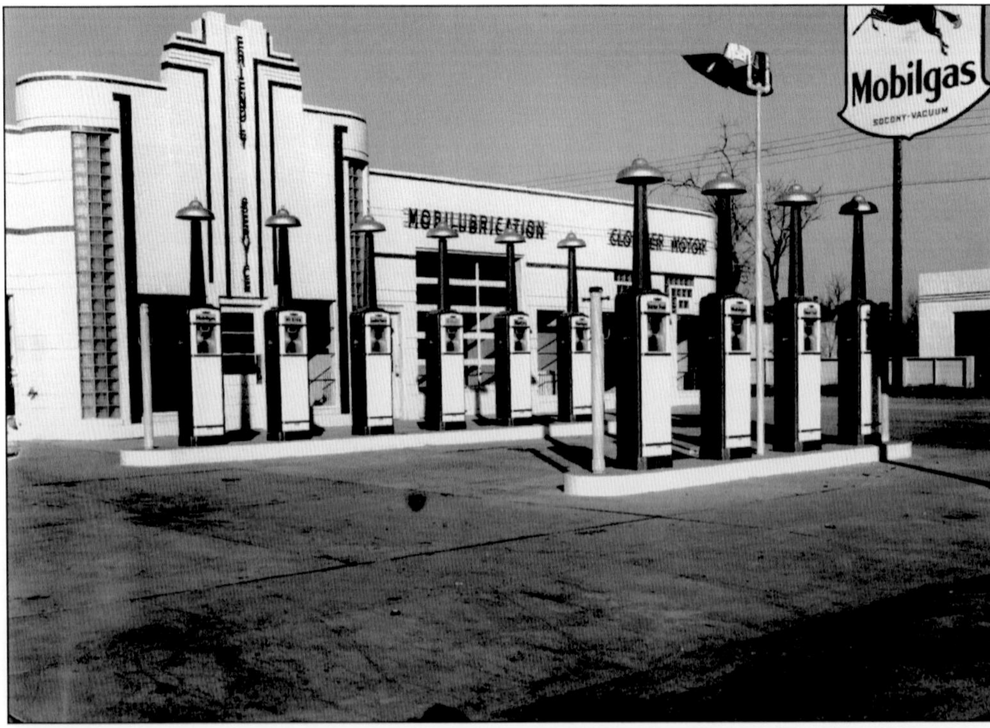

Hinman's Friendly Service was once located at 1008 North Jeffers. This photo was taken in 1943.

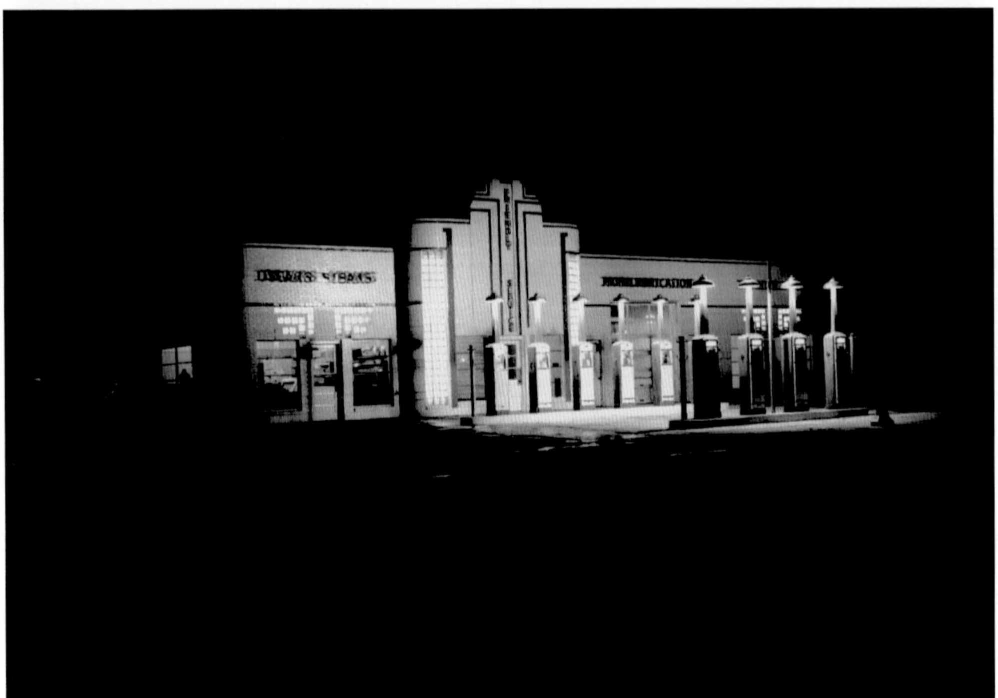

Hinman's Friendly Service (Mobilgas) was also home to the Friendly Inn Café.

Three

Postwar North Platte

1943–1964

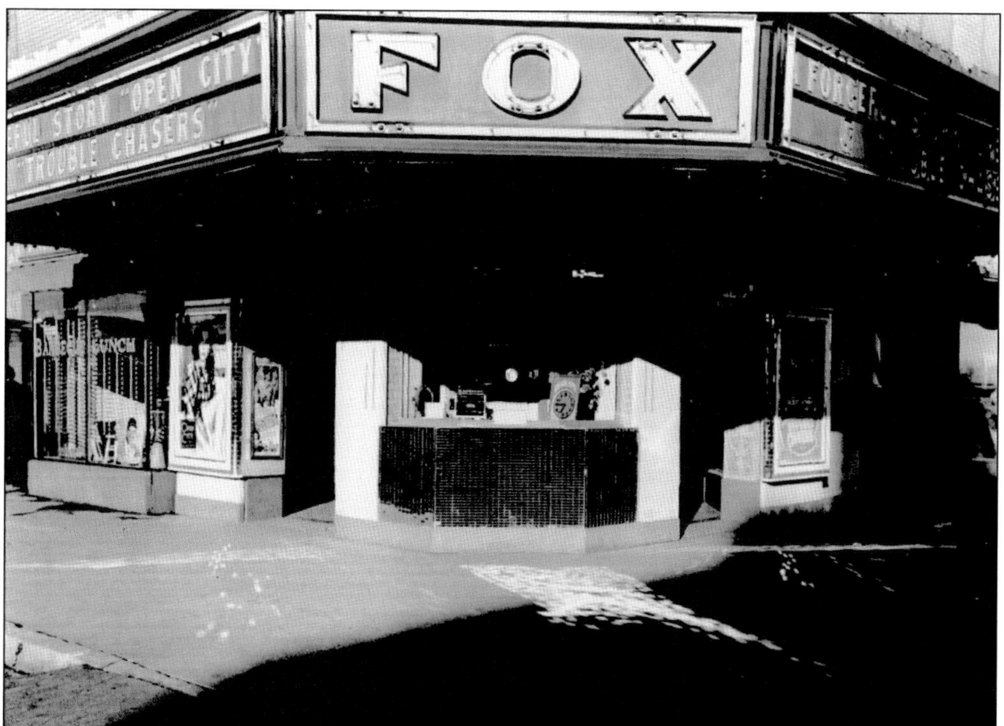

L.F. Newkirk managed the Fox International Mountain Theatre at 301 East Fifth Street. This is how the theater looked in 1943.

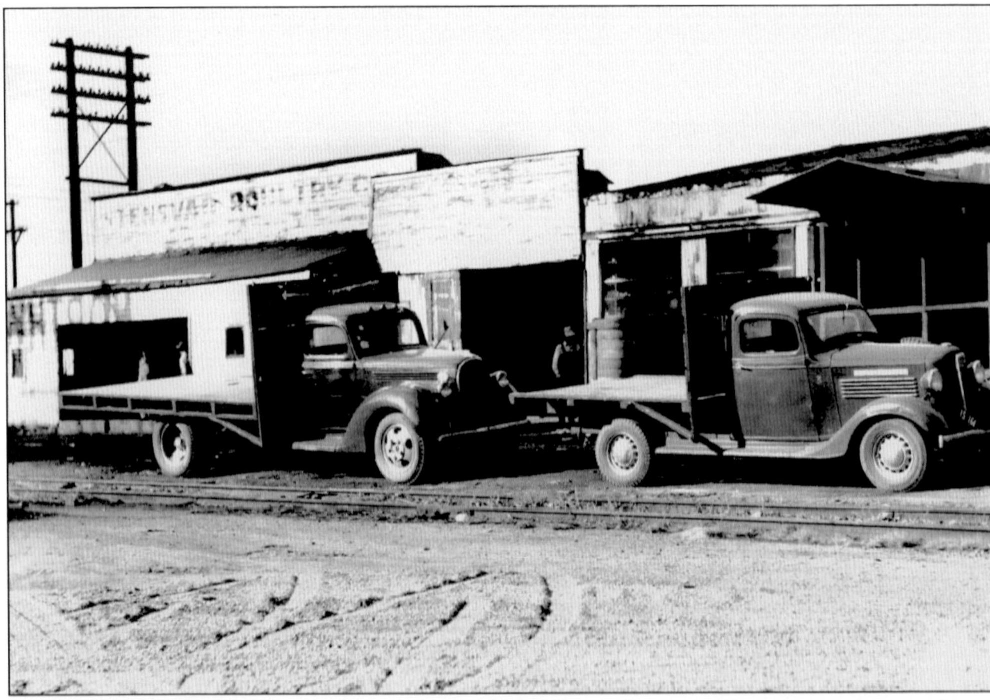

The Stensvad Poultry Company, located at 711 East Front Street, sold cream, poultry, and eggs. Edward A. and Agnes F. Stensvad were the owners.

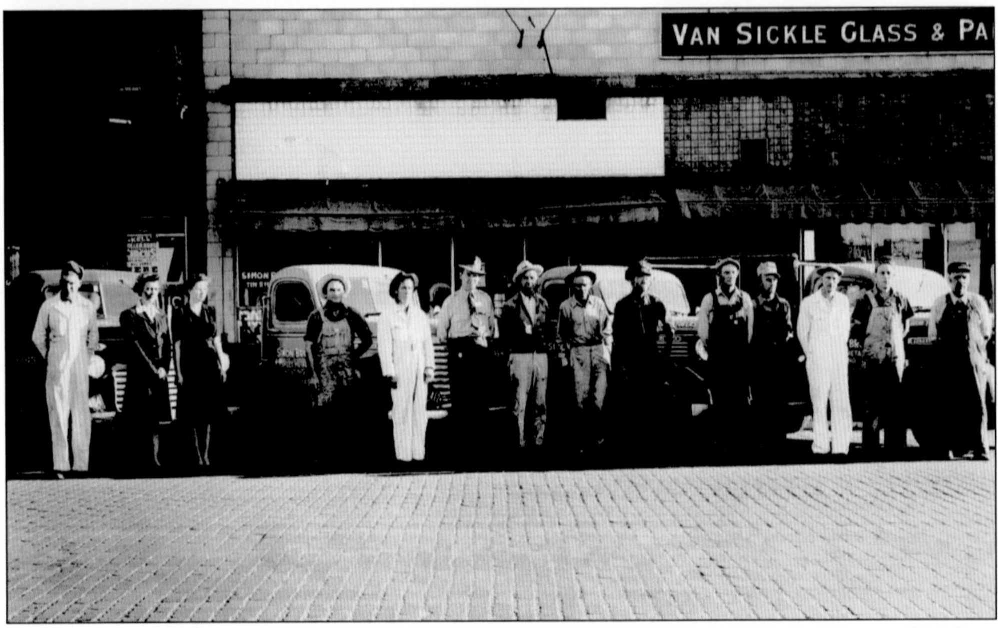

The Simon Brothers Roofing and Sheet Metal Company operated out of a building at 219 East Sixth Street. Pictured here, from left to right, are the following: Wilbur Gosney, Francis Lacy, Pat Simon, George Booth, Bill Howe, William E. Simon, Earl Brown, Earnest Adams, Frank Clark, George Shiltz, John Lloyd, Elmer Hastings, Lynn Fredrick, and Harry Hatisohl. This photograph was taken on August 29, 1944.

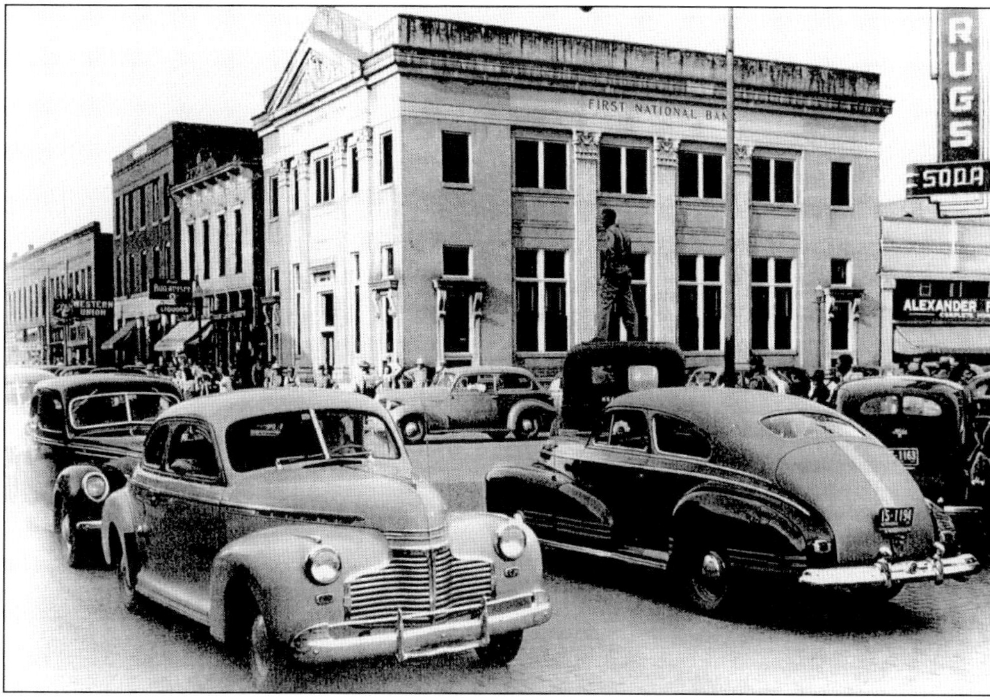

This picture was taken on V-J Day, August 15, 1945, on the corner of Sixth and Dewey. The U.S. Army had sent a squad of the Signal Corps to North Platte to film the North Platte Canteen and were there when the end of the war was declared. One of their men can be seen on top of the carryall.

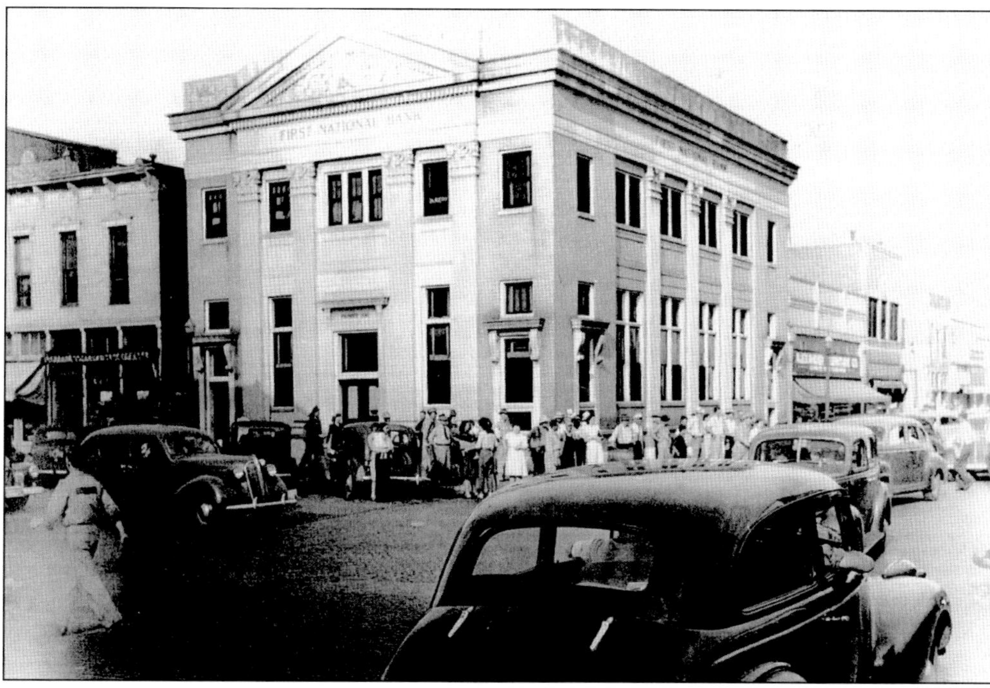

Another photo taken on V-J Day in 1945, this image captures the well-defined brick streets.

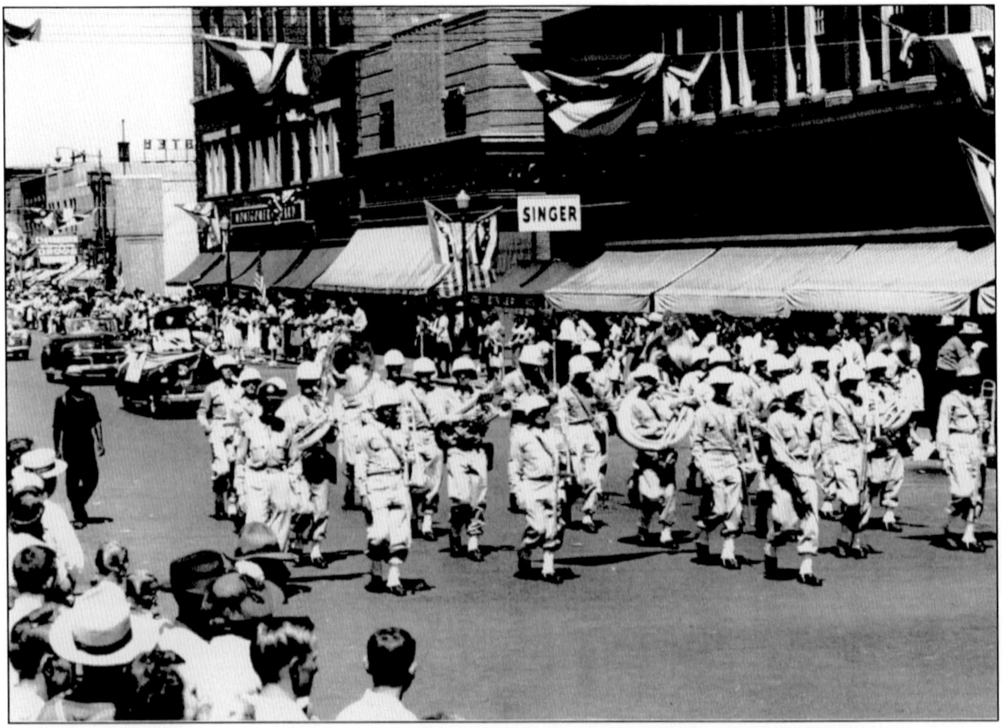

A 1946 parade honored veterans of all wars. This is the 400 block of North Dewey.

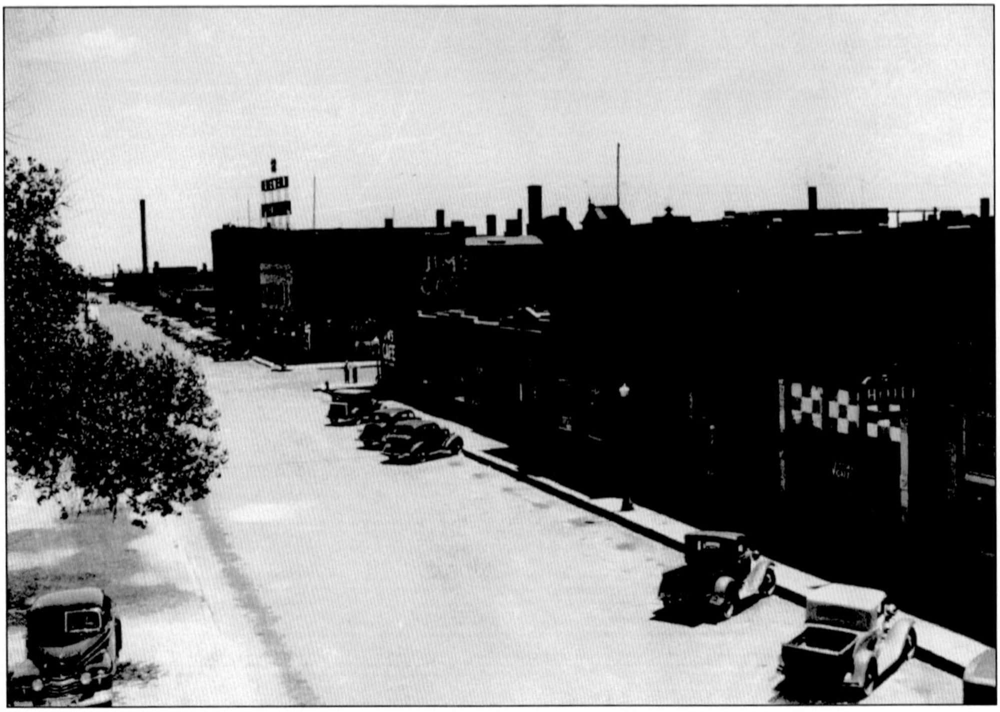
This is a 1946 photo of the 100 block of East Front Street, taken from the Jeffers Street overpass. All of the businesses pictured here were demolished for urban renewal.

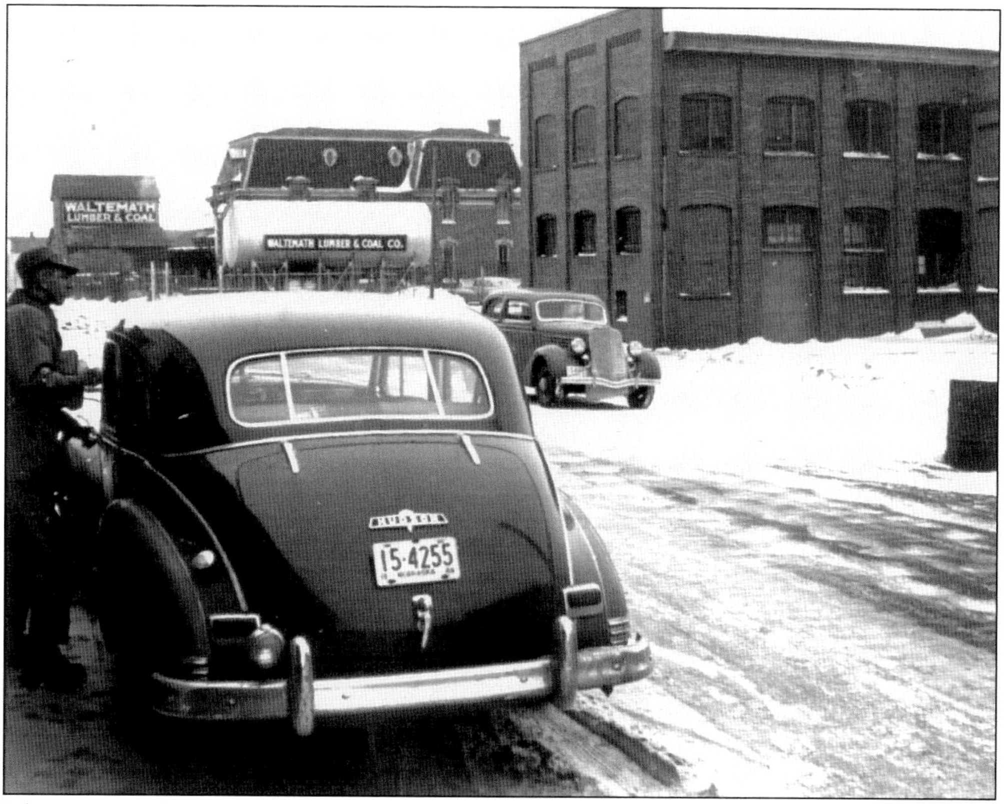

John Stensvad is pictured near the car in front of Stensvad poultry house in this 1946 photograph.

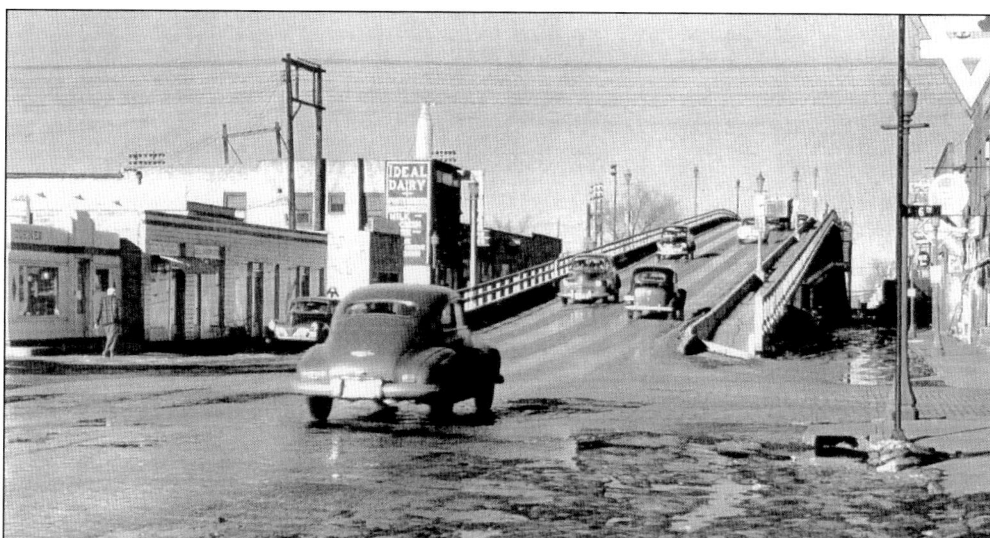

A Standard station once stood here, at Jeffers and Sixth Streets, before the Jeffers overpass was completed. This photograph shows the Cozy Corner Café in 1947. The Conoco station on the opposite corner was also torn down.

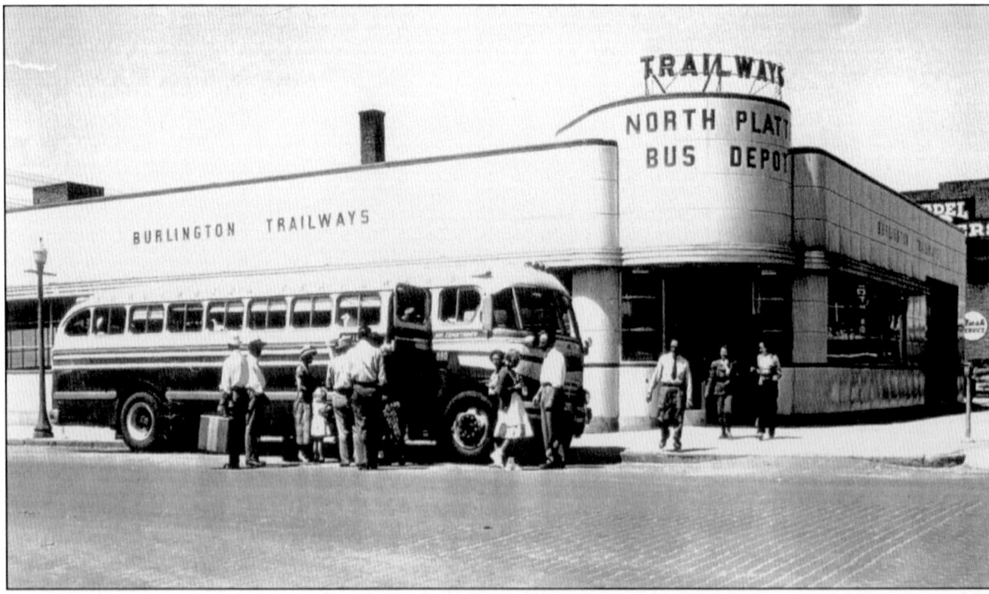

C. Roger Grosh managed the restaurant within the American Burlington Bus Depot on the corner of Sixth and Pine (Bailey). This is how the depot appeared in 1947.

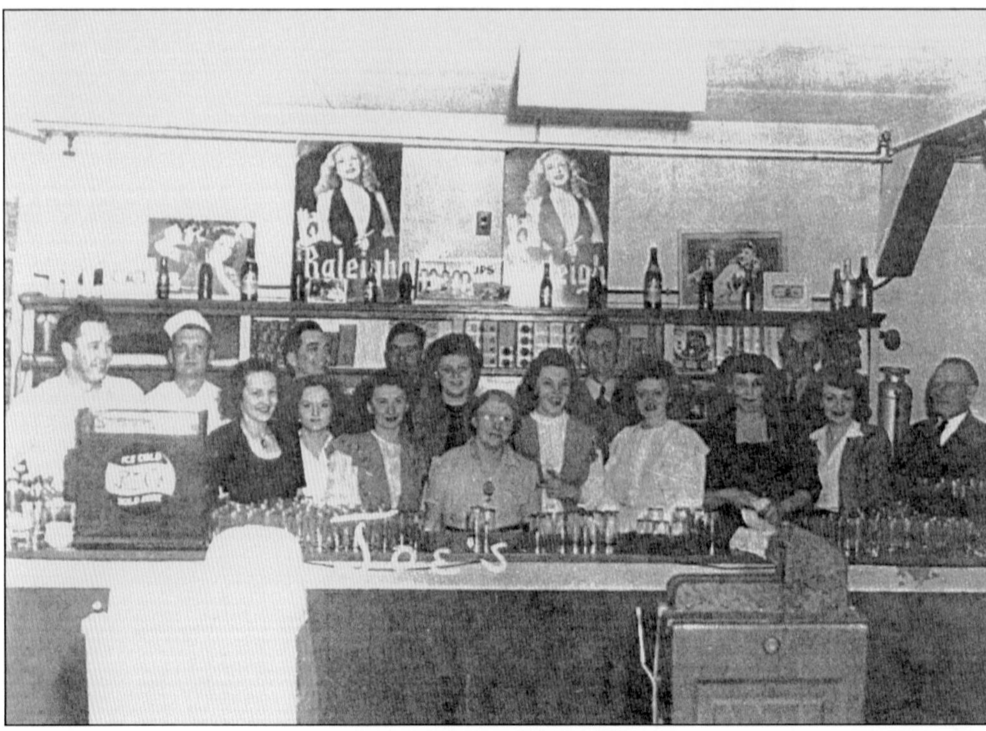

Joe's Supper Club was located three miles west on Highway 30. The ladies pictured in this 1946 photograph are, from left to right, the following: Carrie McCune, Lillian Weldon, Lucille Minor, Letty Schnitker, Mrs. Anthony, Martha Nanan, Inez Schnitker, Bernice Schnitker, and Carrie McCune's sister Martha. The men, from left to right, are as follows: Bob McCune, Harold Mathews, Joe Schnitker, Ed Schnitker, Garrett S. Schnitker (father), and Ray Good.

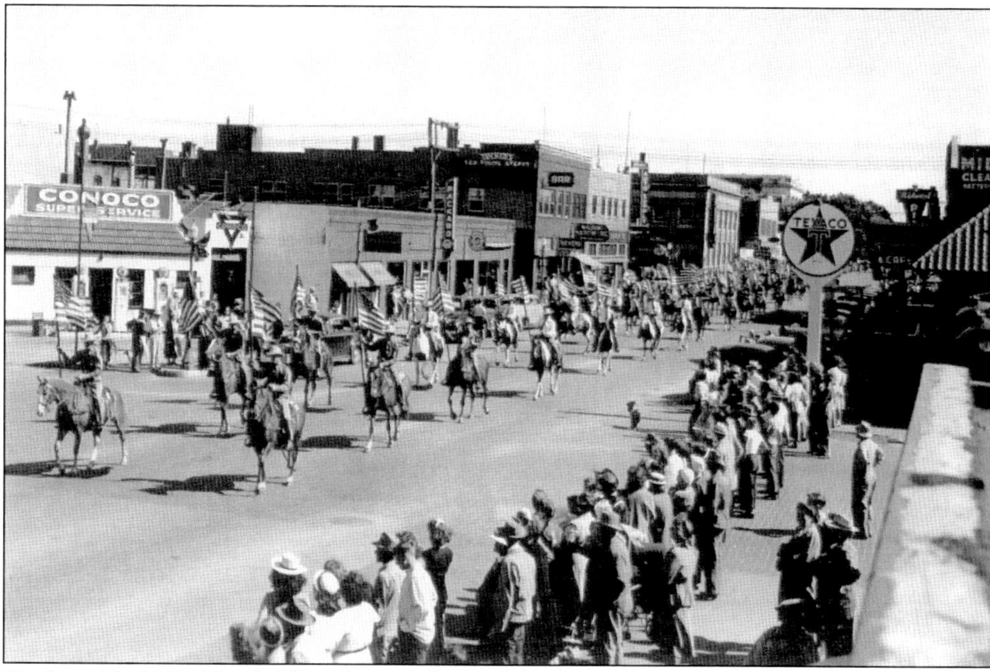

On June 20, 1948, North Platte hosted the Buffalo Bill Blowout Days parade on North Jeffers. Businesses are pictured, from left to right, as follows: Conoco Super Service, Von Goetz Auto Parts, Max Von Goetz Packard Agency, Tucker's Restaurant and Tavern, Wilson Hardware and Sporting Goods, Kinkel Auto Supply, and Evan's Service Station.

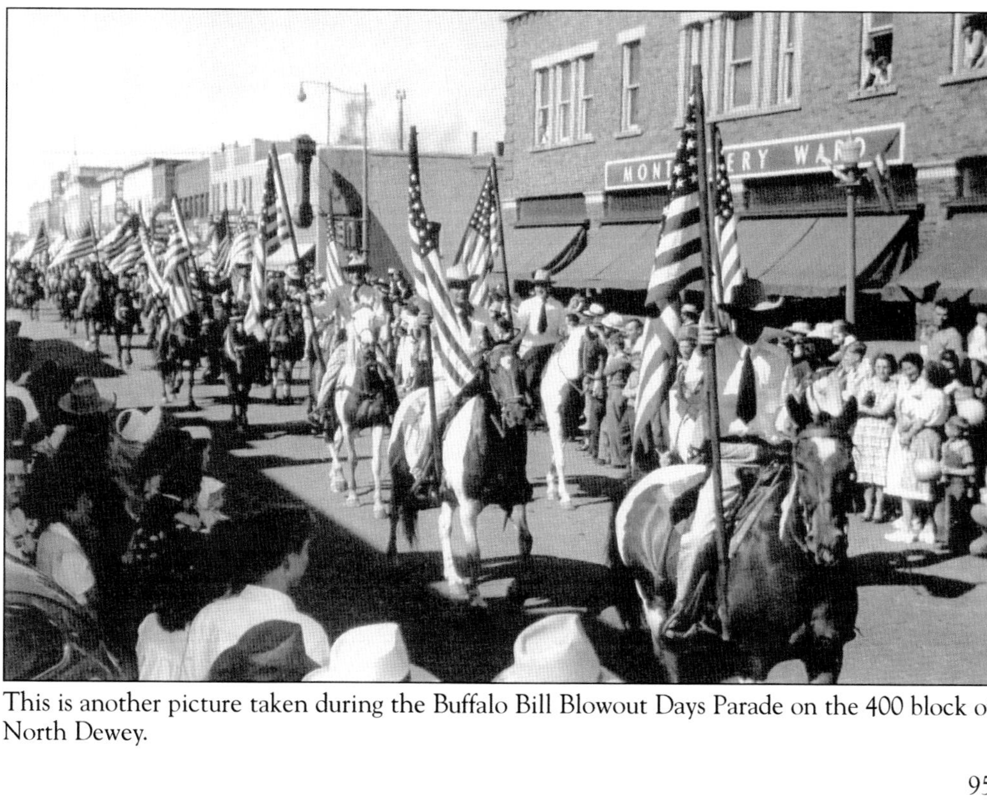

This is another picture taken during the Buffalo Bill Blowout Days Parade on the 400 block of North Dewey.

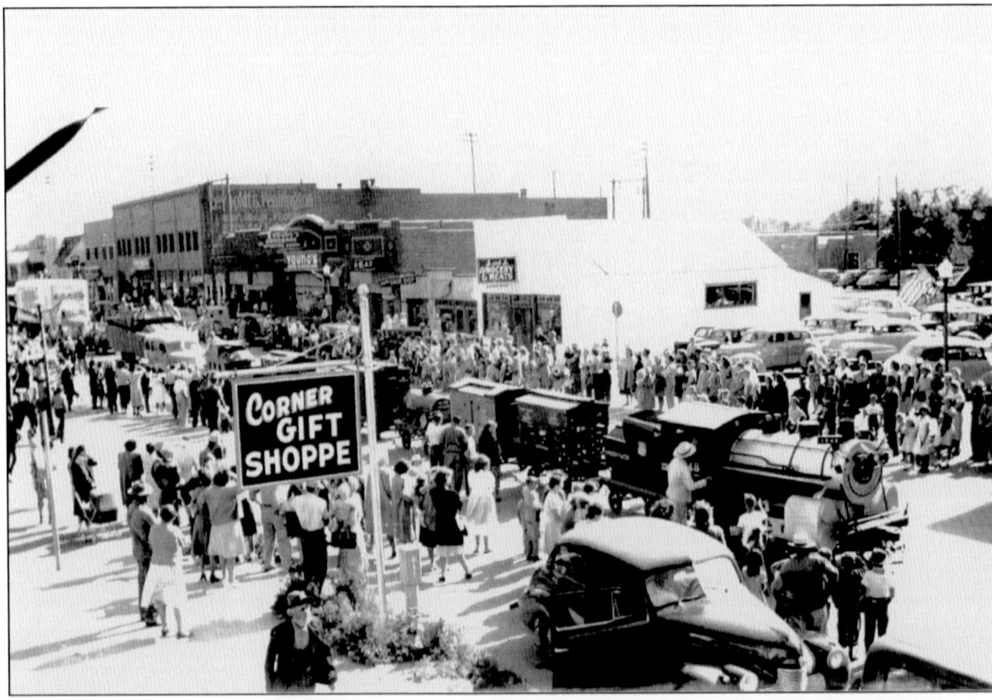

This picture was taken from Mrs. Burton's Rooming House on the corner of Eighth and Jeffers in June of 1948.

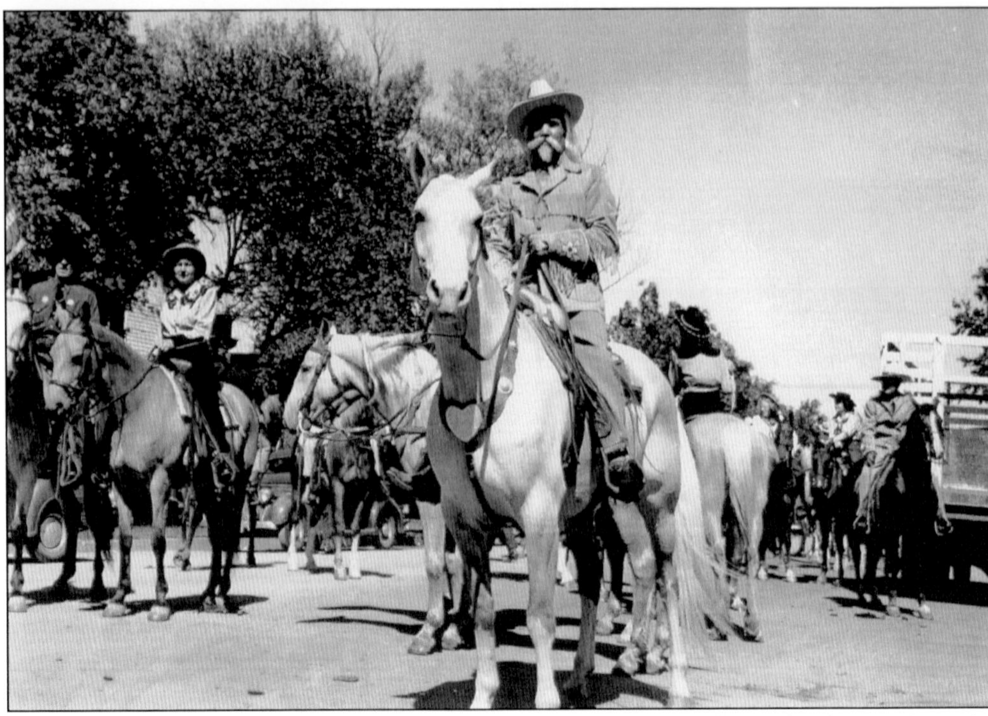

Lee Case from Sutherland was the Grand Marshall of the Buffalo Bill Parade of 1948. Case also furnished the rodeo stock for the celebration.

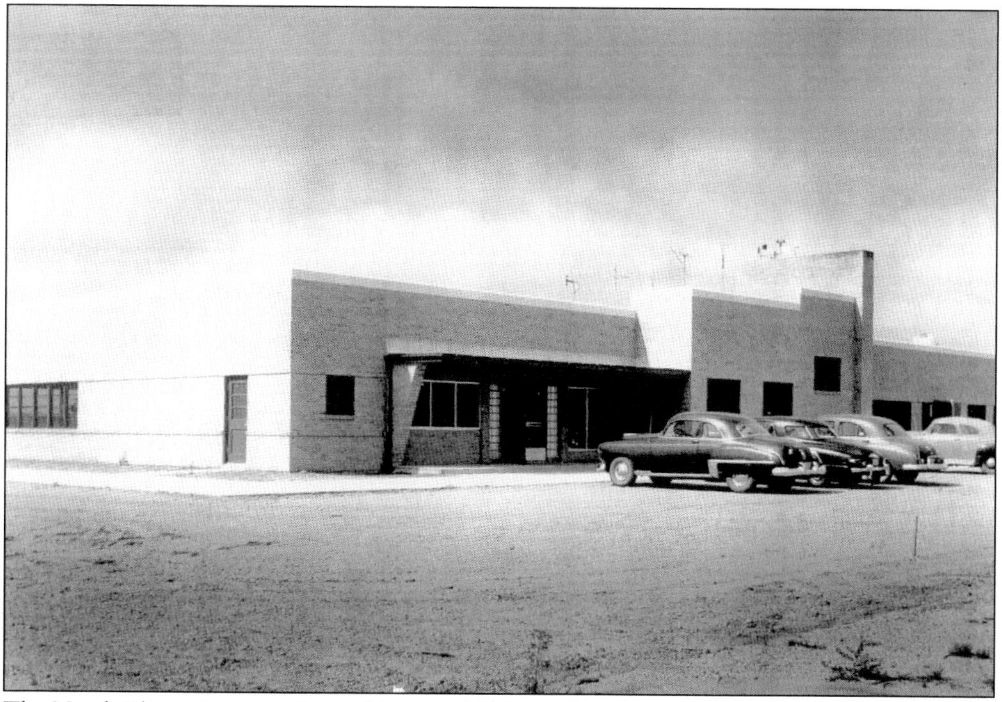

The North Platte Airport, pictured here in 1949, was later renamed Lee Bird Field in honor of the first North Platte flier killed in World War I.

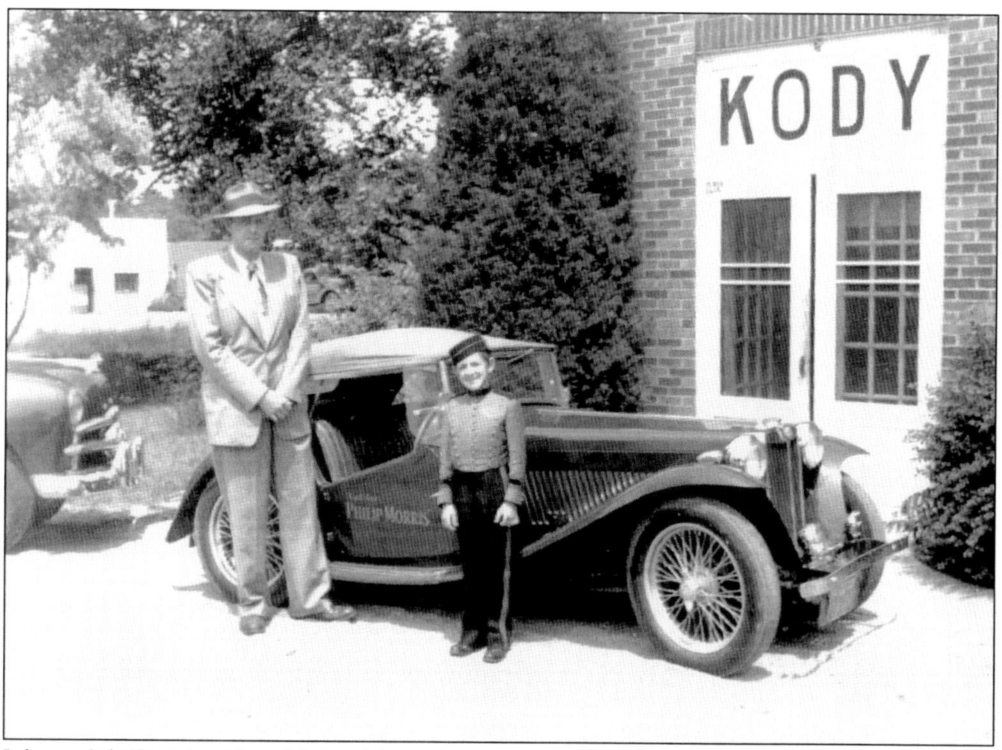

Johnny (Phillip Morris) and John Alexander are pictured at the KODY Radio Station in 1949.

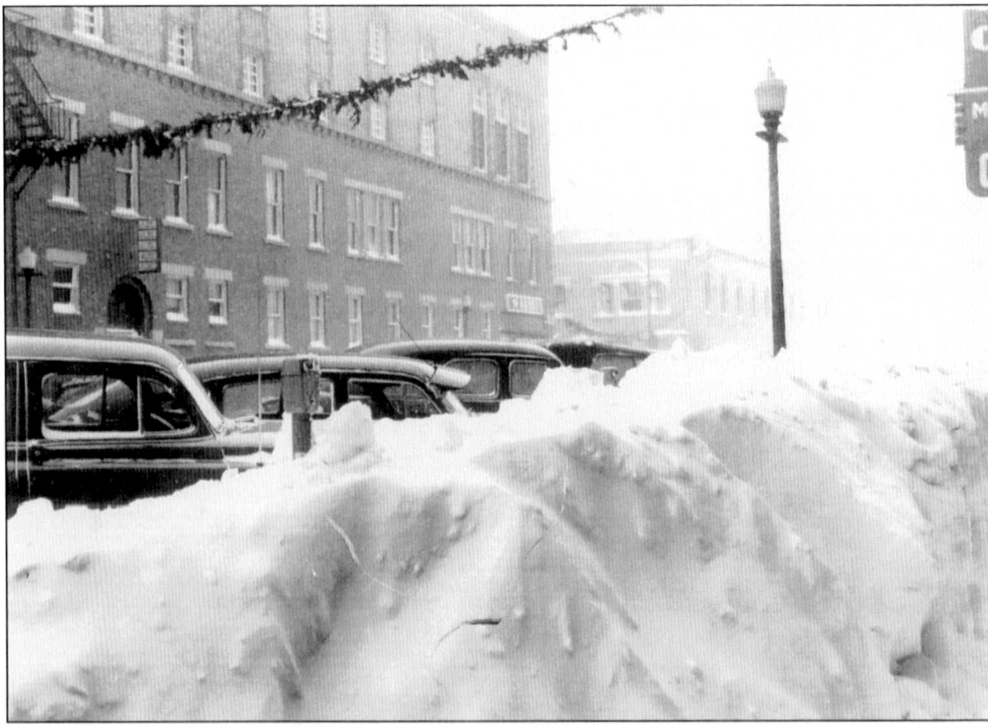

This photograph was taken from the middle of the 200 block on East Fifth Street in front of the Northwestern Public Gas Company, shortly after the blizzard of 1948–1949.

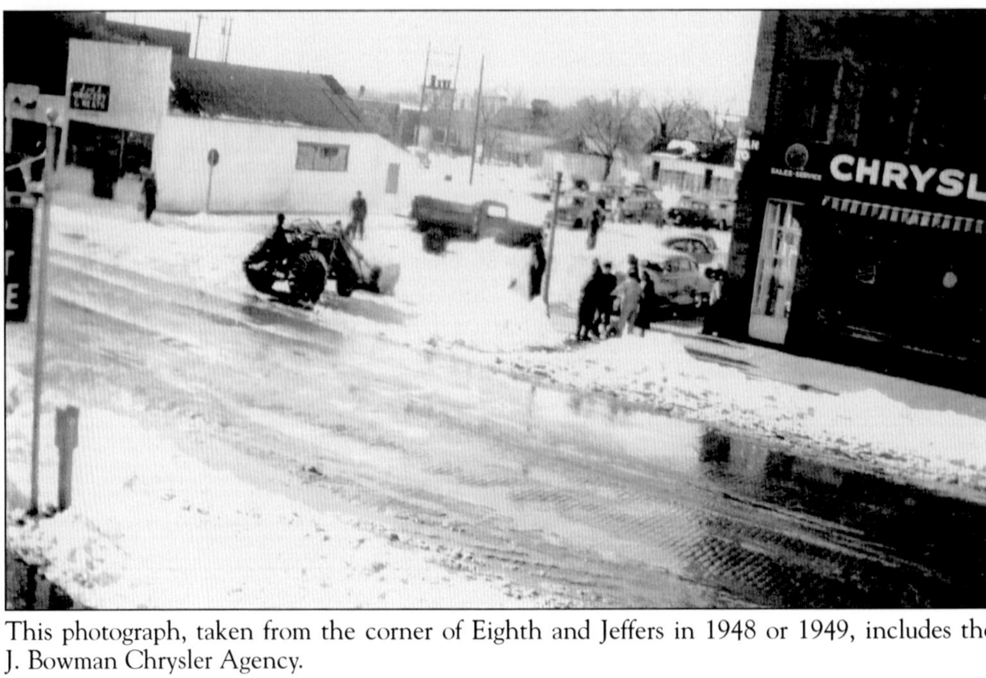

This photograph, taken from the corner of Eighth and Jeffers in 1948 or 1949, includes the J. Bowman Chrysler Agency.

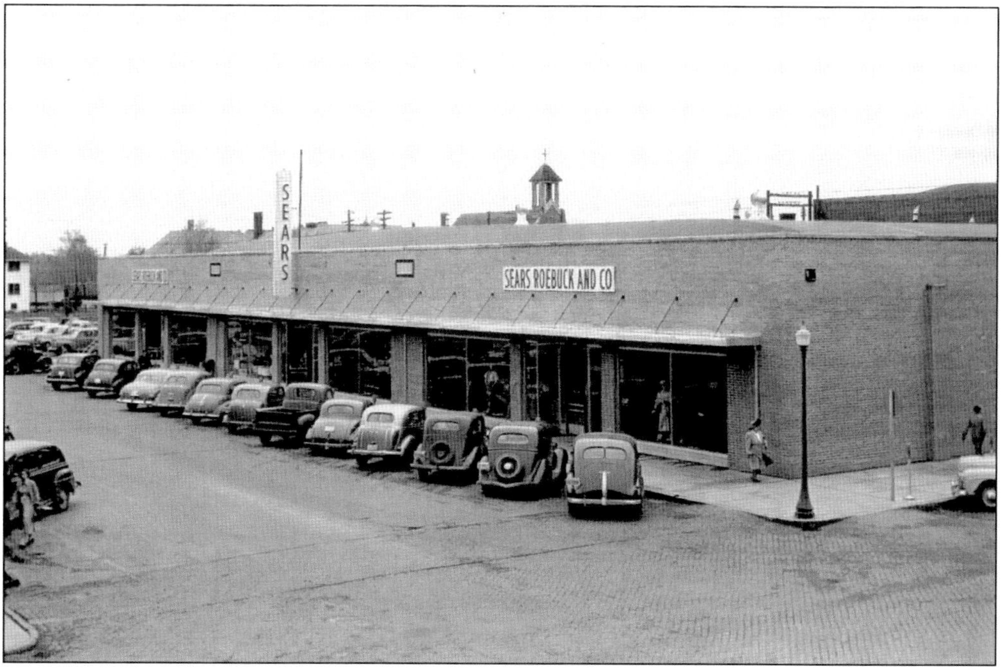

This is a picture of the new Sears and Roebuck Store in the 300 block of East Fifth Street, in 1949. Visible in the background is the bell tower of St. Patrick's Church, which was torn down not long afterward.

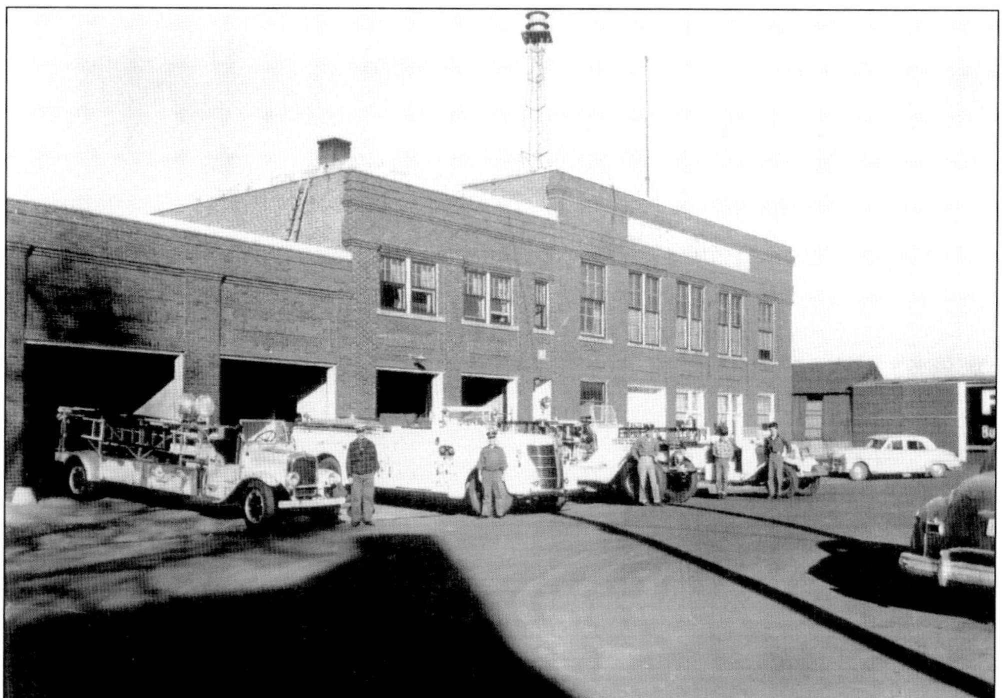

Here is how the Fire Station at Front and Vine Streets appeared in 1950. All if the men pictured are unidentified.

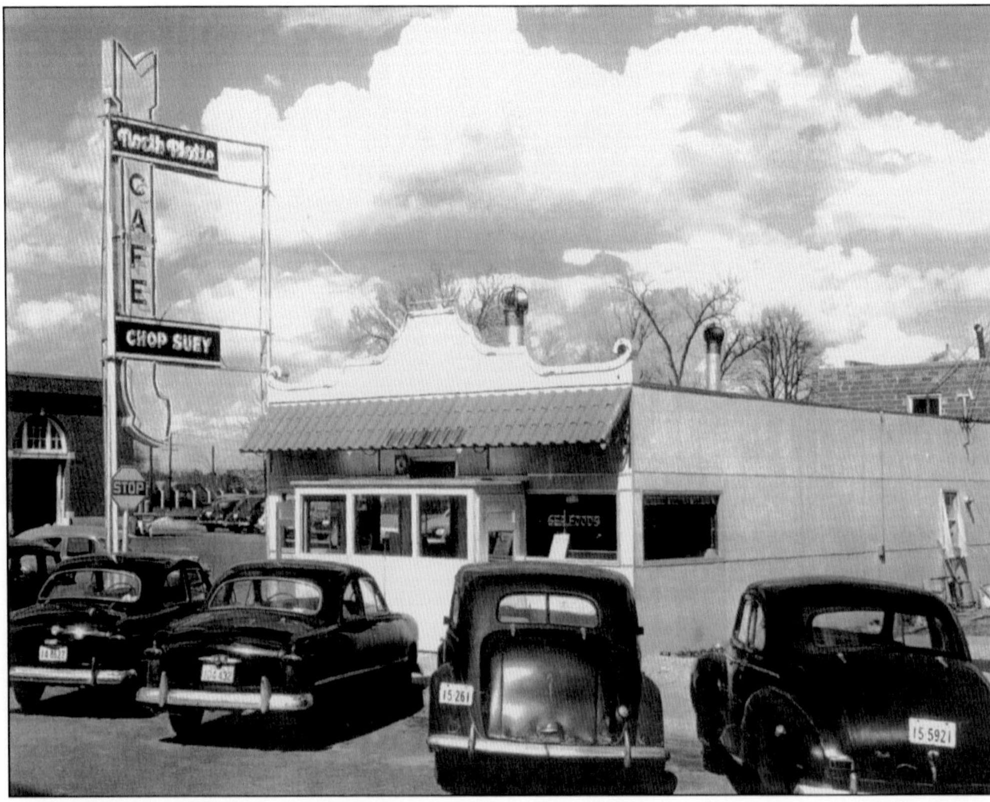

The North Platte Café, owned and operated by Chin Wing, on the corner of East Front and Pine (Bailey) in this 1950 photograph.

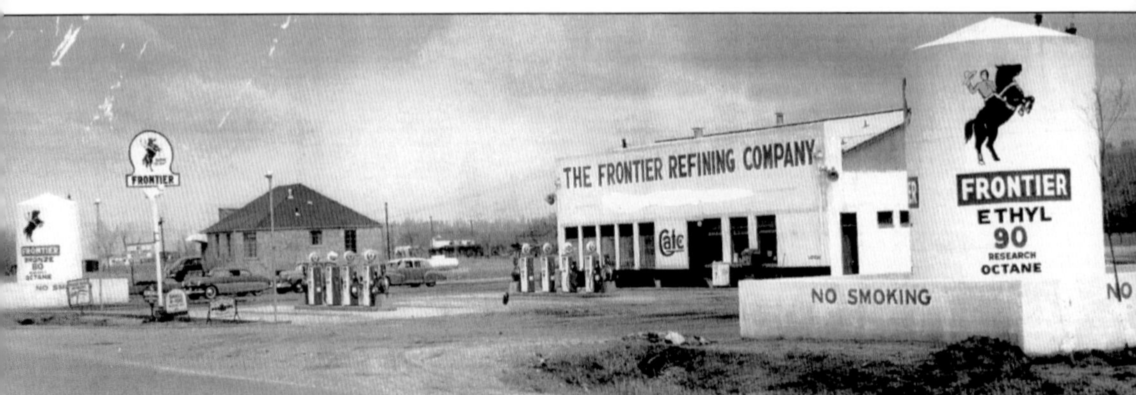

Harold Schaffer managed the Frontier Service Station, Truck Stop, and 24-Hour Restaurant at 3105 West Twelfth Street when this picture was taken in 1950.

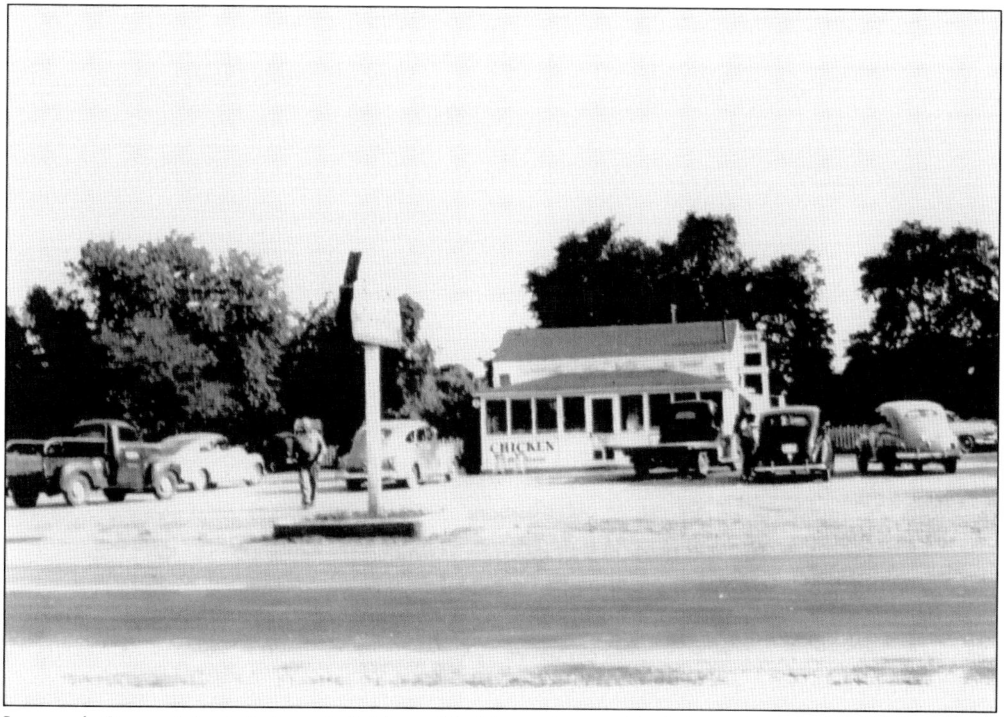

Joe and Grace Merrick founded Merrick's Drive-In, at 1220 East Fourth Street, in 1945. Around 1966, Kris and Louise bought it and renamed it Merrick's Ranch House. Merrick's is now owned by Jacki and Bob Karre. When this picture was taken, in about 1950, it still belonged to its original owners.

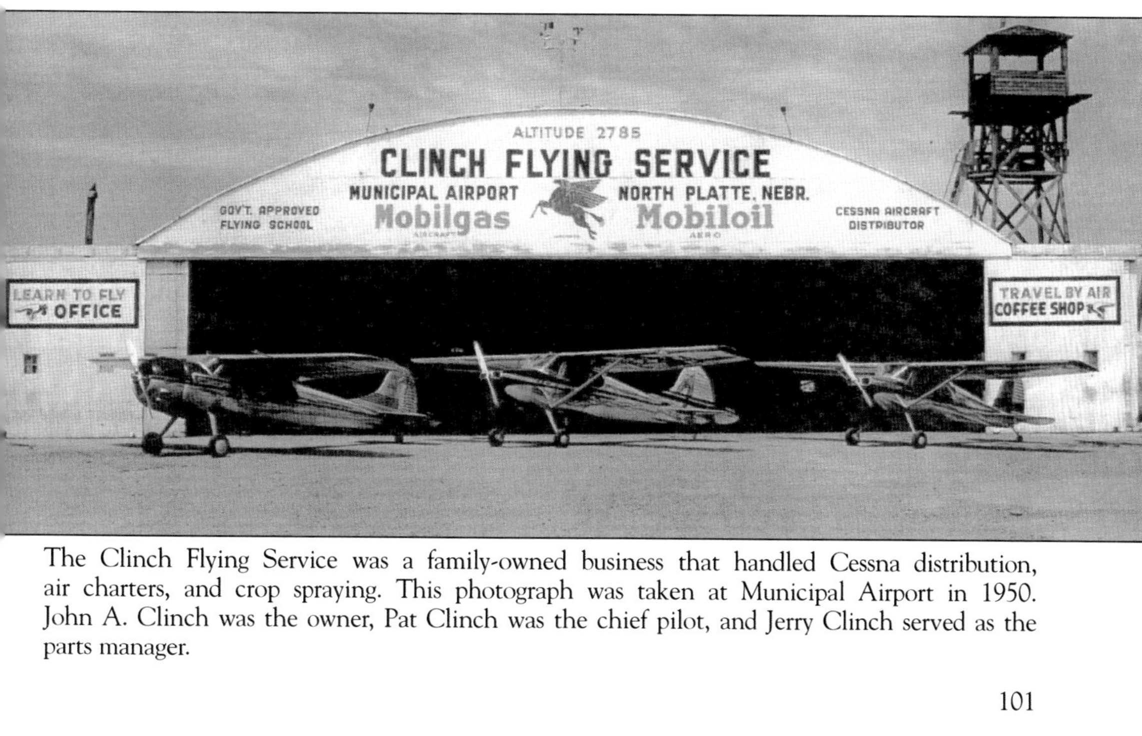

The Clinch Flying Service was a family-owned business that handled Cessna distribution, air charters, and crop spraying. This photograph was taken at Municipal Airport in 1950. John A. Clinch was the owner, Pat Clinch was the chief pilot, and Jerry Clinch served as the parts manager.

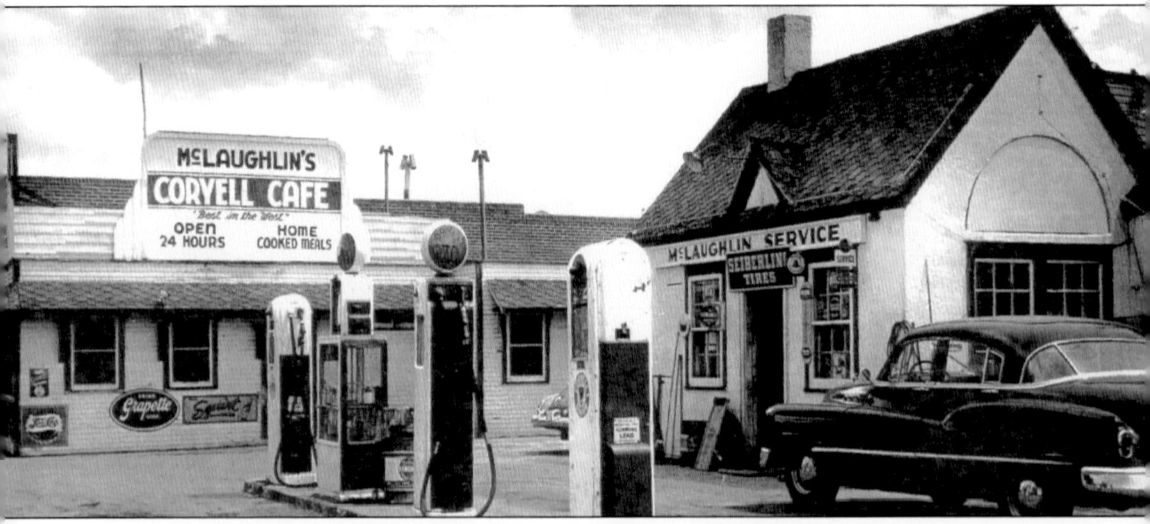

McLaughin's Café and Service Station, at 408 East Fourth Street in this 1951 photograph, is now a vacant lot.

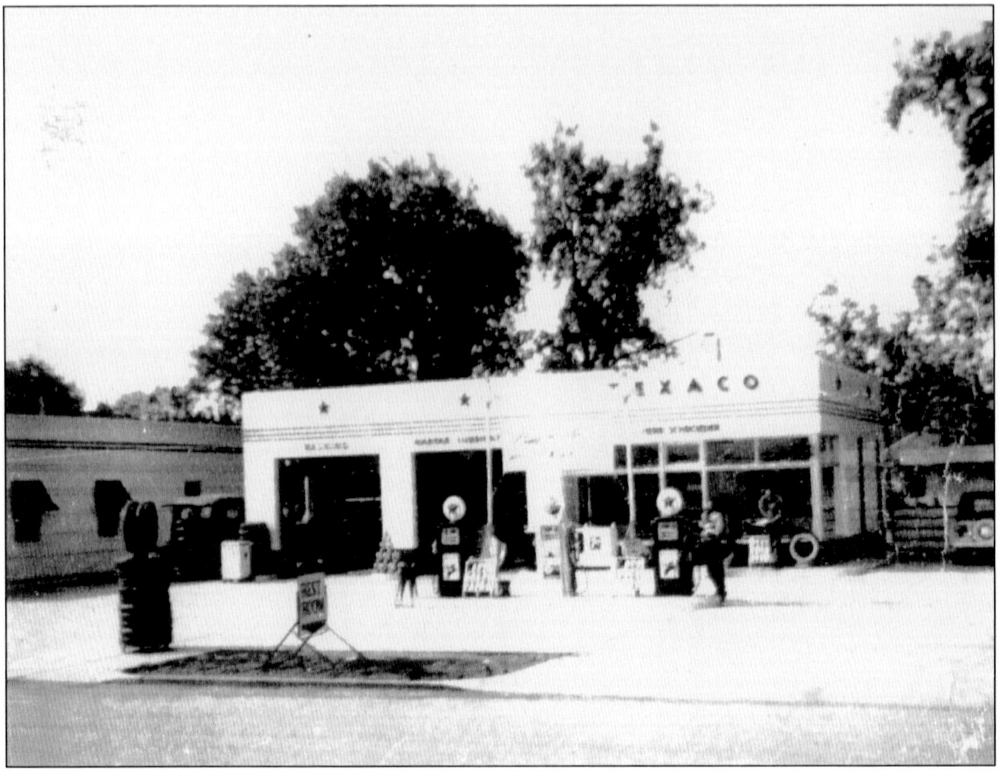

Herb Schroder's Texaco Station on the corner of Twelfth and Jeffers is shown in this 1951 picture. It was owned and operated by Herbert R. and Myrtle N. Schroder.

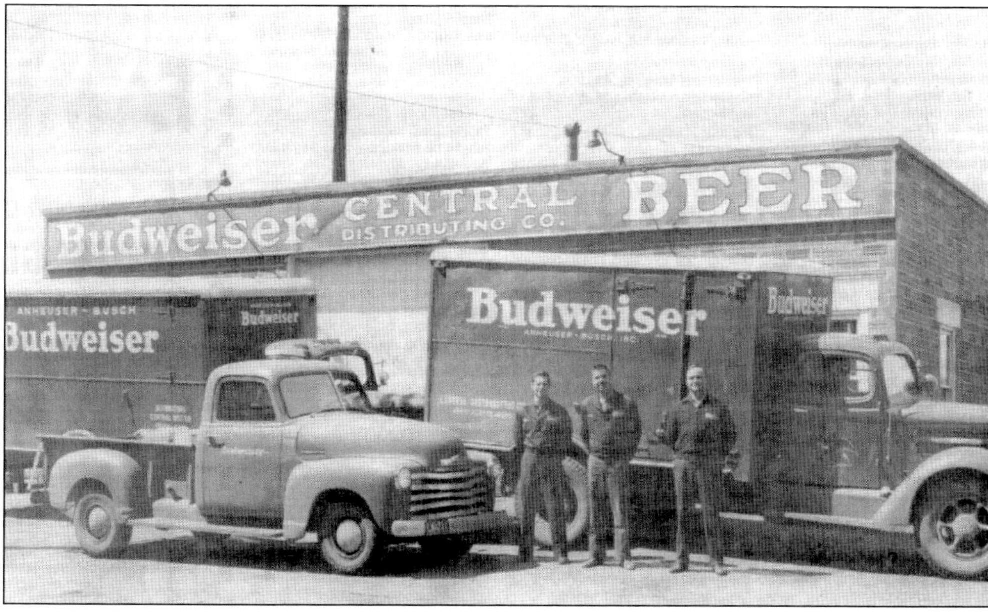

In 1951, the Budweiser Central Distributing Company was located at 523 West Front Street. Pictured, from left to right, are John Humphrey, Chuck Anderson, and Charles (Tot) Anderson.

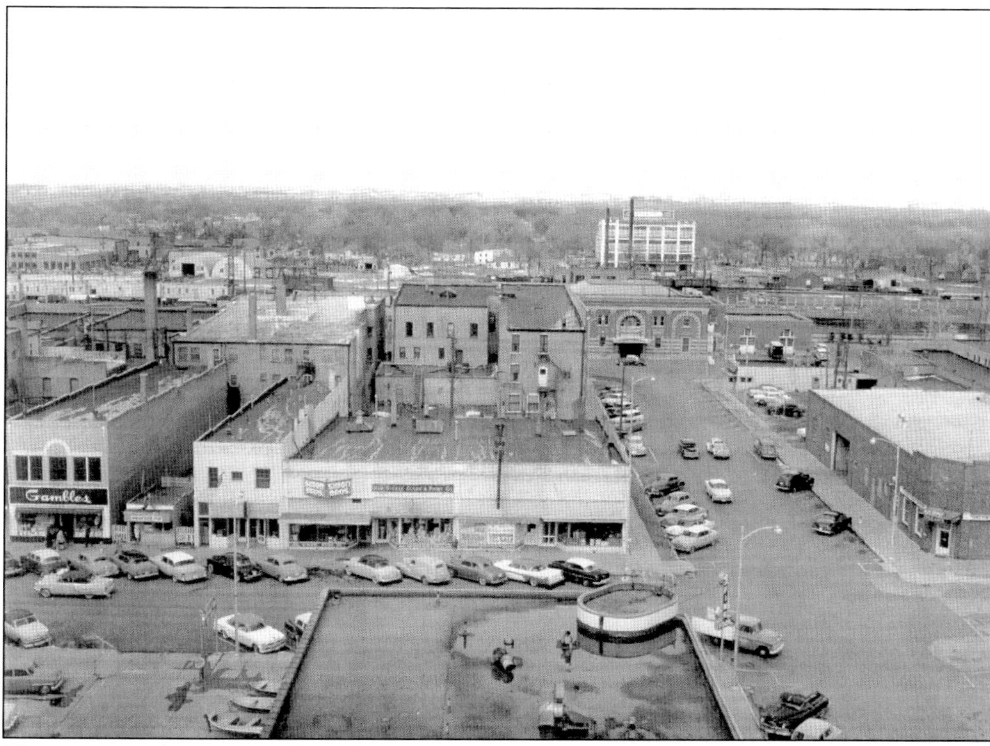

This picture, taken in 1952 from the Pawnee Hotel, provides a look back in time. Every building in this picture fell to urban renewal, except for the 4-story large building in the background, which is the Swift Brookfield Butter warehouse.

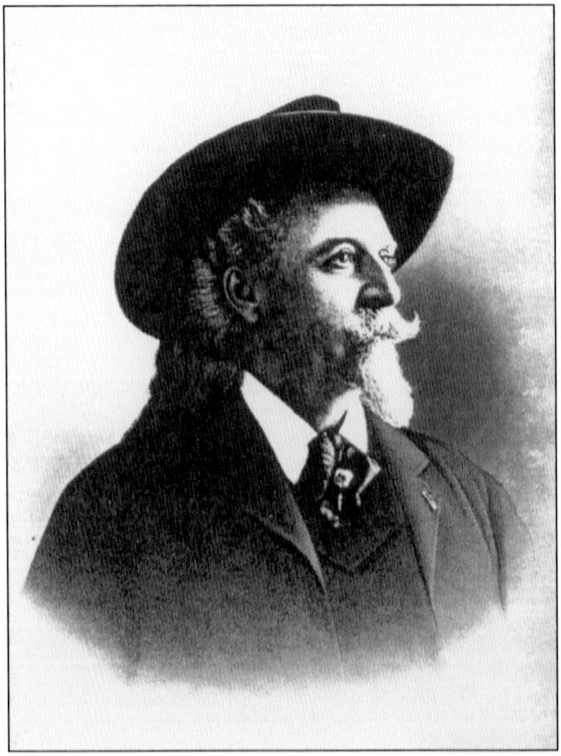

This is a portrait of William F. Cody (Buffalo Bill). He was born in Iowa in 1846 and died in Denver, Colorado, in 1917. He founded the first rodeo ever presented in America on July 4, 1882. His Scouts Rest Ranch still stands about three miles northwest of town.

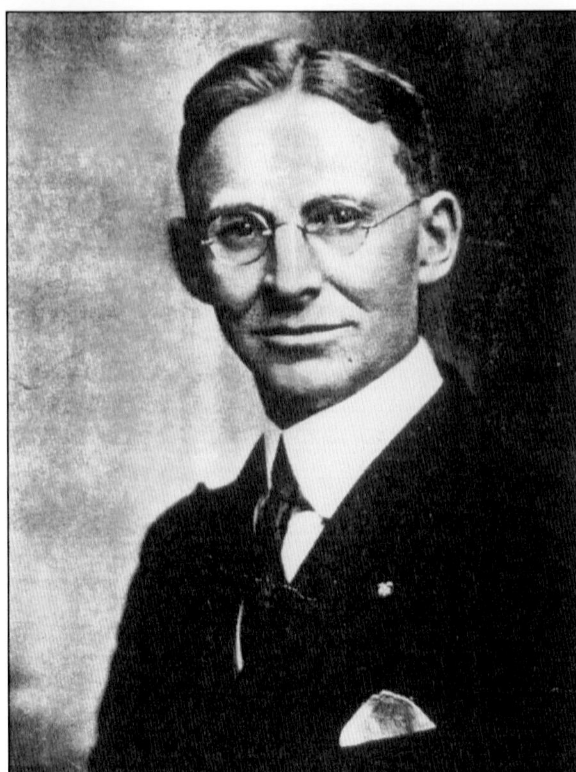

An important figure in North Platte history, William McDonald was the first white child born in Lincoln County (although it was named Shorter County at that time). He was born June 14, 1861, and died on June 14, 1961, at the age of 100. He married Minnie Belton on June 16, 1886. Both are buried in the North Platte Cemetery, along with both sets of their parents.

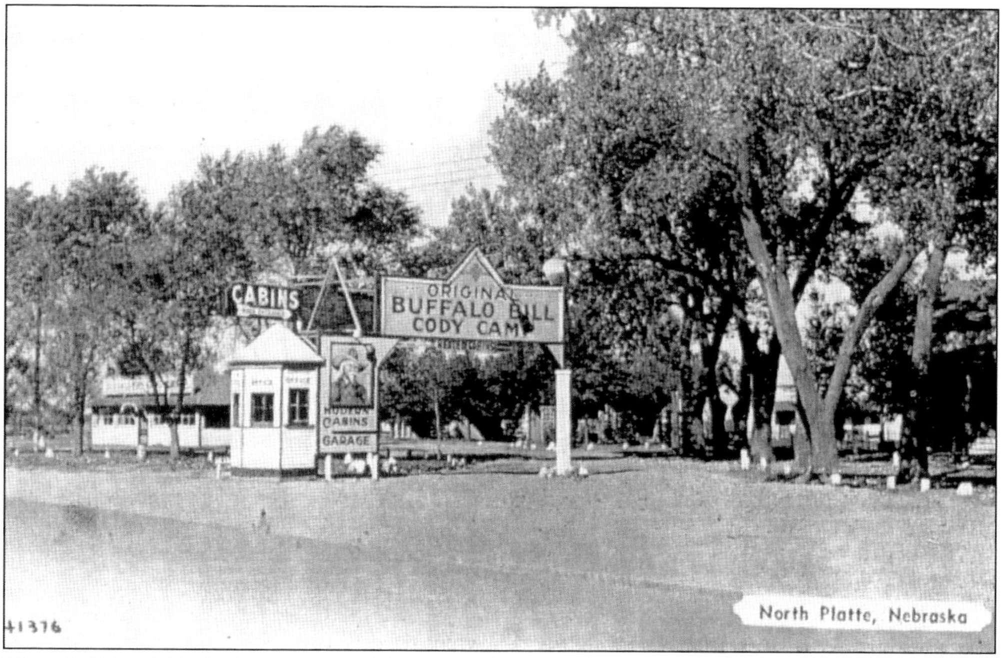

The Buffalo Bill Cody Camp and Trading Post was located at 1301 West Twelfth Street. This picture dates back to 1950.

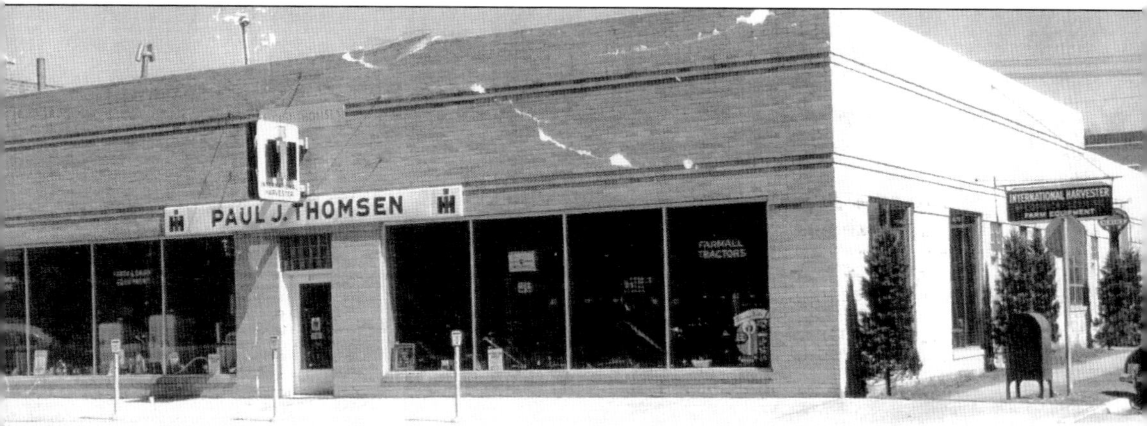

B and D Office Supply now resides at the site originally occupied by Paul J. Thomsen International Harvester and Farmall Tractors. The Thomsen Company, captured in this 1952 photograph, was located at 321 East Fifth Street.

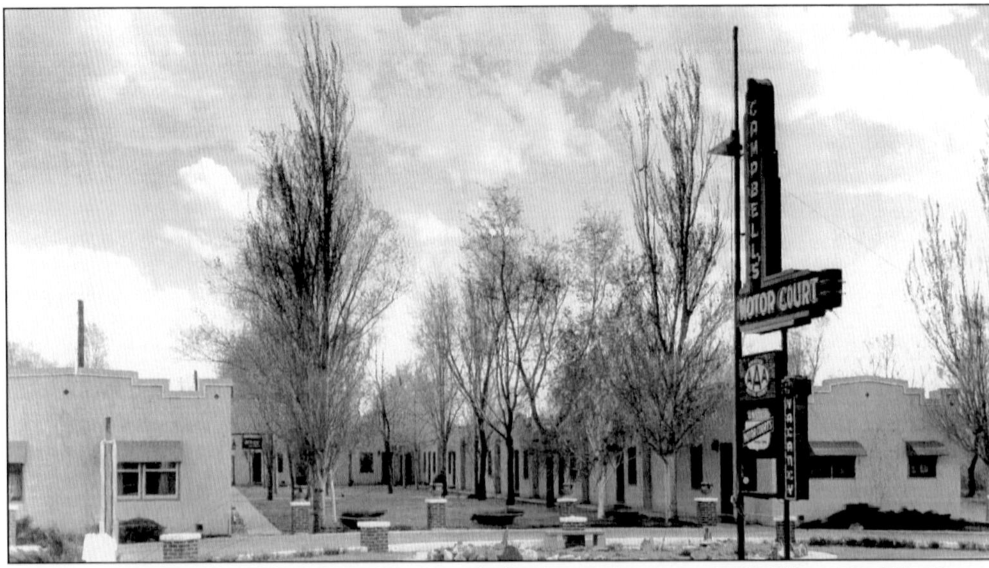

Russell and Mabel Langford ran the Campbell Motor Court at 1400 West Twelfth Street, pictured here in 1952.

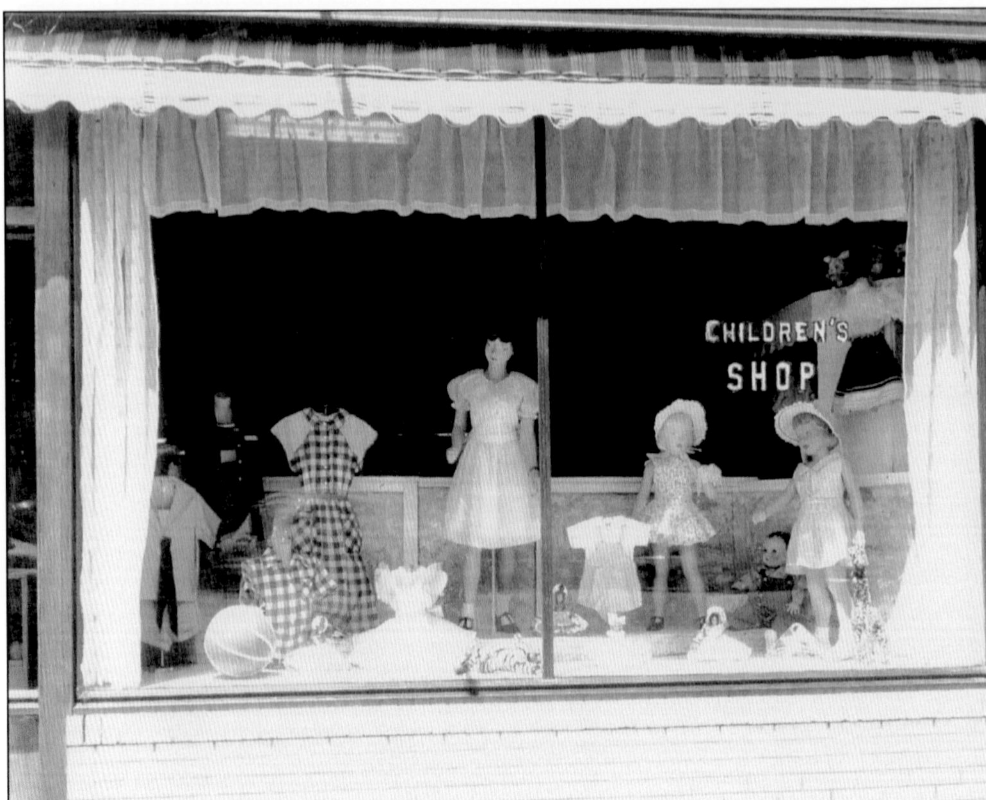

The Children's Shop, which sat at 105 East Fifth Street, was owned by Gertrude Gifford for many years. This is how the shop looked in 1952.

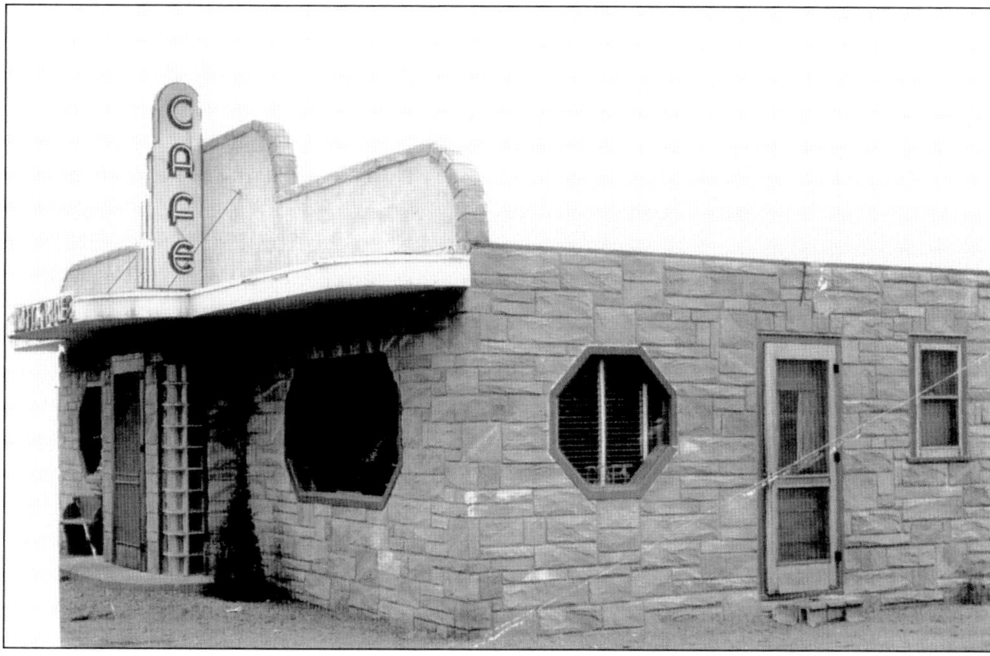

Now home to the Kirby Company, this building at 1300 West Twelfth Street once housed the Knotty Pine Drive-In. Lester and Helene Gunderson were the Drive-In's proprietors. This photo was taken in 1952.

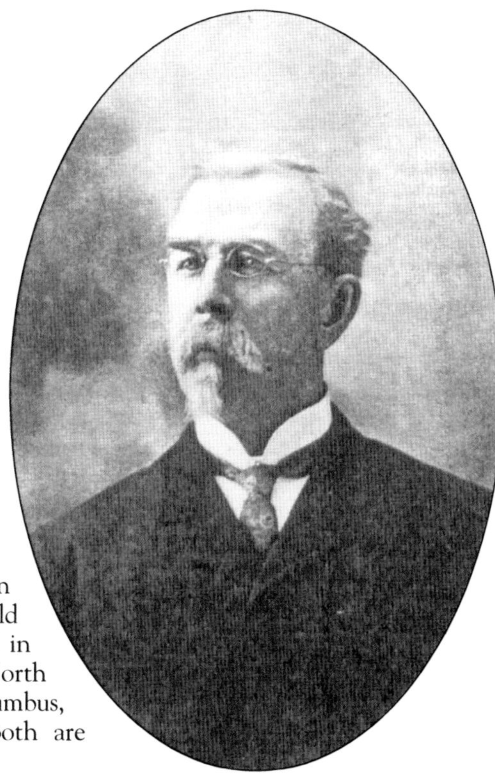

Major Leichester (Lester) Walker built and ran the first light plant in North Platte until he sold it in 1914. He was born September 3, 1836 in Sandusky, Ohio, and died April 9, 1916 in North Platte. He married Georgia Warren of Columbus, Georgia, who died November 15, 1921. Both are buried in the North Platte Cemetery.

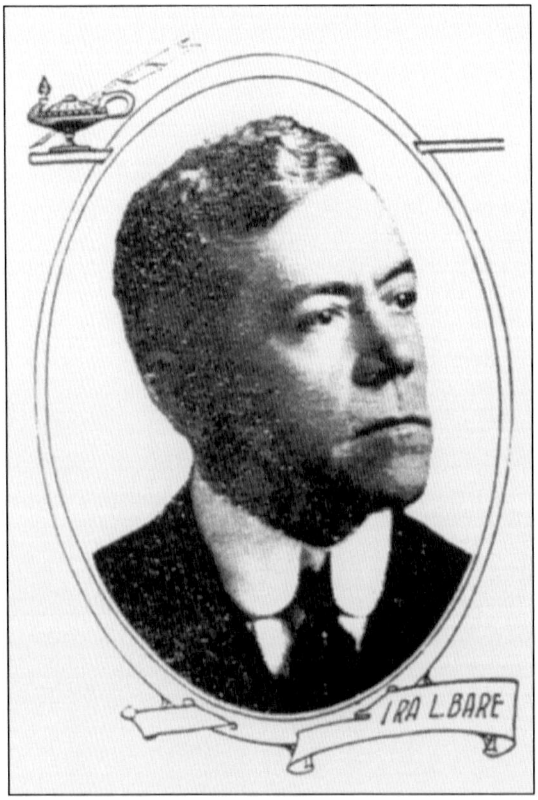

Ira Bare served as Editor and Publisher of the semi-weekly *Tribune and Telegraph*. He was born November 24, 1860 in Huntington County, Pennsylvania, and died December17, 1952. Bare married Mollie Thompson in 1887. She died May 21, 1934. Both are buried in the North Platte cemetery.

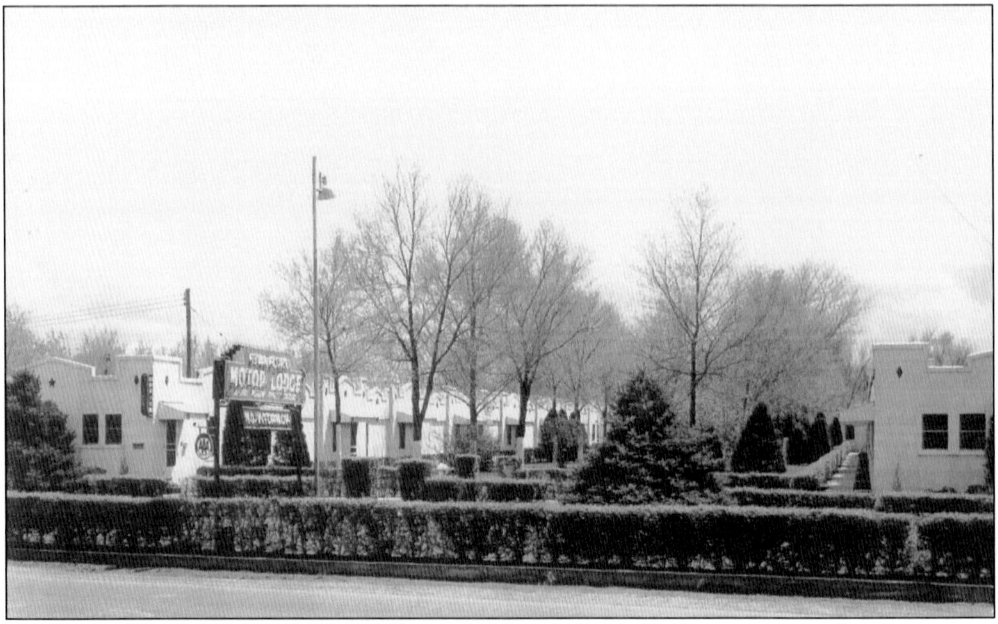

Melvin G. Mueller managed the Stanford Motor Lodge at 1400 East Fourth Street for many years. The lodge is pictured here as it appeared in 1952.

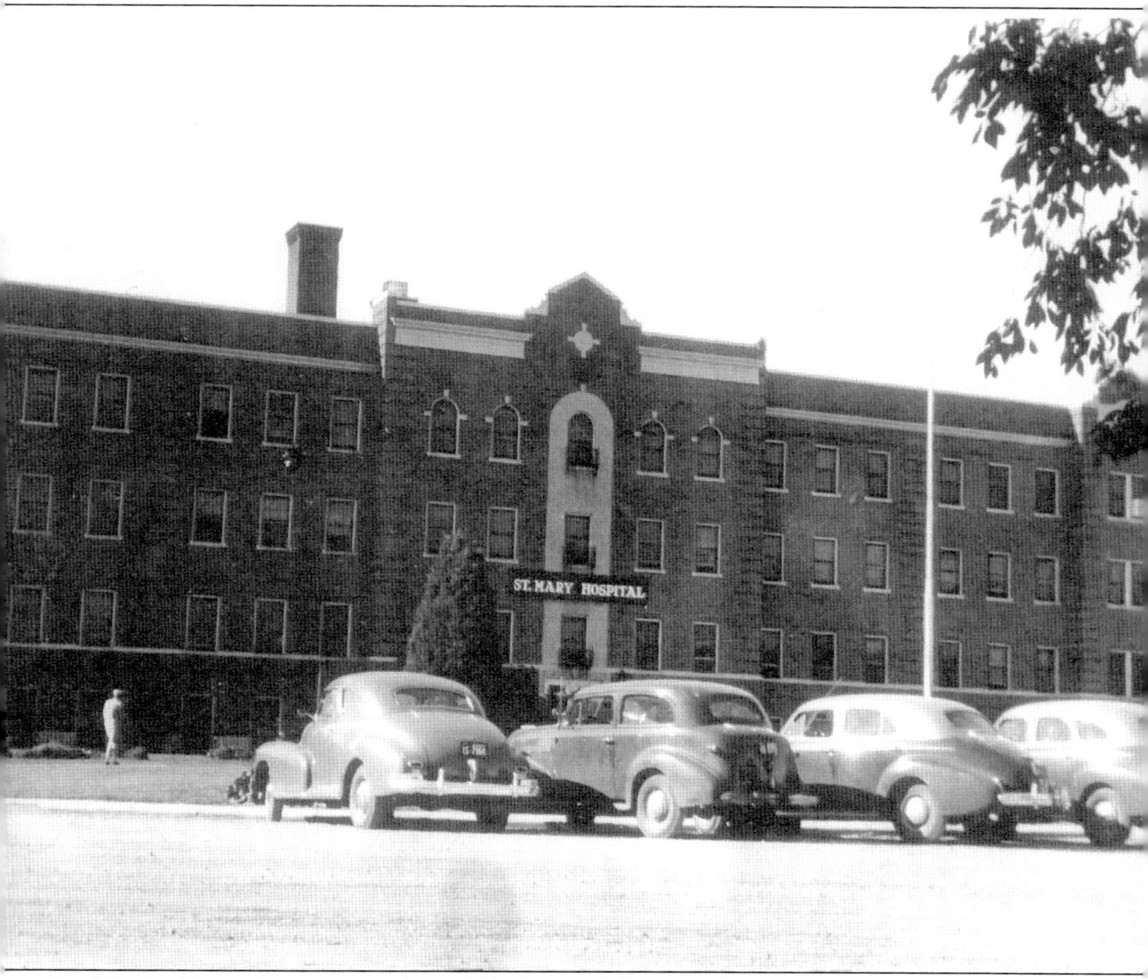

St. Mary's Hospital was located at 200 South Silber Road. Sister Maxantia served as Superintendent of the hospital.

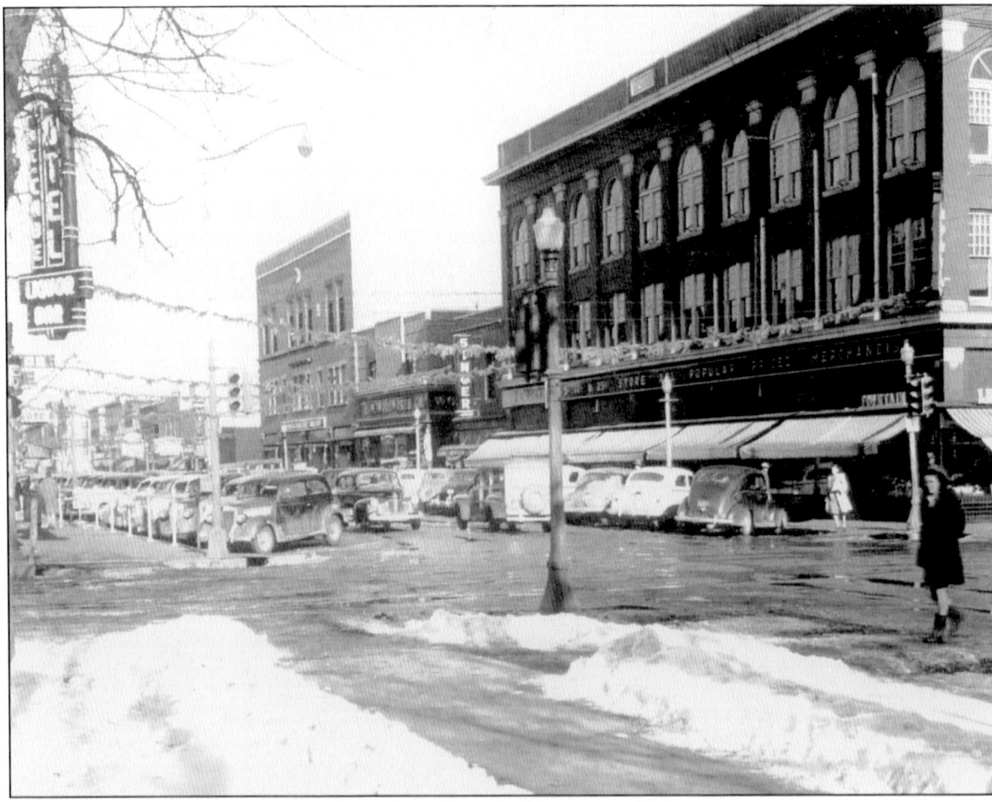

This is a view of Dewey Street from East Fourth Street in 1952.

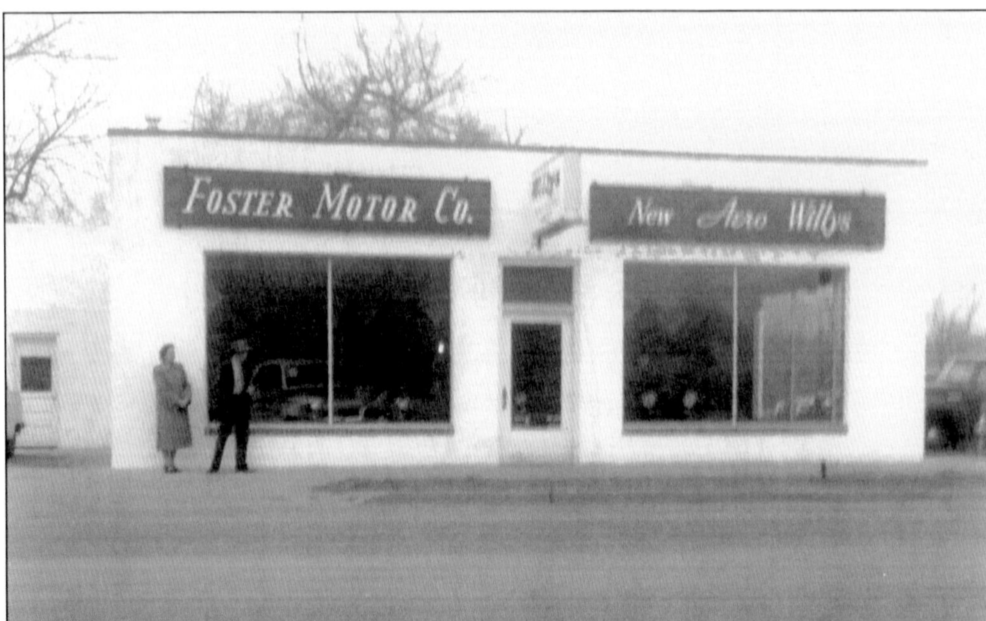

Earl and Sophia Foster owned the Foster Motor Company, located at 1101 North Jeffers, for many years. The company dealt in Willys, Overland, and Jeep sales.

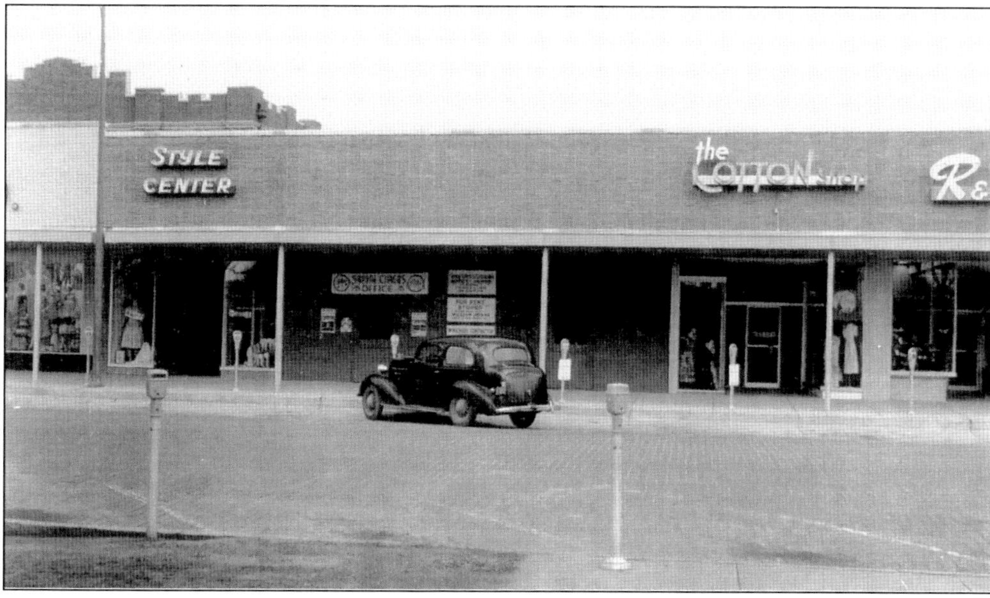

Lincoln Plaza Shopping Center was built between the 300 and 400 hundred blocks of North Dewey. The shopping center incorporated the old Franklin Junior High building and was part of the Grant Department Store. Later, Swan's Furniture Store was located there. Pictured here is the shopping center, as it appeared in 1952.

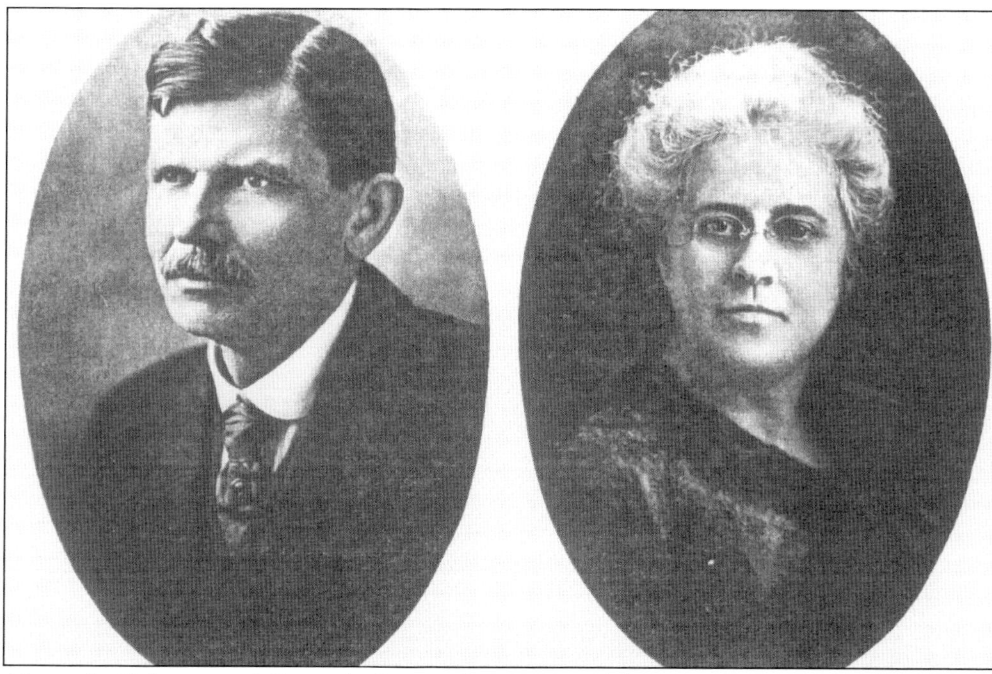

Alexander F. Streitz and Grace A. Stewart Streitz owned the Streitz Drug Store on the corner of Sixth and Dewey. He was born on May 10, 1860 in Michigan, and died on March 22, 1938. Grace Streitz was born on November 20, 1865 in Fort Wayne, Indiana, and died on November 1, 1936. Both were buried in the North Platte Cemetery. Valentine's Book Store later occupied the site of the Streitz Drug Store. Today, it is home to Wilson Photo.

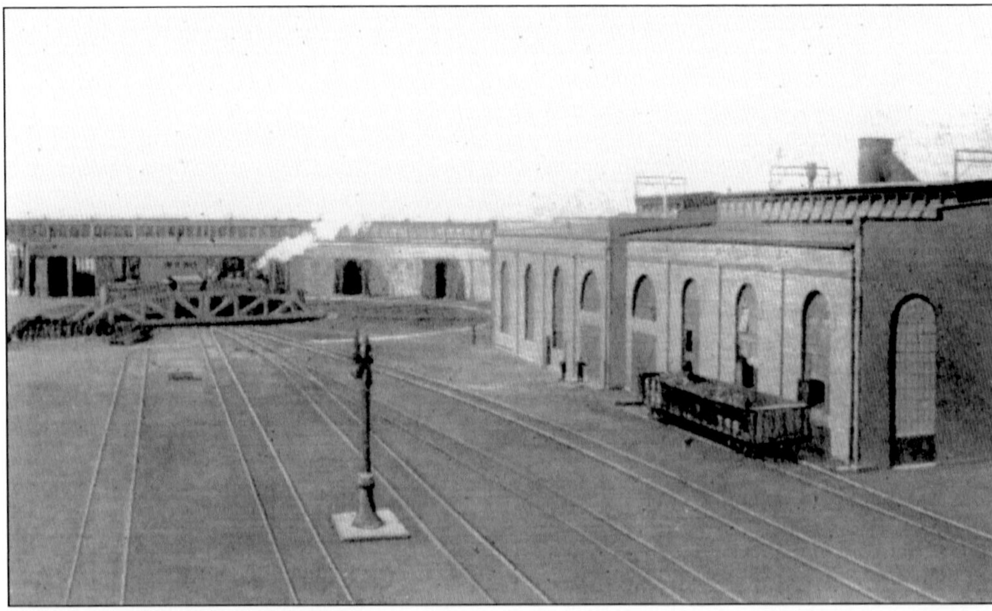

The new Union Pacific shops and roundhouse between Front Street and West Seventh Street were the largest on the U.P. system.

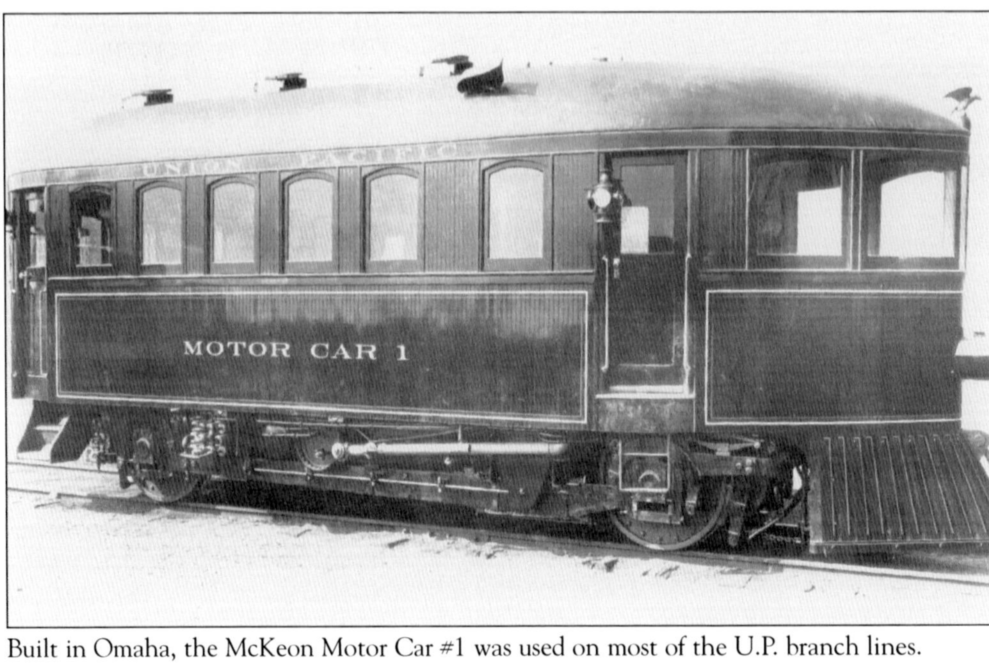

Built in Omaha, the McKeon Motor Car #1 was used on most of the U.P. branch lines.

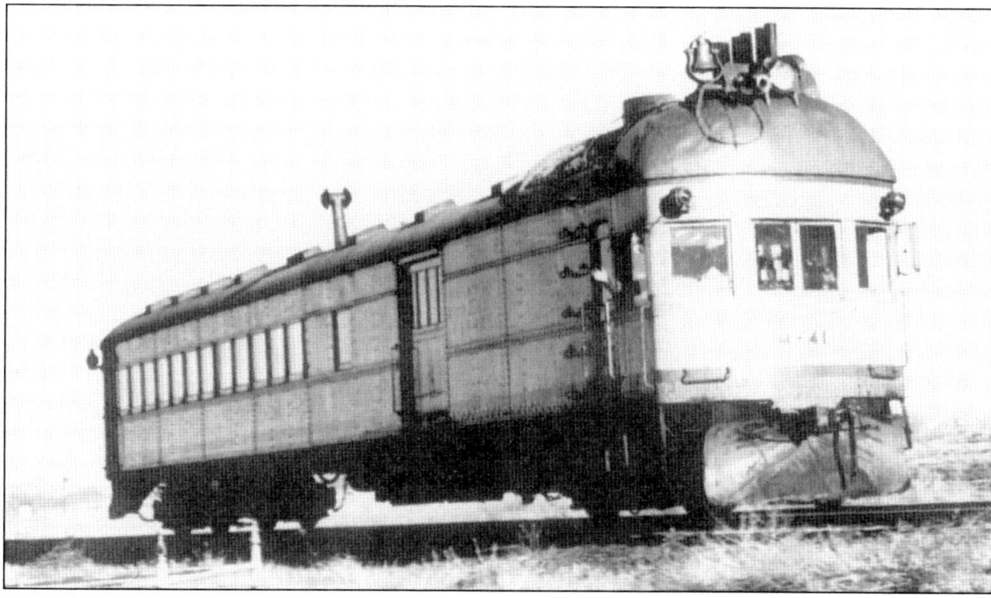

One of the last of the McKeon Motor Cars, this one provided most of its service on the Kearney to Stapleton branch. When it was retired in the 1950s, it was donated to Stapleton and placed on the lot just south of the courthouse. Soon destroyed by vandals, it was cut up for scrap.

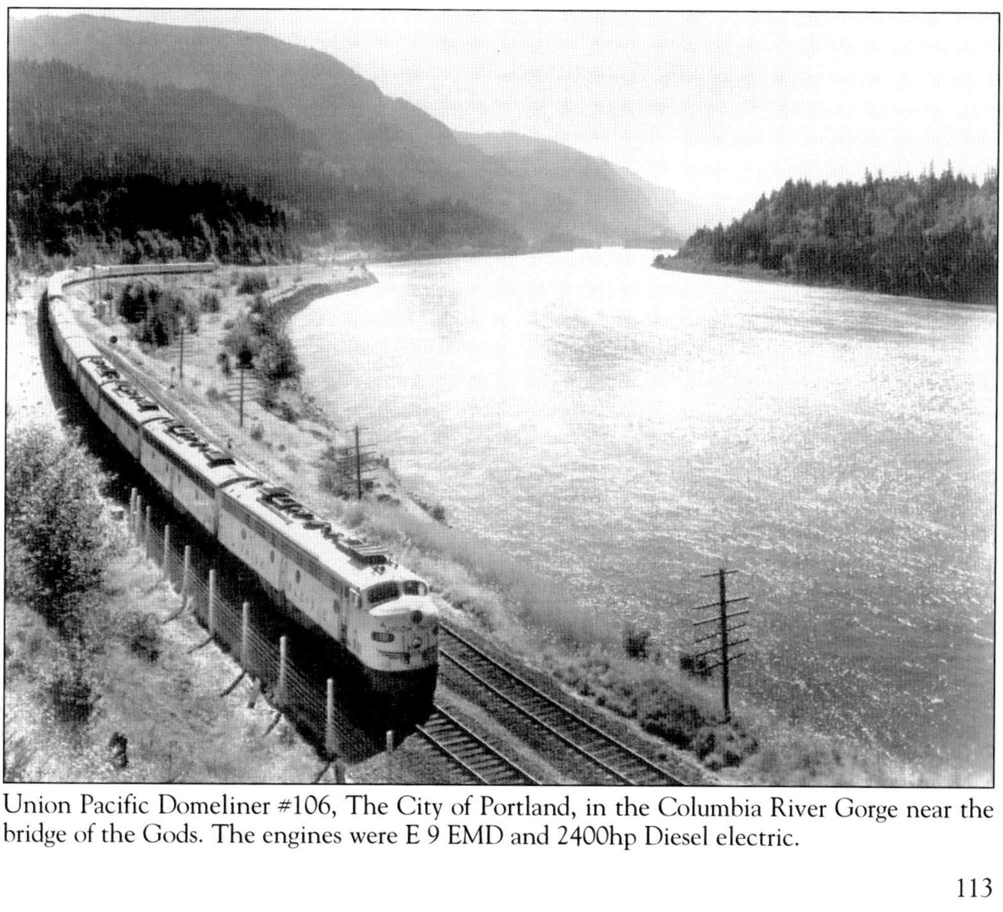

Union Pacific Domeliner #106, The City of Portland, in the Columbia River Gorge near the bridge of the Gods. The engines were E 9 EMD and 2400hp Diesel electric.

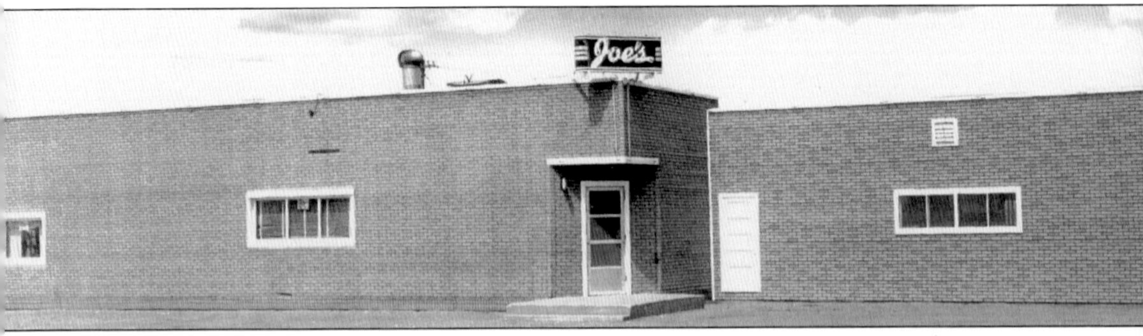

Here is a look at Joe's Supper Club as it appeared in 1952. Located on West Highway 30, it was operated by Joe and Bernice Schnitker for many years.

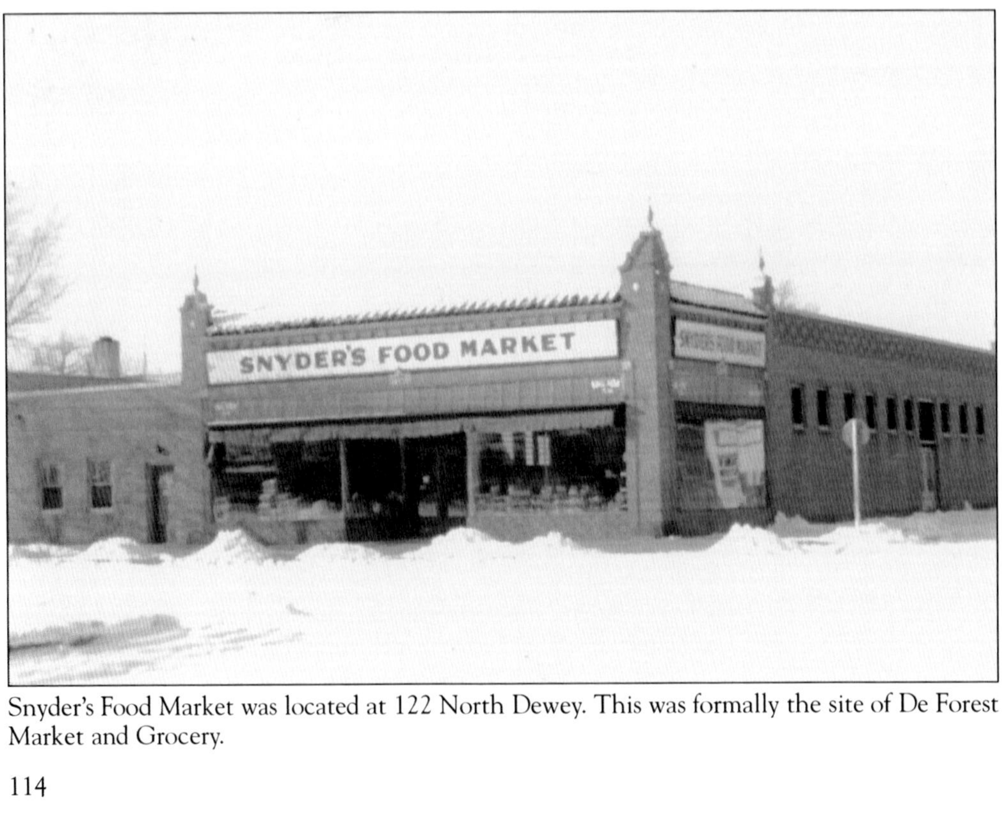

Snyder's Food Market was located at 122 North Dewey. This was formally the site of De Forest Market and Grocery.

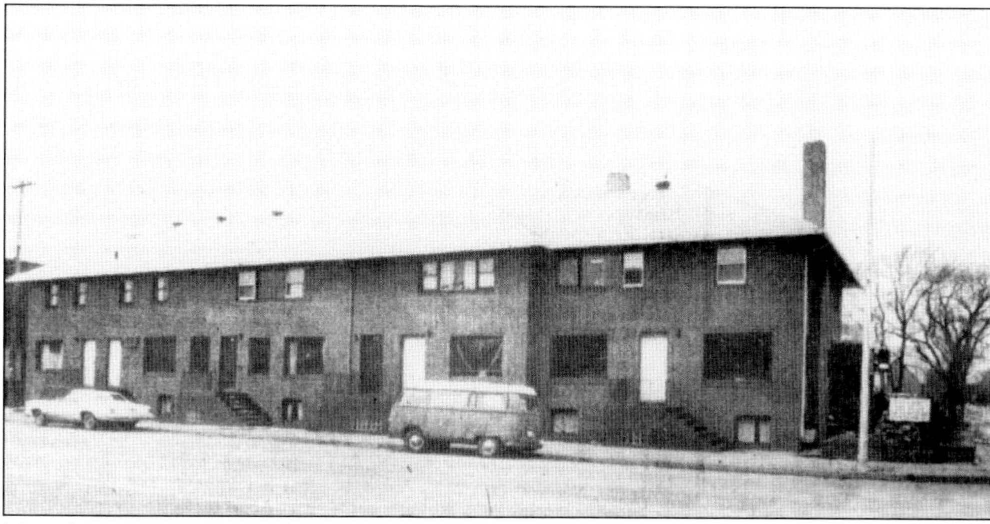

Musselman's Apartments, found at 222 North Jeffers, were eventually torn down by the county in order to make room for a parking lot.

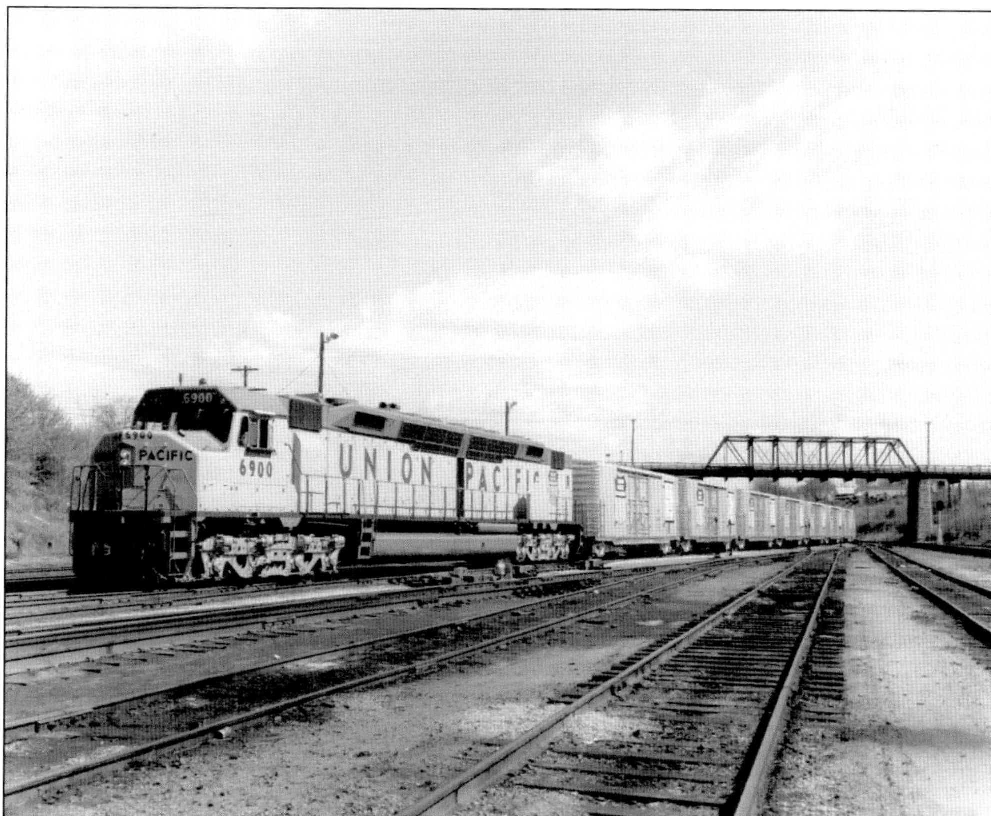

This Union Pacific engine was completed in 1969, upon the 100th anniversary of the Union Pacific meeting Southern Pacific at Promontory Point in Utah on May 10, 1869. This Union Pacific had a 6900 EMD-DDA -40x Centennial 6600 hp engine.

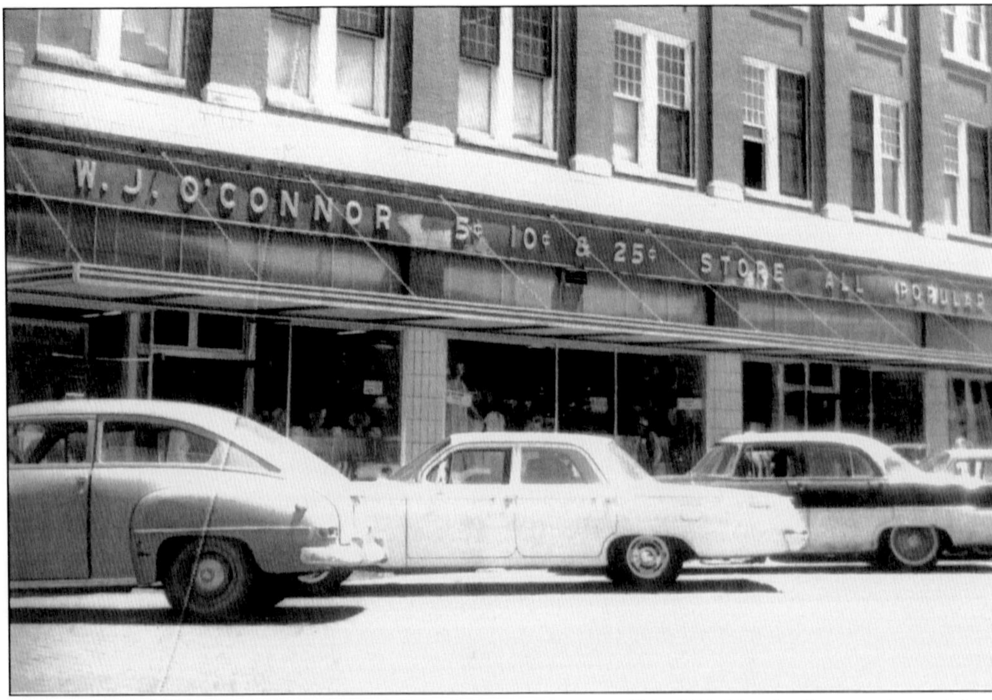

Pictured here is W.J. O'Connor's five-and-dime store at 401–409 North Dewey, its original location. This picture was taken in 1955, the year before the store relocated.

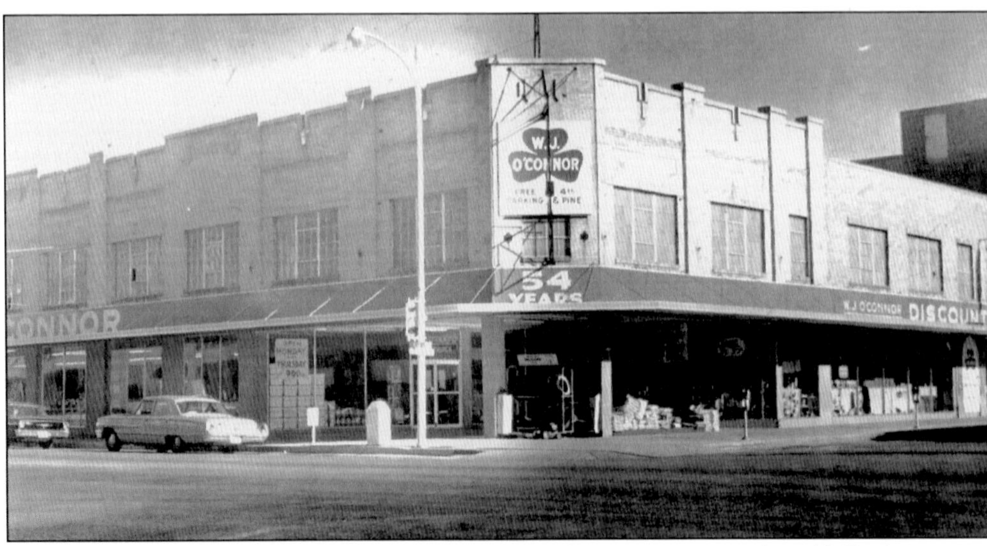

The W.J. O'Connor five-and-dime store in 1956, after moving into the old Ford garage at Fourth and Pine Streets.

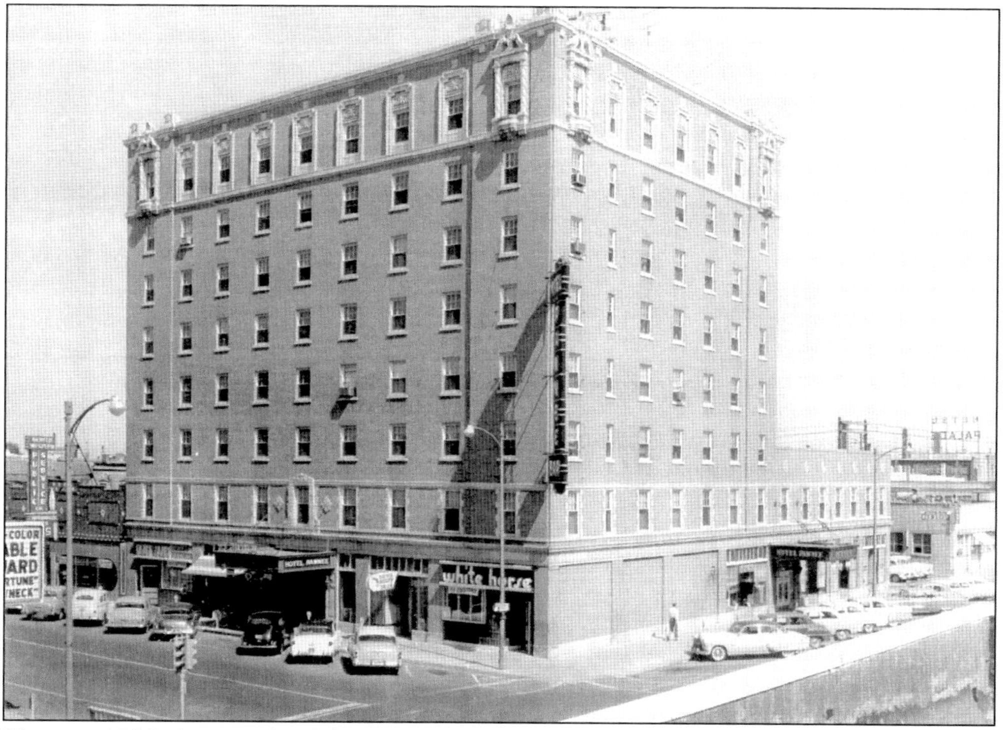

This is a 1956 photograph of the Pawnee Hotel, formerly known as the Yancy Hotel, at the corner of Fifth and Pine (Bailey).

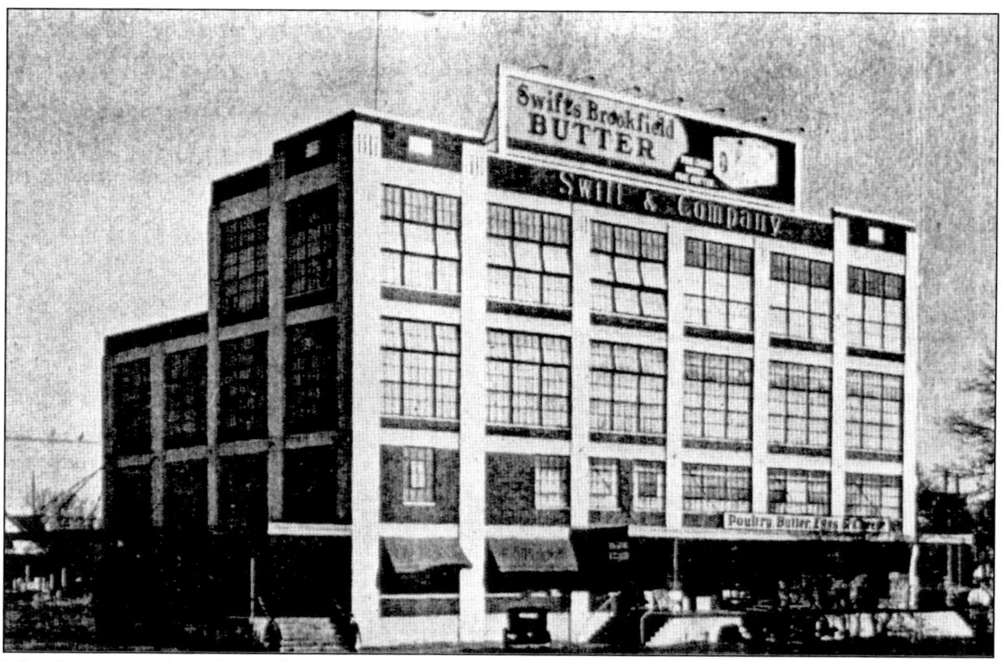

The building that housed the Swift and Company Brookfield Butter Produce Plant was constructed prior to 1929, and sat at Seventh and Pine Streets. The Butter Produce Plant was managed by J.E. Shean for many years.

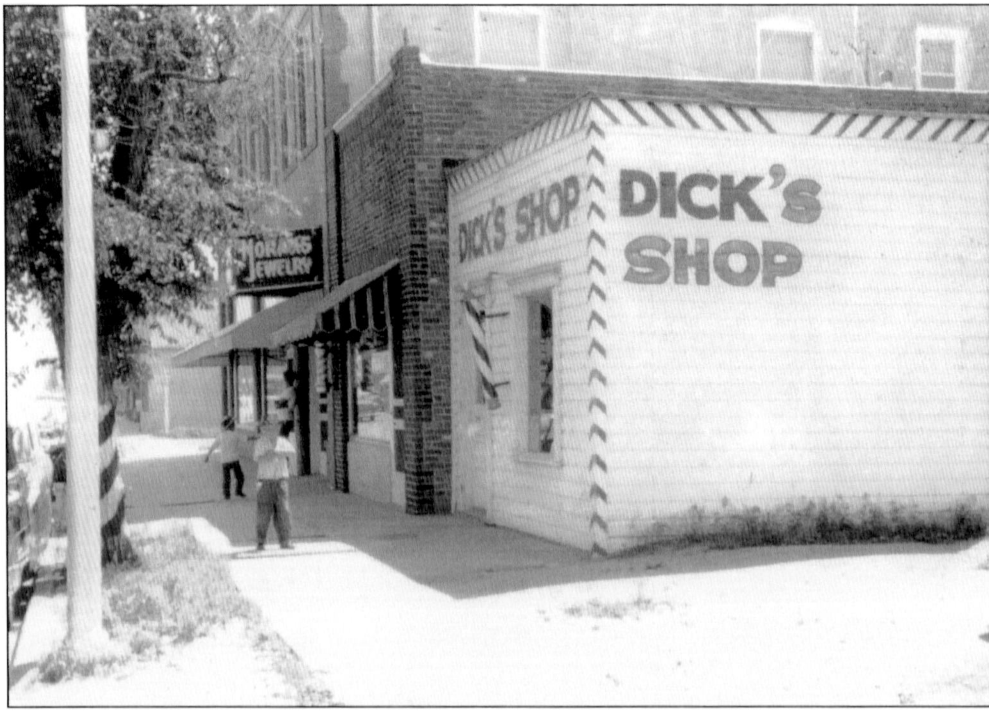

This photograph of Dick Neve's Barber Shop, located at 808 North Jeffers, was taken in 1957.

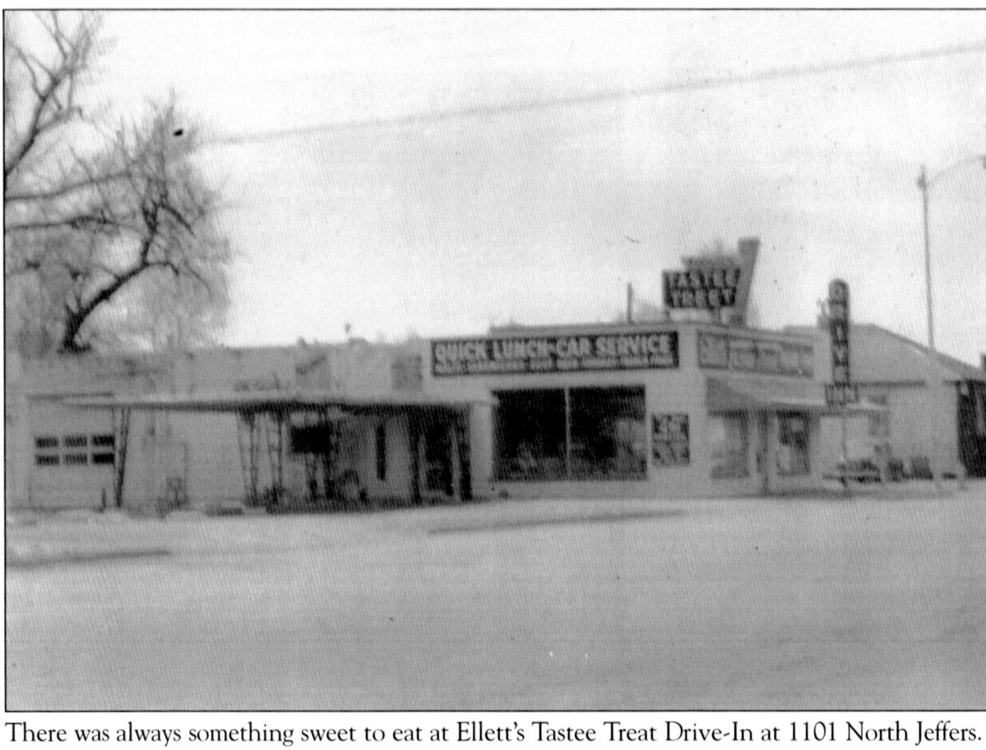

There was always something sweet to eat at Ellett's Tastee Treat Drive-In at 1101 North Jeffers.

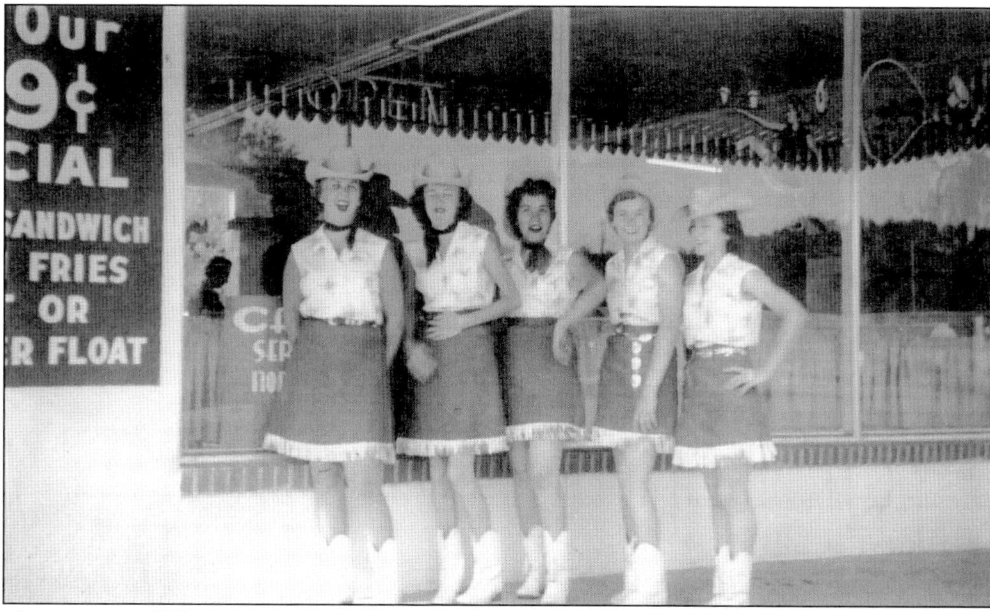

This picture of Ellett's Tastee Treat Drive-In, taken in 1949, identifies carhops, from left to right, as follows: Helen Fitzpatrick, Sue Hansen, Liz Martinez, Rigis Graham, and Bette Hosford.

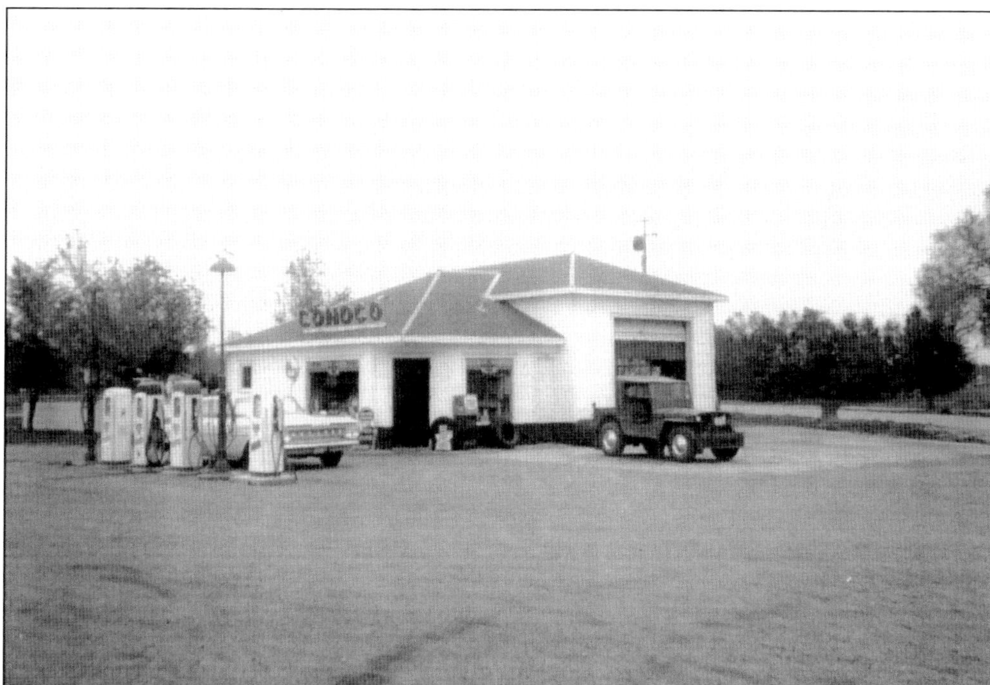

Leroy and Elaine Smith owned the Smith Conoco Station for many years. Located at 1301 South Jeffers, it was removed in 1991 due to the expansion of Francis Street. This photograph was taken in 1962.

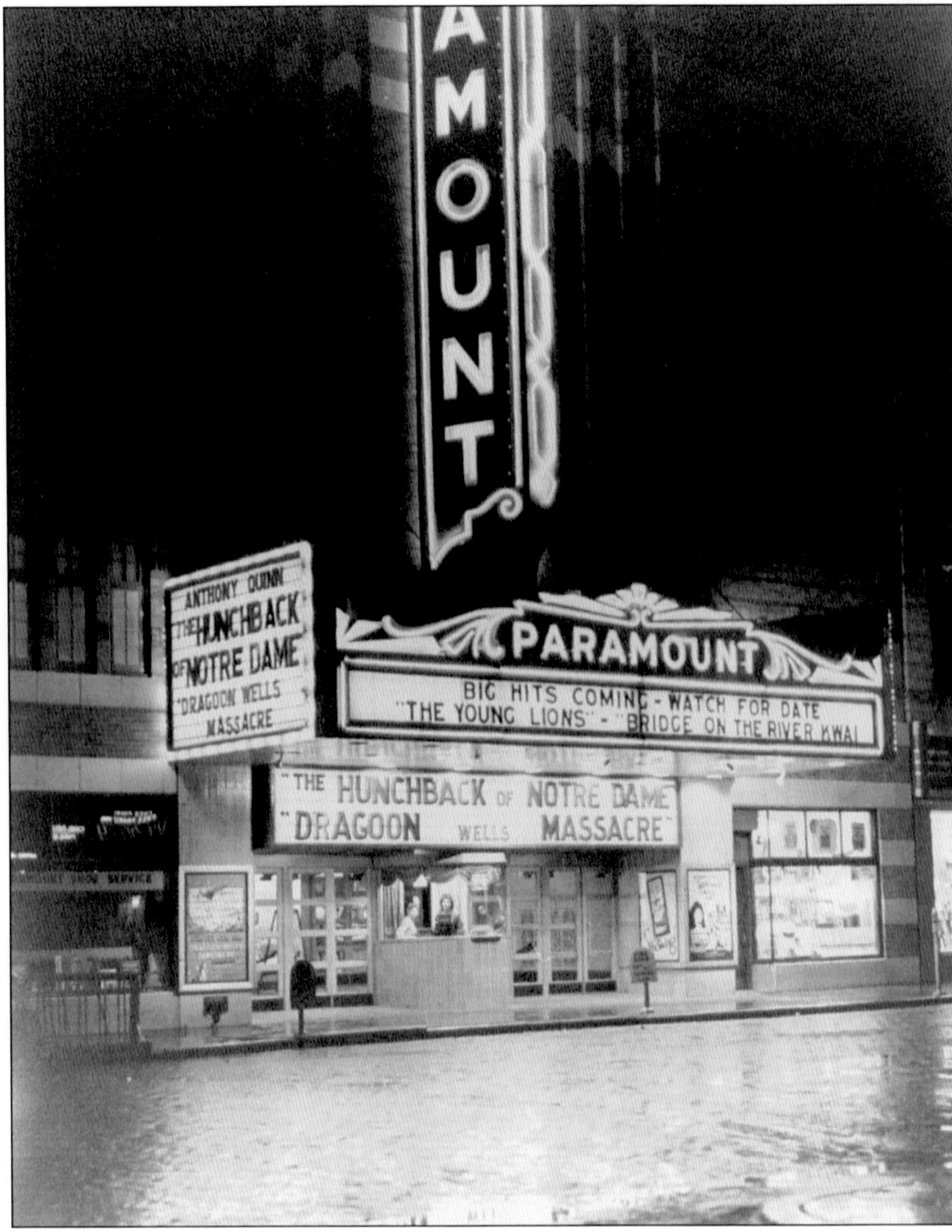

This is a 1957 photograph of businesses on East Fifth Street. The Paramount Theater, located at 222 East Fifth Street, was managed by Frank P. Larson. Walter and Helga Kenney ran Kenney's Karmelkorn shop just a few doors down, at 216 East Fifth. The Paramount Shoe Service, at 224 East Fifth, was owned by Lawrence L. Bobbio.

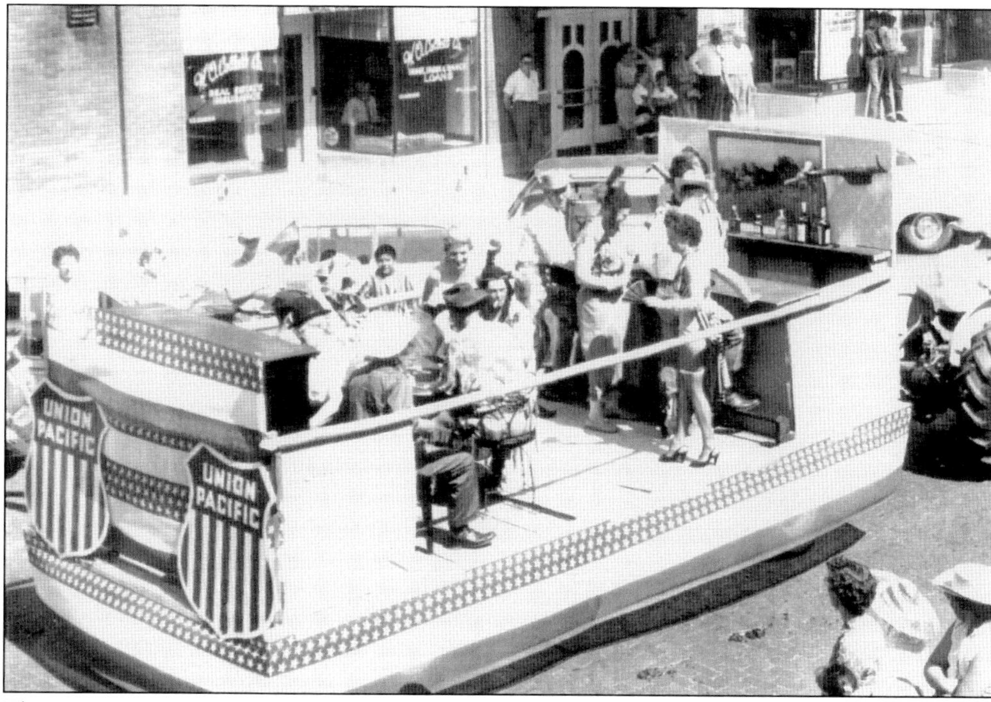

This is a picture of North Platte citizens enjoying the Buffalo Bill Parade of 1959. It was taken on the east side of the Pawnee Hotel. Seated and wearing a flowered shirt is Lyle Hill, and the blonde woman just above him is his wife, Marvia. Standing at the bar on the left is Jim Beckius, the Indian woman is Norma Paustian, and the dance hall girl is Phyllis Beckius. The rest are unknown.

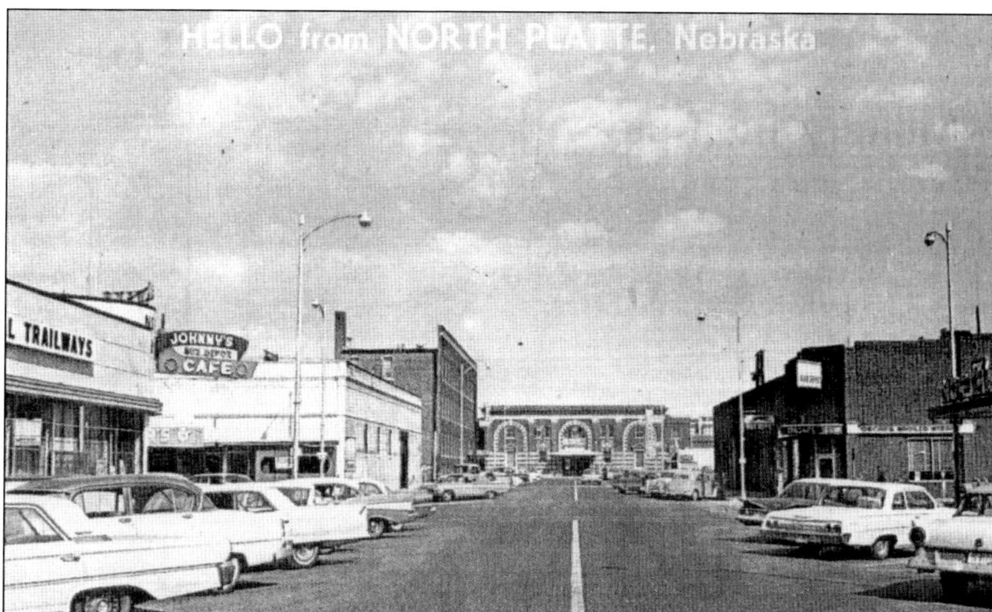

This is a northward view of North Pine Street from the middle of East Fifth and East Sixth. Taken in 1962, all of the buildings in this picture are now gone.

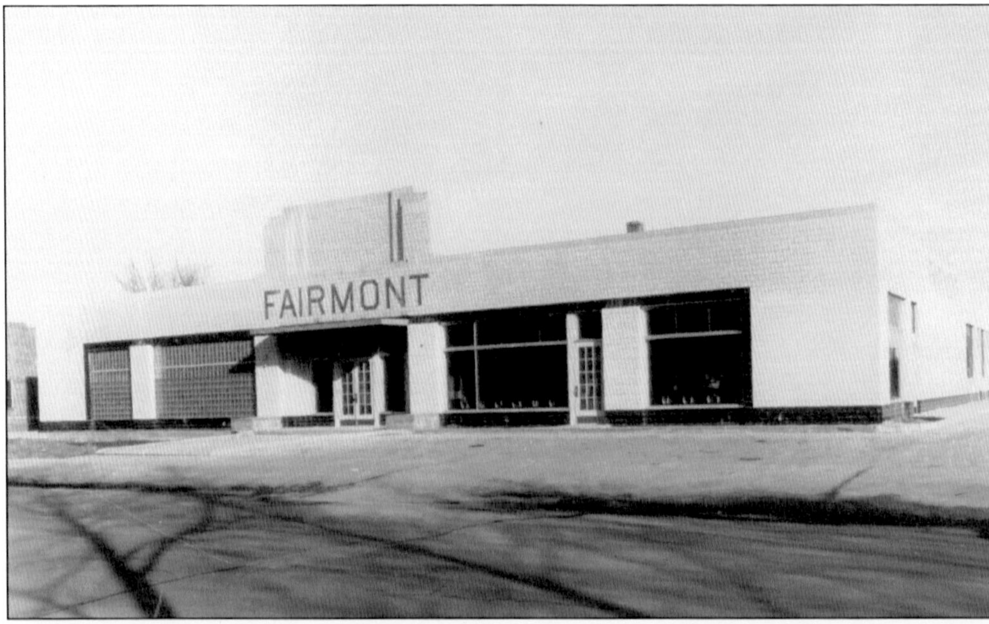

The Fairmont Food Company, at 109–121 South Dewey, was built in 1948 and torn down around 1980.

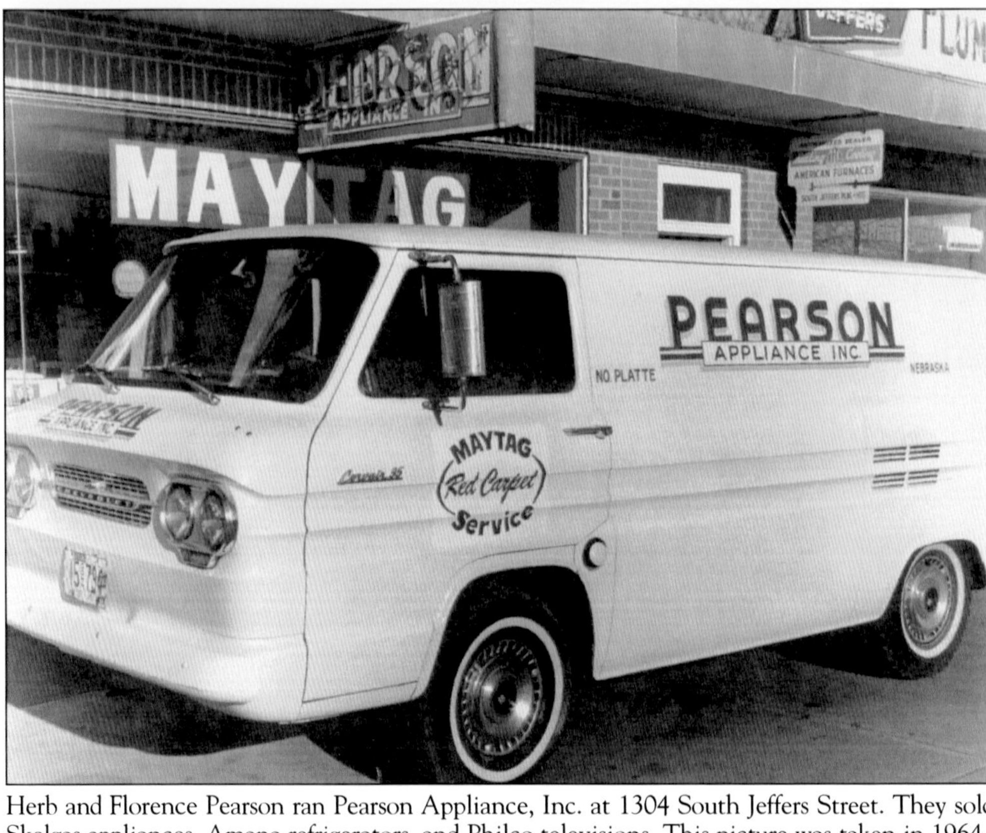

Herb and Florence Pearson ran Pearson Appliance, Inc. at 1304 South Jeffers Street. They sold Skelgas appliances, Amana refrigerators, and Philco televisions. This picture was taken in 1964.

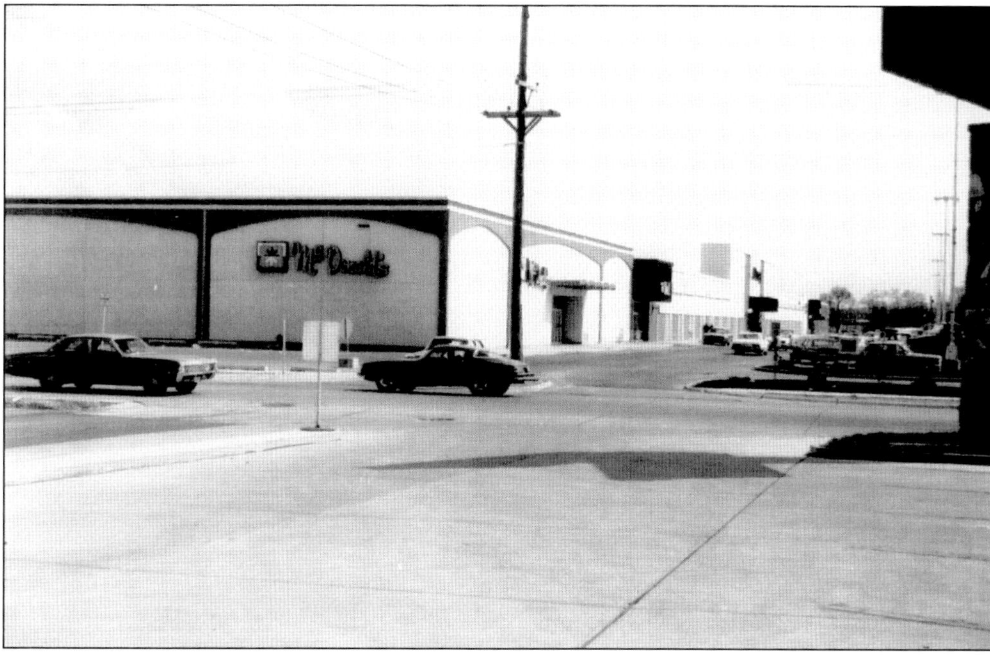

This picture captures the image of the new mall located between the 1000 and 1200 blocks of South Dewey. It was built in 1972.

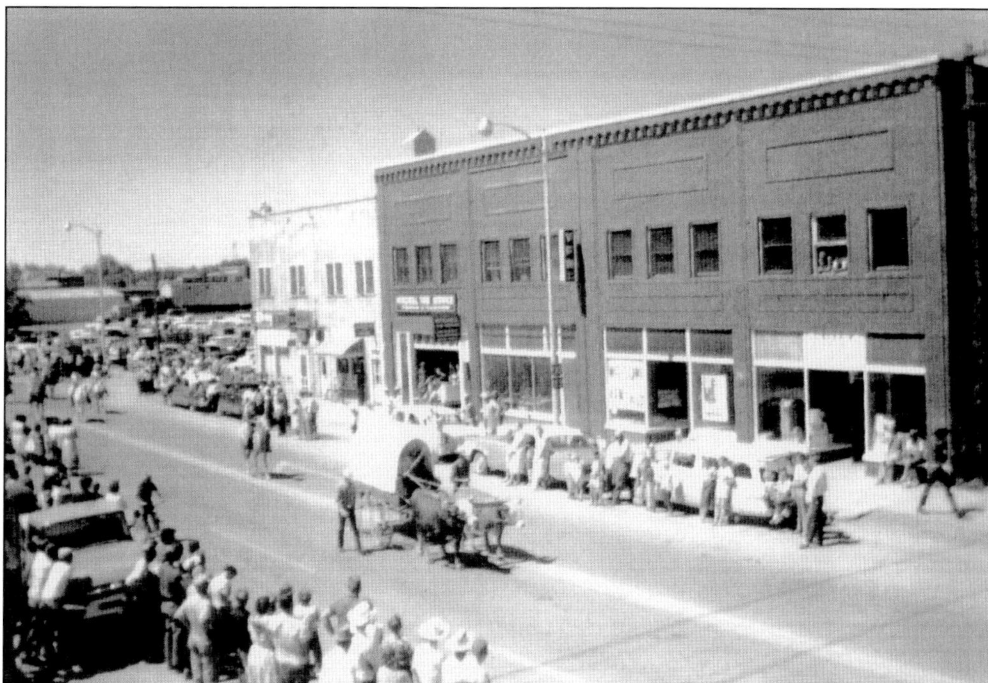

The 700 block of North Jeffers was home to many flourishing businesses in 1956. Among them are The Cozy Corner Café, at 702 North Jeffers; the Hub Bar, also at 702 North Jeffers; the Mitchell Tire Service, at 706 North Jeffers; the VFW Post #1504, at 710 North Jeffers, and Gunnarson Plumbing and Heating, at 712 North Jeffers.

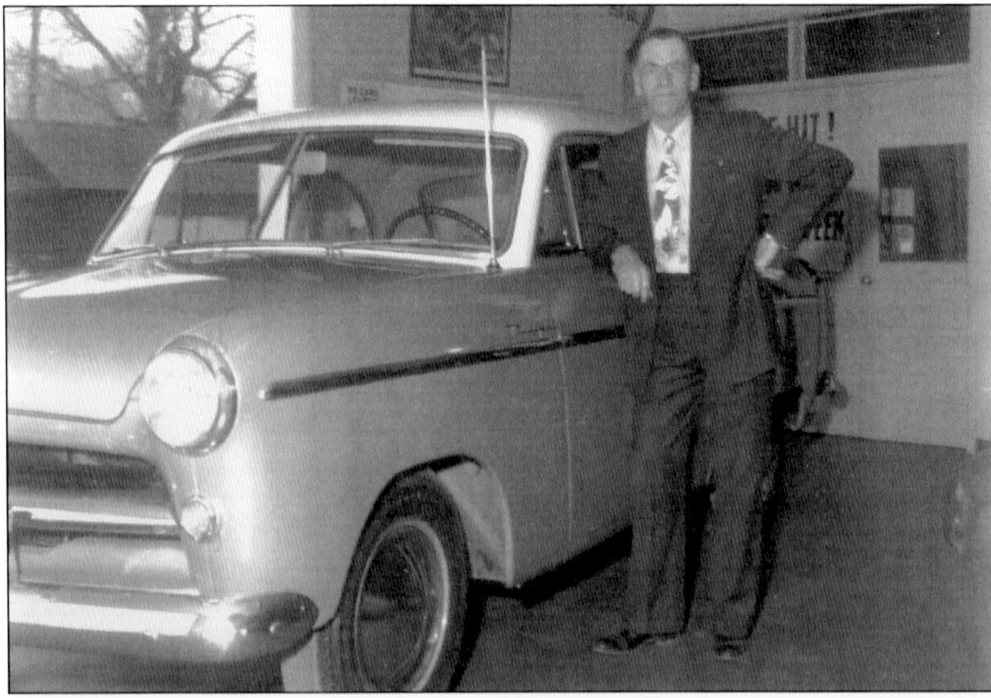

Earl Foster is pictured here with a brand-new 1952 Willys Aero. This photograph was taken in 1952 at the Foster Motor Company at 1101 North Jeffers.

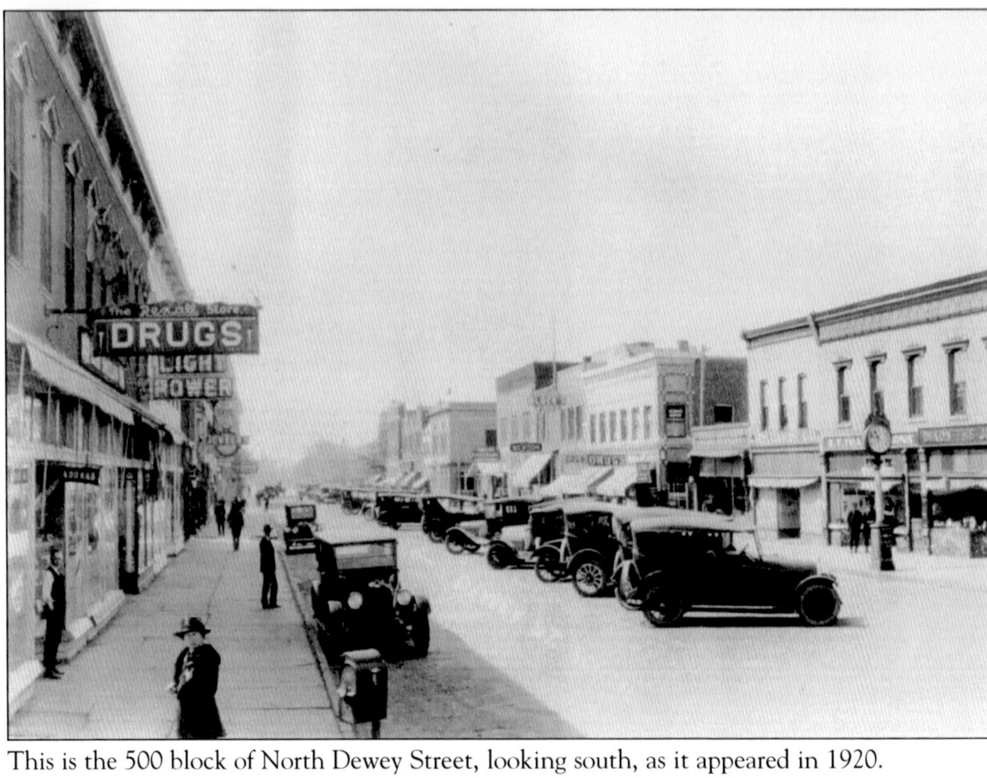

This is the 500 block of North Dewey Street, looking south, as it appeared in 1920.

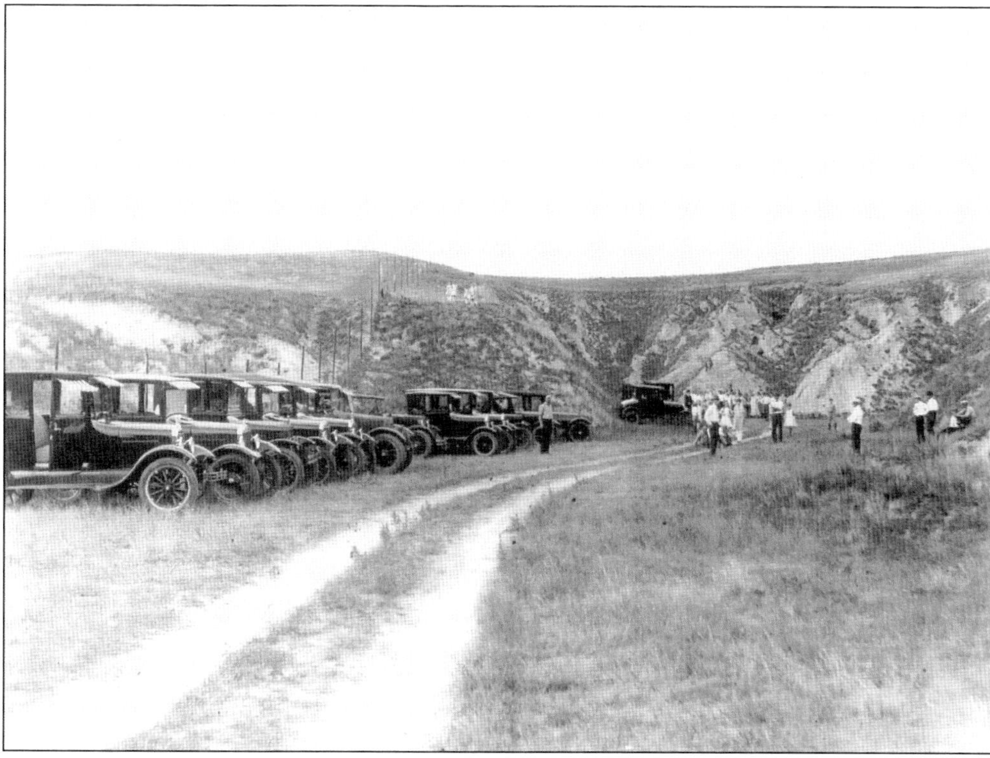

This is a picture of the 1925 Model T rally held in the canyon southwest of North Platte. Note that one Chevrolet is included in the picture.

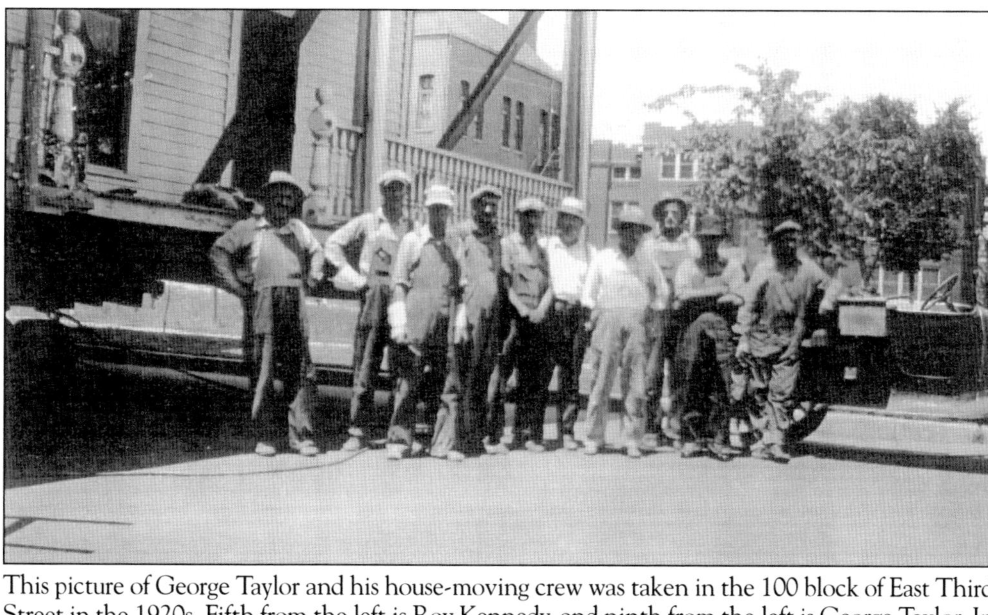

This picture of George Taylor and his house-moving crew was taken in the 100 block of East Third Street in the 1920s. Fifth from the left is Roy Kennedy, and ninth from the left is George Taylor. In the background, the old Senior High (1900–1930) and the Franklin Junior High are still visible.

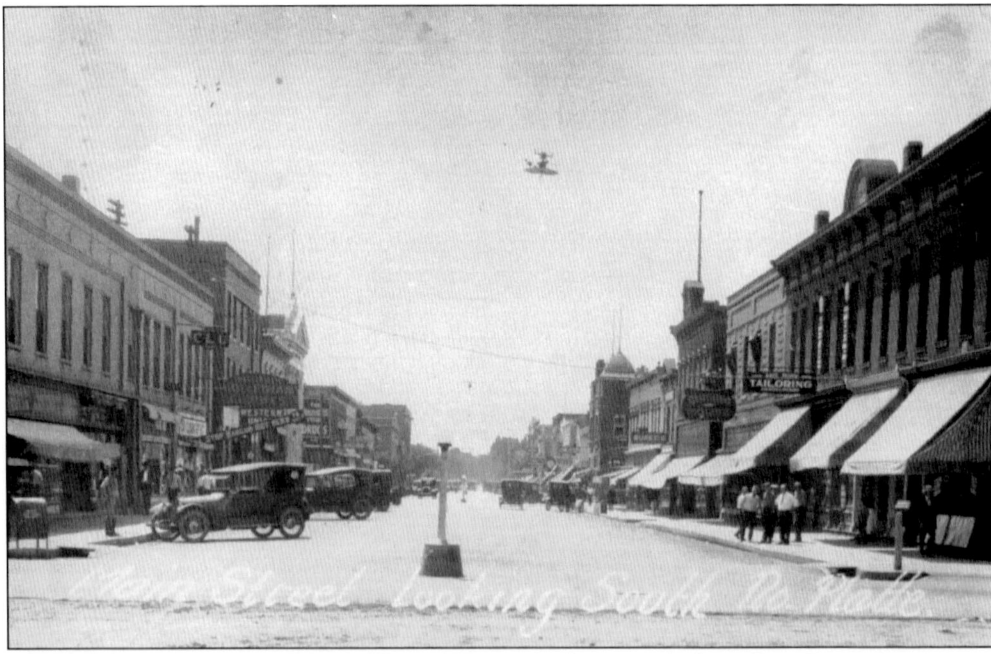

Pictured here is a view of North Dewey Street, looking south from East Front Street, as it appeared in 1926.

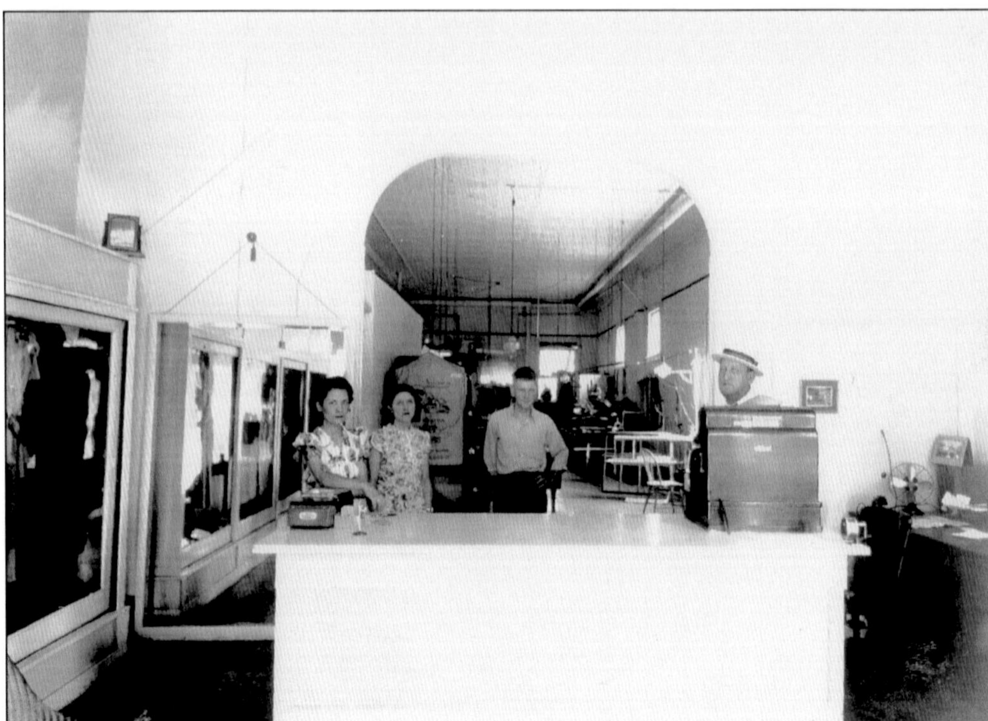

Miles Cleaners at 510 North Jeffers was captured in this 1941 photograph. Pictured, from left to right, are Olga Miles, an unknown woman, Fred Heldenbrand, and George Miles.

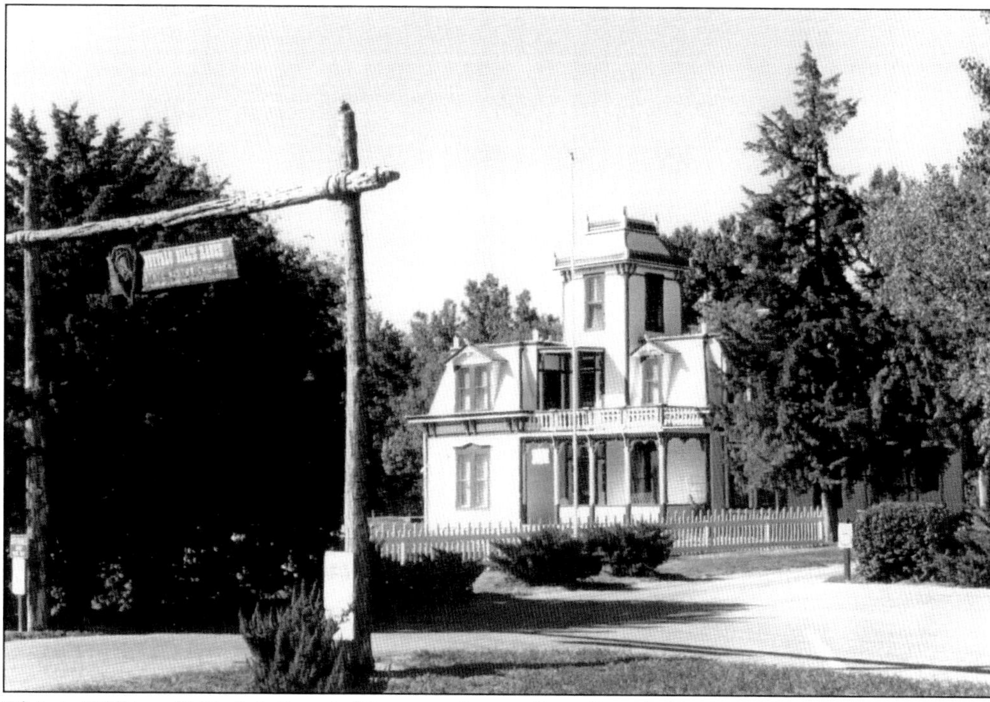

This is William F. Cody's Ranch House at Scouts Rest Ranch. Built in the 1880s, it has been restored to its original condition and is open to the public during the summer. It is now part of the Nebraska Park System.

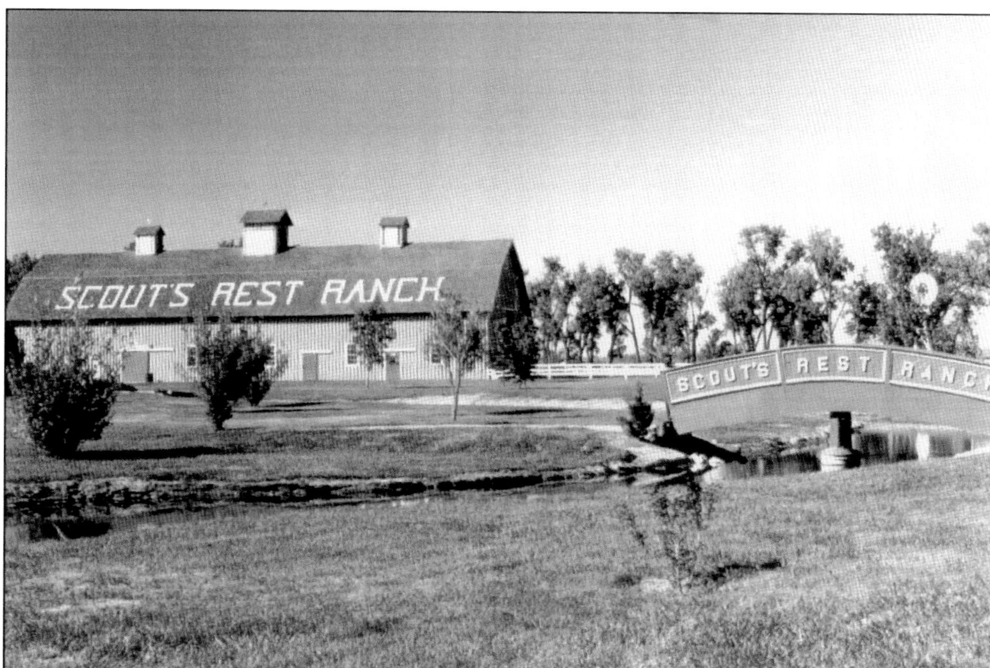

Pictured here is the original barn at Scouts Rest Ranch. It has been preserved according to how it was built in the 1880s, complete with rafters carved in the shape of Winchester gun stocks.

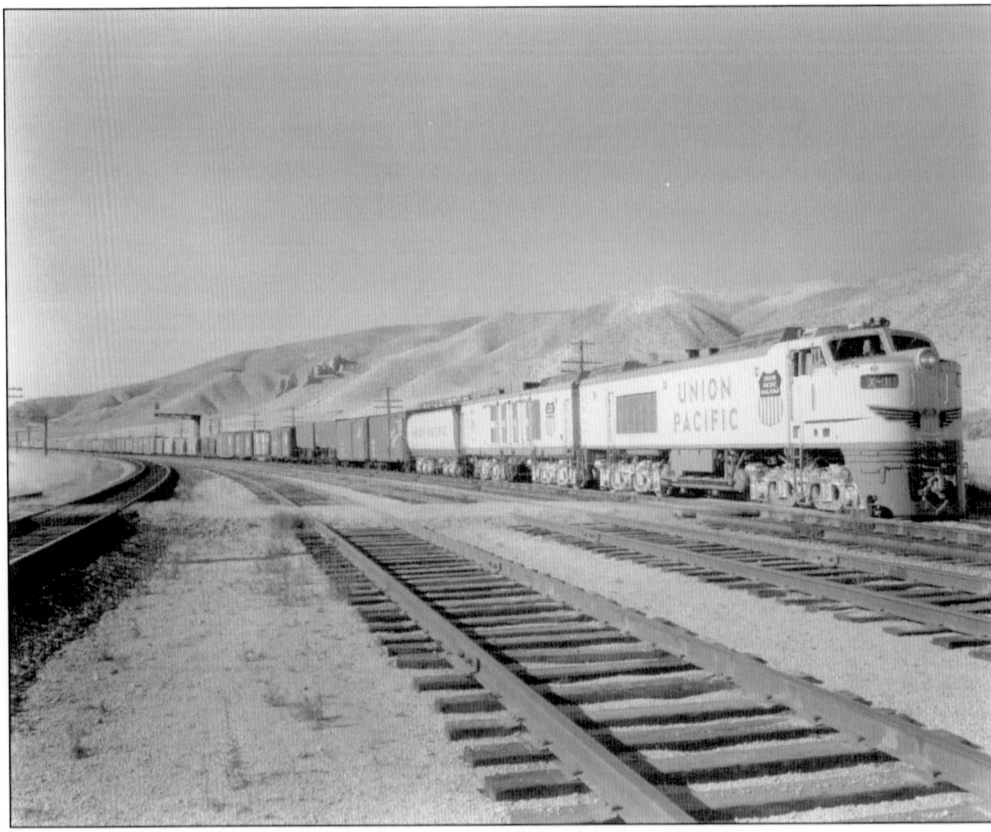

This is the Union Pacific 8500 hp. turbine electric locomotive.

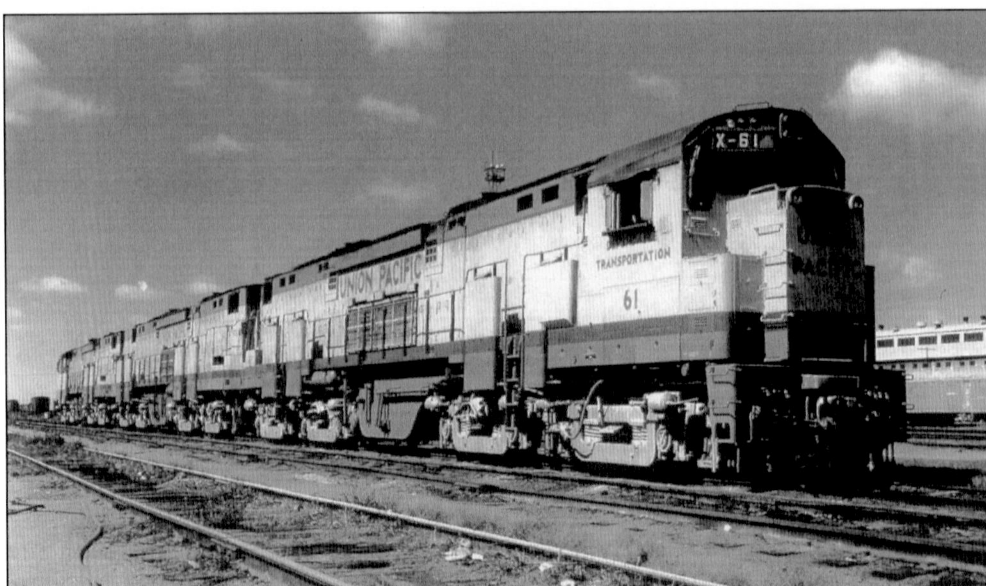

Alco built diesel electric units that had been converted to burn black bunker oil the same way as steam locomotives. You could see the smoke a couple of miles from where they were.